This book is to be returned on or before
the last date stamped below.

1 copy nr.

RESERVE STOCK

10. AUG. 1979

1 5 FEB 1980

2 2 MAR 1980

ANGUSalive

Withdrawn from stock

ANGUSalive

Withdrawn from stock

angus

district

libraries

GAINSBOROUGH

GAINSBOROUGH

ELLIS WATERHOUSE

SPRING BOOKS · LONDON

Originally published 1958 by Edward Hulton Limited
© Copyright Ellis Waterhouse 1958
This edition published 1966 by Spring Books · Drury House · Russell Street · London WC2

The frontispiece reproduces the painting of Thomas
Gainsborough and his Wife and Daughter [296].
By Courtesy of the Marchioness of Cholmondeley

Printed in Great Britain by
Richard Clay (The Chaucer Press) Ltd, Bungay, Suffolk

CONTENTS

ACKNOWLEDGMENTS

To render due acknowledgment to everyone who has helped me in the preparation of this book would risk doubling its size, but the first charge on the gratitude of an author of this sort of book is to all those owners who have generously allowed him to reproduce their pictures, and I am especially grateful to the late Mr James A. de Rothschild and to Mr G. H. Berners for having pictures especially photographed for me. Very many others have responded patiently to requests for information, and both private owners and the custodians of public collections have plunged me in debt in this matter, but I must single out for especial mention the authorities of the National Portrait Gallery in London, and the Registrars of the Museums at Pittsburgh and Worcester (Mass.), who have helped me to clear up difficult points far beyond what one might properly ask of them. Without the Witt Library at the Courtauld Institute in London and the Frick Art Reference Library in New York one could not venture to catalogue with any completeness the works of a painter whose pictures are scattered in every corner of the world: and in pursuing the intricate histories of some of them I have been enormously helped by Messrs Christie's and by the great London dealers through whose hands so many of these pictures have passed. Messrs Agnew, Mr Horace Buttery, Messrs Colnaghi, Duveen, Knoedler, Leggatt and Tooth have provided me with very many essential facts from their archives, and Miss Simpson, of Messrs Knoedler's, has especially been a paragon of patience to my enquiries.

Among colleagues I must first name Dr Mary Woodall, who has herself contributed so much to Gainsborough studies, with whom I have discussed endless problems. In America W. G. Constable, and in Canada John Steegman, have been of the greatest help and answered many questions for me; in England John Hayes has improved and corrected the list of landscapes. I am again, as when I prepared a first check-list of Gainsborough's portraits, deeply indebted to the late Harold Isherwood Kay and to all the Gainsborough material which he collected, which Mrs Kay has allowed me to use. I hope I have not forgotten all the other help that I have received, and that those who are not named here will forgive the omission.

Ellis Waterhouse

CHRONOLOGY OF THE CHIEF EVENTS
IN GAINSBOROUGH'S LIFE

1727   *May* 14.   Baptized at the Independent Meeting House, Sudbury, Suffolk: fifth son of John Gainsborough, cloth merchant, and Mary Burrough. (The date of his birth is not known.)

1740.   He is sent to London by his father to study: he remains there until 1748.

1746   *July* 15. He marries, at Dr Keith's Chapel, Mayfair, Margaret Burr: she has an allowance of £200 a year as (apparently) a natural daughter of a Duke of Beaufort.

1748   *May* 11. The Governors of the Foundling Hospital accept as a gift his painting of *The Charterhouse*.

         October 29. His father dies at Sudbury. About this time he returns to Sudbury and, soon afterwards, settles at Ipswich.

1753   (*c.*) Philip Thicknesse, then Governor of Landguard Fort, visits his studio and is the first outsider to recognize his gifts.

1755   He receives, through the agency of Joshua Kirby, his first London commission (two chimney-piece *Landscapes* for the Duke of Bedford).

1758   He seems to have spent some months as a travelling portrait painter in the Midlands.

1759   *October* 22/23. His house and goods at Ipswich are put up for sale and he takes a house at Bath.

1761   He first sends a portrait (*Lord Nugent*) for exhibition at the Society of Artists in London.

1762   He opens an account at Hoare's Bank in London.

1763   He first sends a landscape for Exhibition at the Society of Artists in London.

1766   He moves to a house in The Circus, Bath.

1768   He is invited to become a founder-member of the new Royal Academy in London.

1769   He exhibits at the first Royal Academy show in London.

1772   His nephew, Gainsborough Dupont, who had already lived in his house for some years, is apprenticed to him (his only recorded pupil).

[8]

1773   He has a disagreement with the Royal Academy over hanging his pictures and sends nothing to the Exhibitions for 1773 to 1776 inclusive.

1774   He leaves Bath and settles in London: taking a part of Schomberg House, Pall Mall, in the summer.

1777   He returns to the Royal Academy Exhibition (including his first portraits of members of the royal family).

Rev. Henry Bate (later Sir Henry Bate-Dudley) first becomes Gainsborough's supporter in the Press (which he continues to be for the rest of Gainsborough's life).

1781   He exhibits his first seapieces, his first fancy picture, and portraits of the King and Queen at the Royal Academy.

1783 (*c.*) He makes his show-box (now in the Victoria and Albert Museum).

He goes on a sketching tour to the Cumberland Lakes.

1784   He has his final disagreement about hanging with the Royal Academy, withdraws his pictures and never exhibits there again.

July. He opens an exhibition of his pictures at Schomberg House, which he repeats annually until his death.

1788   *August* 2. Dies. He lies buried in Kew Churchyard.

★ ★ ★ ★ ★

1789   From 30 March, the great part of his remaining pictures, and his collection of old masters, is exhibited for private sale at Schomberg House (some twenty of the landscapes and fancy pictures are sold).

1797   *April* 10/11. Sale at Christie's of the unfinished portraits from Gainsborough's studio and of landscapes and fancy pictures by Gainsborough and Gainsborough Dupont decd. (Transcription of the catalogue with prices and buyers' names in *Walpole Society*, vol. V.)

GAINSBOROUGH

The character of the man

GAINSBOROUGH was so nearly the exact opposite in temperament to Sir Joshua Reynolds, whose bent of mind was intellectual and worldly, and whose preference went towards the society of men of letters, that some knowledge of the man is of considerable help before making the attempt to analyse his style. His character shines forth from his letters to intimate friends, especially the series to Unwin,[1] the lawyer, and to Jackson,[2] the musician: and we have Jackson's own account of him,[3] published in 1798, as well as the impulsive obituary pamphlet by the eccentric Philip Thicknesse,[4] penned at a single sitting soon after Gainsborough's death. Mr Whitley, in his biography, oddly under-stresses the evidence of these two friends of long standing, partly because other biographers of Gainsborough had used them before, and partly because he thought them spiteful and biased. Thicknesse was certainly a spiteful character, but his genuine affection for Gainsborough (though not for his wife) was clearly sincere: and Jackson, who probably makes a little malicious fun over Gainsborough's musical pretensions—which touched his own profession—may well have been right in his assertion that Gainsborough's character "was, perhaps, better known to me than to any other person". All the scattered fragments of evidence from other sources confirm the essential validity of the impressions given by these two friends.

Thicknesse says of Gainsborough that "of all the men I ever knew, he possessed least of that worldly knowledge, to enable him to make his own way into the notice of the Great World". He gives good evidence of his impulsive generosity and of the general benevolence of his nature, and there is other evidence to justify his remark that, at home, Gainsborough "seldom had his own way, but when he was roused to exert a painful authority for it, and then he flew into irregularities, and sometimes into excess, for when he was once heated, either by passion or wine, he continued unable and unwilling also, to do business at home".

From Jackson's two essays on the "Character" of both Gainsborough and Reynolds we get a complementary picture. The following extracts are not consecutive, but their rearrangement seems to me to be fair: "Gainsborough avoided the company of literary men, who were his aversion—he was better pleased to give, than to receive, information

... so far from writing, [he] scarcely ever read a book—but, for a letter to an intimate friend, he had few equals and no superior. It was like his conversation, gay, lively—fluttering round subjects which he just touched and away to another—expressing his thoughts with so little reserve, that his correspondents, considering the letter as part of their friend, had never the heart to burn it. . . . He detested reading; but was so like Sterne in his letters, that, if it were not for an originality that could be copied from no one, it might be supposed that he had formed his style upon a close imitation of that author. . . . His conversation was sprightly but licentious—his favourite subjects were music and painting. . . . The common topics, or any of a superior cast, he thoroughly hated, and always interrupted by some stroke of wit or humour." These judgments, which can partly be checked from Gainsborough's own letters to Jackson, give a vivid and engaging picture of the man, and help to explain how difficult it was for Reynolds and Gainsborough to meet on common ground.

Beginnings and early training

In the obituary notice by Bate-Dudley which appeared in the *Morning Herald*[5] on the Monday after Gainsborough's death, we have what must be Gainsborough's own statement to his friend, which is that "after painting several landscapes from the age of ten to twelve, he quitted Sudbury in his 13th year, and came to London". This was in 1740. To corroborate or conflict with this is the puzzling remark in a letter of 1788 to Bate-Dudley, in which he is speaking about the picture known as *Gainsborough's Forest* (pl. 22). "It is in some respects," he says, "a little in the *schoolboy stile*—but I do not reflect on this without a secret gratification; for, as an early instance how strong my inclination stood for Landskip, this picture was actually painted at Sudbury in the year 1748; it was begun *before I left school*; and was the means of my Father's sending me to London."[6] It is generally taken to mean that this picture was begun in 1740 and its promise was such that Gainsborough's father sent him to London for training, but that it was painted in the main (or entirely repainted) at Sudbury in 1748, where Gainsborough may be presumed to have returned at the time of his father's death. It gives the impression of having been painted all at one time and it is hard to believe that this can have been earlier than 1748—but it remains true, and worth stressing, that Gainsborough's statement would really only make sense if 1748 had been printed in error for 1740 in his letter. By accepting 1748 as the date, we can get a quite reasonable sequence of his works in order, and it is better to assume that we have, in fact, no knowledge at all of his real "schoolboy" style. But that he had a bent towards landscape when he came to London can be accepted. This agrees also with the genuine signature and date of 1747 on the picture at Philadelphia (pl. 23).

Certainly his schoolboy period was partly spent in drawing from nature, and it is even likely that he may have copied some little Dutch landscapes before coming to London. In another letter written at the end of his life (22 May 1788, to Thomas Harvey of Catton [7]), he writes from his bed of sickness: "I feel such a fondness for my first imitating of little Dutch Landskips that I can't keep from working an hour or two of a Day." This imitation had been, at the time, an original thing to do, and the only other painter of the middle of the century who deliberately imitated the Dutch was Nicholas Tull (d. 1762), an almost unknown painter some of whose works were engraved in the 1760s, together with some early Gainsboroughs for the Ipswich dealer Panton Betew. They are curiously similar to early Gainsboroughs and it seems reasonable to suppose that a taste for such Dutch landscapes survived in East Anglia, which did a certain amount of direct trading in pictures with Holland.

Jackson remarks that Gainsborough's "first manner was an imitation of Ruysdael": the obituarist of the *London Chronicle* (7 August 1788), who was well informed about the painter's early years, says more accurately and precisely—"The first manner he studied was Wynants, whose thistles and dockleaves he frequently introduced into his early pictures. The next was Ruysdael" (by whom, of course, Jacob Ruisdael is intended) and we can in fact observe this progression. By 1748 he seems to have graduated to the Ruisdael manner and his earliest works are thus those little pictures with large foreground weeds, which can sometimes almost be mistaken for the work of Wynants. He kept up this self-taught method of study during his early years in London by repairing pictures for the art trade, for an unusually candid sale catalogue of 1762 (of Mr Oldfield's pictures) has the entries: 17. *A Dutch landscape, repaired by Mr Gainsborough. 56. Wynants, a landscape, the figures by Mr Gainsborough.* But this was the only aspect of his art which he taught himself. The same *London Chronicle* obituarist gives the following account of his first years in London: "He made his first essays in the art by modelling figures of cows, horses and dogs, in which he attained very great excellence: there is a cast in the plaster shops from an old horse that he modelled, which has peculiar merit. He soon afterwards became a pupil of Mr Gravelot, under whose instructions he drew most of the ornaments which decorate the illustrious heads so admirably engraved by Houbraken. . . ." Until recently no casts from Gainsborough's model of the old horse were known to survive, but Dr Mary Woodall has published [8] one of them, which belonged to the painter John Constable, and is still in the possession of his descendants. It already almost sets the style for the animals which were to animate his landscapes throughout his whole life, and he probably used models of this sort to help in arranging his compositions more often than has been supposed. The story that Gainsborough drew the decorations for the 1743 edition of Birch's *Lives of illustrious persons in Great Britain* (the London version of "Houbraken's heads") is confirmed by the fact that a copy of this book was among the small number of volumes from Gainsborough's possession sold in 1799, and some of what seem to be the original drawings survive in the Ashmolean Museum at Oxford. A certain facility in drawing rococo frames in the backgrounds of his portraits (such as the *Lord Clare*, pl. 57), can no doubt be derived from this youthful experience.

The apprenticeship (if such it was) to Gravelot was of fundamental importance to the young Gainsborough for the development of his personal style. Hubert Gravelot (1699–1773) was primarily a draughtsman and engraver, thoroughly trained in the French rococo style, who had designed the plates for the second edition of Theobald's Shakespeare, which came out in 1740, the year Gainsborough came to London. At any rate in 1744 (and probably for some years earlier) he was the drawing teacher at the Academy in St Martin's Lane, and Bate-Dudley, in his obituary, says that Gravelot introduced Gainsborough there. Francis Hayman was the teacher of painting at the Academy and Hayman and Gravelot, in almost inextricable combination,[9] were jointly responsible for designing and painting what was the most important commission for a public place in London during these years—the pictures for the adornment of Vauxhall Gardens. A dozen of these were already engraved in 1743. It was this world of draughtsmen, engravers and illustrators, with a mannered style which owed its chief allegiance to the French rococo, which surrounded the young Gainsborough during his apprentice years, and it pulled in an opposite direction from the naturalistic study of nature, which he had learned from Dutch landscape painting. Gravelot taught drawing from dressed-up dolls and the bottle-like appearance of some of Gainsborough's small full-length portraits reveals this tradition (*Mr and Mrs Browne*, pl. 11). It may well be that Gainsborough's continued use throughout his life of artificial models for landscapes as well as figures derived from this source. It has been plausibly but tentatively suggested by Professor Gowing that Gainsborough may even have worked on one of the Vauxhall pictures,[10] and his wholesale assimilation of the Frenchified Vauxhall style can be most clearly seen in the picture of a courting couple (Cat. no. 752: pl. 17) which has appropriately found its way to the Louvre. I am inclined to believe the early tradition that this shows Gainsborough and his wife (with whom he made a runaway marriage in 1746) and that the picture was painted as a sort of private joke to celebrate the occasion, "with all the high French . . . seasoning of affectation", as Fielding was to describe the novelist's occasional treatment of human nature in his introduction to *Tom Jones* (1749). This wholly artificial sort of landscape backdrop, which alternates rather confusingly with the more agreeable Dutch naturalistic manner in Gainsborough's early small-scale portraits (compare Cat. nos. 753 and 754—which are companions), owes its origin to this training. A blend between the two styles, with more or less Dutch tree forms but put together with a rococo art, was not original to Gainsborough but was common form in the artistic *milieu* in which the young Gainsborough was brought up. It can be seen in the engravings after Hayman to Moore's *Fables for the female sex*, first published in 1744, and, even more curiously, as a backdrop for an arrangement of cones, squares and polyhedrons in the edition of Brook Taylor's *Perspective*, published by Gainsborough's friend Joshua Kirby at Ipswich, for which subscriptions were invited in 1751.

Gainsborough's years of training may be considered to close with the view of *The Charterhouse* (pl. 1) which he presented to the Foundling Hospital in 1748. To have made such a gift, as the companion to the work of older and more established painters,

The Charterhouse [861] *Foundling Hospital Offices, London. By Courtesy of Apollo Magazine*

shows that Gainsborough was then practising as an independent painter: and, since these gifts were in the nature of an advertisement, it shows the kind of picture that he most liked painting, and that he hoped that those who saw it would commission from him. It owes its quality—and, in its modest way, it is one of the most beautiful pictures he ever painted—equally to the Dutch tradition and to his own genius. There is something of Van der Heyden and something of Jacob Ruisdael in it, but Gainsborough has added a personal poetry and a personal feeling for the picturesque to the old topographical tradition. It seems to have met with no response and it remains, with the exception of the lost *Landguard Fort*, the only picture that he painted with a specific topographical content.

Gainsborough's views on landscape

At this point, before considering the stylistic development of Gainsborough's mature years, it may be helpful to collect the clues which the artist himself and his contemporaries have given us, as to how he regarded the composition of landscapes. His attitude certainly had nothing in it of the inspired and direct meditation on the natural scene which we have come to expect of the landscape painter since the age of Constable and Turner. Eighteenth-century taste liked topographical painting and it liked certain kinds of artificial landscape. It was not until the close of the century, with the appearance of the theorists of the "picturesque", that anything like a modern feeling for landscape appears, and eighteenth-century British collectors of the upper classes considered the extremely artificial compositions of Vernet the only modern landscape paintings worthy of their consideration.

Gainsborough was determined to avoid the topographical tradition at all costs. Writing to Lord Hardwicke, probably about 1764,[11] he declined a request to paint a specific view in the following unequivocal terms: "Mr Gainsborough presents his humble respects to Lord Hardwicke, and shall always think it an honour to be employed in anything for his Lordship, but with respect to real views from Nature in this country he has never seen any place that affords a subject equal to the poorest imitations of Gaspar or Claude. Paul Sandby he believes is the only man of genius who has employed his pencil that way. Mr G. hopes that Lord Hardwicke will not mistake his meaning, but if his Lordship wishes to have anything tolerable of the name of Gainsborough, the subject altogether, as well as figures &c., must be of his own brain; otherwise Lord Hardwicke will only pay for encouraging a man out of his way, and had much better buy a picture of some of the good Old Masters." From this it is clear that Gainsborough not only knew what sort of landscape he wanted to paint, but was also determined that his landscapes should be judged and valued as works of the creative imagination on a level with the great masters of landscape who were admitted by the connoisseurs of the age.

In the first of his letters to Jackson in the Royal Academy (probably of 1767) he makes an even more valuable comment on his aims in his own landscapes: "but to be serious", he writes, " (as I know you love to be), do you really think that a regular composition in the Landskip way should ever be filled with History, or any figures but such as fill a place (I won't say stop a gap) or create a little business for the eye to be drawn from the trees in order to return to them with more glee". It will be noticed that he speaks of "a regular composition in the Landskip way" which is perhaps not altogether the same as what we often mean when we speak of a "Landscape". This is borne out by the method he certainly often employed in "composing" his landscapes, which seems to us very far from natural, but of which there is a variety of contemporary evidence. Sir Joshua Reynolds, in his Fourteenth Discourse (1788), which is still the most striking account of Gainsborough's genius, says of him that "from the fields he brought into his painting-room stumps of trees, weeds, and animals of various kinds; and designed them, not from memory, but immediately from the objects. He even framed a kind of model from landscapes on his table; composed of broken stones, dried herbs, and pieces of looking-glass, which he magnified and improved into rocks, trees, and water." And William Jackson[12] says: "He made little laymen for human figures. All the female figures in his Park scene he drew from a doll of his own creation. He modelled his horses and cows, and knobs of coal sat for rocks—nay, he carried this so far, that he never chose to paint anything from invention, when he could have the objects themselves. The limbs of trees, which he collected, would have made no inconsiderable wood-rick, and many an ass has been led into his painting room." Whitley gives a third variant, from a letter by an unnamed "Amateur of Painting", in the *Somerset House Gazette*, 1824, p. 348, which shows that this practice was certainly used by Gainsborough at Bath as well as in his London years: "I . . . have more than once sat by him of an evening [at Bath] and seen him make models—or rather thoughts—for landscape scenery on a little old-fashioned folding oak table, which stood under his kitchen dresser. . . . This table, held sacred for the purpose, he would order to be brought to his parlour, and thereon compose his designs. He would place cork or coal for his foregrounds; make middle grounds of sand or clay, bushes of mosses and lichens, and set up distant woods of broccoli."

Just as he learned the use of a dressed doll from Gravelot, I suspect that Gainsborough acquired this model-landscape habit very early. It has automatically been assumed that this was only an occasional pastime with him, but it seems to me more likely that his whole mature output of landscapes (with the exception of the handful of seapieces, which have a freshness often lacking in the woodland scenes) owe a great deal to this procedure. The great output of drawings for landscape composition in his last years may well almost all have been produced in this way of an evening—and indeed it is the only way we have of explaining how he found time to do them. A certain insensibility to the ordering of the seasons, in which trees in spring, summer and autumn foliage all appear in the same picture (e.g. Cat. nos. 906, 919, etc.), is also to be explained in this way. He did of course also make many figure studies and drawings from nature, which he no doubt used in the preparations of his compositions or "thoughts".

Robert Andrews and Mary, his Wife (Detail) [18] *Reproduced by Courtesy of the Trustees, The National Gallery, London*

This evidence of Gainsborough's landscape methods will prepare us for the paintings of his Suffolk period.

Gainsborough's years in Suffolk

Gainsborough presumably settled in Suffolk about 1748, soon after painting the picture of *The Charterhouse*. It is generally assumed that he spent a few years at Sudbury before settling in Ipswich, but it is likely that, in order to earn a living, he moved to Ipswich as soon as possible and was established there before 1750.[13] Although no doubt anxious to paint landscape as much as possible, no painter of the time could survive without a portrait practice, and he evolved his mature portrait style during the period he spent at Ipswich before settling at Bath at the end of 1759. Although his London training had made him quite accomplished at the small full-length in a natural or artificial landscape (a genre much popularized by Hayman in London from about 1745 onwards, which certainly served as the model for this type of Gainsborough), he was still extremely gauche in portraiture on the scale of life. The obituarist of the *London Chronicle* (conceivably his early Suffolk friend, Samuel Kilderbee) remarked that his earliest portraits had "very little to recommend them", and Thicknesse, on first visiting the painter's studio about 1753, speaks of seeing a number of portraits "truly drawn, perfectly like, but stiffly painted". Among those which Thicknesse saw was the *Admiral Vernon* (pl. 45), which proves the truth of what he says. The *Unknown Officer* dated 1756 (Cat. no. 765: pl. 26) is still very stiff in the body, though the portrait of a brother officer, *Charles Hamilton* (pl. 27) is a great deal more free and competent. The *William Mayhew* of 1757 is, as far as I can judge, still decidedly gauche, but from 1757 to 1759 he clearly made an enormous advance, and, by the time he settled in Bath in 1759, he could cope with the human figure on the scale of life, even at full-length, with freedom and ease. He taught himself to some extent on portraits of himself and his own family, most of which he did not bother to finish. For both the groups of his daughters in the National Gallery (pls. 51, 52) were probably painted just before he moved to Bath. The only life-size full-length that he may have completed at Ipswich is the *William Wollaston* (pl. 61). Though the sitter was M.P. for Ipswich, I am inclined to think that this was painted after Gainsborough's move to Bath.

It is in the rather small number of miniature full-lengths, especially the *John Plampin* (pl. 13), which owes its composition to the engraving after Watteau's *Antoine de la Roque*, that Gainsborough was able to experiment with the intimate and informal style, which he attempted to introduce, on the scale of life, during his first years at Bath. It may be to a small extent an accident that certain of these small-scale pictures, notably the *Mr and Mrs Andrews* (pl. 10), by being combined with a landscape background of just the same degree of fresh informality, should happen to be rightly seen as masterpieces by modern eyes.

In landscape composition Gainsborough was a great deal more advanced than in the field of portraiture. The key to what he was doing lies in the two pictures at Woburn (pls. 39, 41), which were paid for in 1755 and are specifically described in the invoices as landscapes "for a chimney piece". The "chimney piece" was, in fact, about the only kind of landscape which a British patron would buy at home. It was regarded as hardly more important as a work of art than the plaster ornaments by those who commissioned them. By tradition they were artificial compositions, peopled with vaguely rustic figures, whose actions were not sufficiently particularized for the result to be a "History". What Gainsborough did was to give works of this kind a new dignity, not composing them out of old clichés, but putting them together from the freshly observed motives of the rural scene, of which he made little oil studies, perhaps direct from nature. It is doubtful if there was any sale for these little pictures and they were mainly given to friends. At the same time the finished result was given a dash of the high French affectation, so that it had something of the air of a naturalized Boucher "Pastoral". In addition to the Woburn pictures, it is at least probable that nos. 826, 827 and 835 were all painted as chimney-pieces for Suffolk houses and the same may well be true of all the larger landscapes of these years. We know that this was true of no. 886 *A view of Landguard Fort*, now known only from engravings, for Thicknesse relates that he invited Gainsborough to dinner with him and desired him "to take down in his pocket book the particulars of the Fort, the adjacent hills, and the distant view of Harwich, in order to form a landscape . . . of the size of a pannel over my chimney piece", and even this was adorned with markedly rococo figures and foreground.

These compositions are little anthologies of motives observed from life, put together in a landscape composed according to ornamental rules. Many of the motives were to be constantly used throughout the whole of Gainsborough's life—such as the boy letting his horse drink which first appears in no. 827 (pl. 37) with a number of other motives which were taken up again in the 1770s. In the same picture the cliff to right seems originally to have been much lower, but to have been heightened in the interests of rococo design (and the tree to left given a correspondingly spindly form) so that the whole scene is as far from Suffolk as possible. Donkeys are also constantly inserted into these pictures, often along a horizon, which reminds us that, later in the century, the donkey, no doubt because of its varied silhouette, was considered the most "picturesque" of animals. The pleasing contrast between a prevailing romantic and artificial air and sharply and even humorously observed local nature is clearest in the Woburn picture (pl. 41) where the aged ploughman in the background has his shirt sticking out through a hole in the seat of his pants. The last of the pictures which may have been painted with a chimney-piece intention is the so-called *Sunset* in the Tate Gallery (pl. 65). A drawing in private hands at Oxford (which may be a copy) inscribed as by or after Gainsborough in 1759, is sufficiently close in style to the *Sunset* to make that date probable. After moving to Bath Gainsborough seems to have been determined that his landscapes should stand on their own and that he would do no more chimney-pieces.

Gainsborough's prices

The evidence available for Gainsborough's scale of prices at different moments of his career is almost wholly derived from the far too small number of receipts which have so far been discovered. For portraits Thicknesse asserts that he at first charged five guineas a head and raised it to eight. For a half-length in 1758 he was charging fifteen guineas (*Mr Wayth*), and the year he moved to Bath and his first few months there, he still charged only eight guineas for a head (*Mr Lee* and *Mr Lucy*). At some date in the 1760s, perhaps fairly soon after settling in Bath, since the rush of clients seems to have been very considerable from the beginning, he raised his prices to twenty guineas for a head, forty for a half-length, and presumably eighty for a whole-length. Between 1770 and 1772 he again raised his prices to thirty, sixty and one hundred guineas, and this scale seems to have remained constant until 1787, when he again raised them to forty, eighty and one hundred and sixty guineas.

We are less well informed of his landscape prices. For the chimney-piece for Thicknesse in 1753 he wanted to charge fifteen guineas, and the two for the Duke of Bedford of 1755 were fifteen for the smaller and twenty-one guineas for the larger (43 ×51 in.). An upright landscape (57 ×47 in.) was sold to Sir William St Quintin in 1766 for forty guineas. For a large landscape for the Prince of Wales he charged a hundred guineas in 1785, and for the three landscapes bought by the Duke of Rutland about 1785 (which may have been on his hands for some time) he charged two hundred and twenty guineas. His late fancy pictures, as works of greater original invention, he valued more highly than his other works, and it is probable that the prices put upon the pictures at the private exhibition for sale at Schomberg House in 1789, after Gainsborough's death, were his own prices. A few of these pictures were probably cheap because they were unfinished. The average for the small landscapes (about 11 ×13 in.) was thirty guineas: the next size varies from fifty to eighty guineas, and the large landscapes of his last period range from one hundred and fifty to two hundred and two hundred and fifty guineas, while *A peasant smoking at a cottage door* (Cat. no. 1011) was priced at five hundred guineas. The fancy pictures which remained unsold were the Newcastle *Two boys* (eighty guineas); the *Boy with a cat*—probably unfinished, two hundred and fifty guineas; its finished companion four hundred guineas. For the *Woodman* he seems to have received five hundred guineas.

Portraits of the Bath period (1760-1774)

Before settling in Bath in October 1759 Gainsborough seems to have more or less exhausted the possible patronage for portraits in Suffolk, and there is some evidence that he was travelling round painting portraits in noble houses. A letter from the poet Whitehead (Harcourt MSS.) speaks of him as at the Earl of Jersey's house at Middleton in December 1758, and 19 April 1759 is the date of the receipt for two portraits of the Lees of Hartwell not far away. From the moment he settled in Bath a steady flow of sitters came to his studio, and an examination of the family connections of many of the sitters of the early 1760s shows that some sort of friendly grapevine must have been active among interrelated families in Bristol and Somerset. Gainsborough soon made personal friends with certain families such as the Prices of Foxley (later, in the person of Sir Uvedale Price, who was twenty years younger than Gainsborough, to play an important role in the theory of the "picturesque"), Lord Bateman and Sir William St Quintin: and he was given an opportunity, such as he had never had before, to see, in the collections of the West Country, old masters and especially the works of Van Dyck. During the Bath years he merely developed the modified rococo vein of landscape which he had practised before—and he had less time to paint landscapes than either before or after—but, as a portraitist, he became a new man. The first portraits of 1760 (*Mr Lucy* and *Mr Wise*) are still timid and inexperienced, but a small group of half-lengths of about 1760/61 show an enormous stride forward. The best of these are of oldish men of strong character—*Lord Nugent* (pl. 57), *Sir William St Quintin* (pl. 59), *Mr Coward* (pl. 58) and the elder *Uvedale Price* (pl. 60). In these the figure almost bulges out of the picture plane, and the modelling of the features by a sort of hatching method is very pronounced. This recalls his remark, in a letter of 1758 (Whitley, p. 20) to a patron, about "the touch of the pencil which is harder to preserve than smoothness": but in fact the prevailing taste gradually forced Gainsborough to conceal this.

Gainsborough's chief aim in portraiture during the next few years was to try to graft all the elegance he could learn from Van Dyck (and we know that he visited Wilton amongst other houses) on to his own native, informal style. Admirable as are some of his heads at this time, and a great number of his half-lengths, it is by the full-lengths of these years that we can best watch his development and judge of his quality. Public exhibitions in London began (at the Society of Artists) only in 1760 and these were a new means by which a painter living in the provinces could make himself known. In 1760 he does not seem to have felt that he had a work of sufficient importance to send to London, but, from 1761 onwards, he sent a series of full-length portraits (and a very few landscapes) which are perhaps his finest and most original achievements. He probably visited London annually and arranged appointments for sitters during his stay there, for there is a letter (Woburn MSS.) of 7 January 1765 to the Duke of Bedford's agent in which he writes: "I should be much obliged if you would also acquaint the Duchess that 'tho' my Ill Health forbids my following Business in London (to which I have frequent invitations) Her Grace may nevertheless command me at any time to paint *any of The Family* there."

The series of exhibited full-lengths of these years is:

Society of Artists 1761. *Earl Nugent* (pl. 64).
1762. *Mr Poyntz* (pl. 63).
1763. *Mr Quin* (pl. 69).
Mr Medlycott (pl. 68).

Portrait of Mrs Kilderbee (née Wayth) [416] *The Ipswich Museum and G. Oliver and Sons, St. Catherine's House, Portsmouth Road, Guildford, Surrey. By Courtesy of The Connoisseur*

Society of Artists 1765. *General Honywood* (pl. 83).
Colonel Nugent (pl. 89).
1766. *Garrick* (pl. 86).
Dr Charlton (pl. 87).
Mr and Mrs Byam (?) (pl. 82).
1767. *Lady Grosvenor* (now cut down).
Duke of Argyll (pl. 95).
Lord Vernon (pl. 97).
1768. *Earl of Bristol* (pl. 105).
Hon. T. Needham (pl. 104).
Royal Academy 1769. *Countess of Sefton* (pl. 111).
Lord Rivers (pl. 110).
1770. *Lady Eardley and child* (pl. 126).
The Blue Boy (?) (pl. 127).
1771. *Lady Sussex and child* (pl. 128).
Lady Ligonier (pl. 131).
Lord Ligonier (pl. 130).
Captain Wade (pl. 129).
1772. *Lady M. Fordyce* (pl. 136).
The Linley sisters (?) (pl. 145).

At least a further two dozen life-size full-lengths date from this period of fourteen years, including such masterpieces as the *Lord* and *Lady Howe* (pl. 88), *Mrs Portman* (pl. 70) and *Mr Truman* (pl. 117). The one piece of evidence we have for how long it took Gainsborough to paint a full-length is in his letter to Unwin of 10 July 1770, referring to the two Ligonier pictures, where he describes a visit to George Pitt (Lord Rivers) "who had got two whole length canvasses, and his son and daughter . . . in readiness to take me prisoner for a month's work".

The way in which Gainsborough refined his style under the guidance of Van Dyck can best be seen by comparing, for instance, the *Mrs Thicknesse* (pl. 62) of 1760, which Mrs Delany saw in the painter's studio and described to her sister as "a most extra-ordinary figure, handsome and bold. but I should be very sorry to have any one I loved set forth in such a manner", with the *Lady Sefton* (pl. 111) of 1769. The latter is an eighteenth-century version of Van Dyck of hardly surpassable refinement. In the same way the male portraits of 1761/63, which show the most delightful variety of informal poses, carried on from the small-scale full-lengths of his Suffolk period, give way to the Vandyckian elegance of *Captain Wade* (pl. 129). No doubt this change was partly due to the prevailing taste of his patrons, but Gainsborough taught himself how to do it by a study of the old masters, especially Van Dyck, just as he modified his landscape style under the influence, partly of Rubens, and partly (one presumes) of Watteau.

The habit of painting his figures in a subdued light—and, in consequence, to be seen, under ideal conditions, in subdued lighting—probably grew on Gainsborough during these years. The portraits of *Earl Nugent* and *Mrs Portman* show more or less the way in which the light was admitted into his studio in the earlier 1760s. But he increasingly became interested in the play of reflected lights in silks and satins and the prodigious painting of Lady Sefton's dress involves a much more subdued lighting. Indeed a number of such pictures come to life in a remarkable way when seen by artificial light. The consequence of this is that Gainsborough's pictures more and more needed sympathetic hanging to show them off to proper advantage, and the conditions of public exhibition in eighteenth-century London were as unfavourable to them as possible. Gainsborough's successive quarrels with the Royal Academy (the first was in 1773) all centred round this point. Alone of painters of any consequence Gainsborough resisted the temptation to modify his style for exhibition purposes.

Studio method

The normal practice in Gainsborough's time was for portrait painters to employ assistants in painting their draperies and other accessories. In the tenth of his letters to Jackson Gainsborough speaks of this practice, certainly without disapproval, and almost as if he employed it himself: "There is a branch of Painting", he says, "next in profit to portrait, and quite in your power without any more drawing than I'll answer for your having, which is Drapery and Landskip backgrounds. Perhaps you don't know that whilst a face painter is harrassed to death the drapery painter sits and earns five or six hundred a year, and laughs all the while." Yet the consensus of contemporary evidence is that Gainsborough himself did not employ one. I can only point to two examples which seem to show the intervention of a drapery painter (*Miss Cunliffe* and *Lord Harborough*) and I suspect that one of these was left unfinished when he left Ipswich and the other when he left Bath and that the client was probably responsible for calling in outside help.

Reynolds speaks with admiration of Gainsborough's method "of forming all the parts of his picture together; the whole going on at the same time, in the same manner as nature creates her works". This may have been true of his last years, but the unfinished *Captain Matthew* (pl. 151) shows that, in fact, at any rate in his portraits, he entirely completed the face before bringing the rest of the picture to anything but the sketchiest condition. And the immense delays in finishing certain portraits, such as the *Mrs Awse* and the *Mrs Unwin* (the latter of which was on hand for eleven years!) suggest that this was his normal method.

We hear of no studio assistant beyond his nephew, Gainsborough Dupont, who seems to have lived with the painter and his family from about the time when they settled in Bath, when Dupont was about five. He was formally apprenticed to his uncle at the age of seventeen (in 1772), but he no doubt made himself useful about the studio for some years before that, and the existence of certain contemporary replicas of some

[22]

of Gainsborough's Bath period portraits suggests that there may have been other helpers. There are, for instance, no less than three versions of each of the two portraits of *Thomas Prowse* and *Mrs Prowse*. Comparing the photographs one can perhaps come to the conclusion that one of them is *the* original, but the others seem at least to be exactly contemporary and done under Gainsborough's own eye. Similarly, in 1765, an original and two copies were ordered from the artist of the portrait of the *Duke of Bedford*. In view of the great amount of business Gainsborough had during these years, and the slightly inferior quality of the repetitions, it seems pretty certain that he did, to a limited extent, employ a studio assistant.

Landscapes of the Bath period

We are very much less well documented on the sequence of Gainsborough's landscapes than we are on his portraits. At the Society of Artists he exhibited only "A large landskip" in 1763; "A large landscape with figures" in 1766 (which can be identified with some certainty with pl. 92); and "A landskip and figures" in 1767. There are, of course, also the landscape backgrounds of the dated portraits to help us, but I am not sure whether Gainsborough's landscape-background style quite kept pace with his style in pure landscape, since there is a certain difference in intention between the two. There is also a clue to a possible influence in the portrait of *Uvedale Tomkyns Price* (pl. 60), who died in 1764 and must have been painted soon after 1760.

Price was the father of Sir Uvedale Price (1747–1829), who later became famous from his *Essay on the Picturesque*, 1794, in which he came out strongly in favour of natural beauty. It is possible, however, that the father was the originator of the younger Price's ideas, for, in Gainsborough's portrait, he is holding a crayon in his hand, and a drawing of trees, and another drawing, in the same style, hangs on the wall behind. Gainsborough sometimes puts pictures which are clearly fragments of his own landscapes on the back walls of his portraits, but nowhere else does he put a drawing, and it seems reasonable to suppose that Price was the author of the drawings in the portrait. We know that Gainsborough made drawings of trees in Price's park at Foxley and the younger Price, in later life, speaks of often walking with Gainsborough round the countryside. If the elder Price really was the originator of a movement in favour of admiring the natural beauty of the English scene, it would help to account for the curious way in which Gainsborough, in his painted landscapes of the 1760s and 1770s, seems to anticipate the younger Price's theorizing of the 1790s.

The obituarist of the *London Chronicle*, who names Wynants as the first model for Gainsborough, says the second of the artist's landscape styles was based on Ruisdael. This has generally been supposed to refer to his later Suffolk manner, since the largest of his Suffolk landscapes (pl. 46) is in fact a free copy in reverse from a Ruisdael in the Louvre. But I think a much more intimate influence from Ruisdael is visible in what appear to be the important landscapes of the early 1760s. The largest and grandest is that at Worcester, Massachusetts (pl. 66), which could well have been the picture shown at the Society of Artists in 1763. This is a study of a storm of wind among thick foliage, with a lowering grey sky and a lurid white light on the distant hills. The shadows of the main tree masses are very dark, as in Ruisdael, and Gainsborough is attempting something much more impressive and poetical than in any of the Suffolk landscapes. Thick masses of foliage are also found in the Scampston picture of 1766 (pl. 92), though the figures, a rustic dallying with a milkmaid, belong to the same pastoral world as in the Woburn chimney-pieces. Soon after this, however, the rival influence of Rubens begins to make itself felt. The *Harvest Waggon* (pl. 99), which may well be the picture shown in 1767, has its main figure group adapted from the group in Rubens's *Deposition from the Cross*, of which Gainsborough is known to have seen and copied (pl. 291) the reduced version which was then at Corsham and is now in Lady Lee's collection. A letter to Garrick of 1768 (Whitley, p. 62) reveals that Gainsborough had lately seen and admired Rubens's *Watering Place* (then at the Duke of Montagu's and now in the National Gallery in London) and the influence of that picture is visible in the Toledo *Returning from market* (pl. 98). These last two pictures have a much higher key of colour than the Worcester and Scampston ones, and the character of the figures has also changed. They are no longer merely rustic-pastoral but have a sort of ideal elegance, which is neither of the purely rustic world nor yet of the world of fashion. They are, as it were, the sort of human beings who are worthy of Gainsborough's trees and encourage the eye to "return to them with more glee". We shall perhaps learn the sort of beings they are when we come to consider Gainsborough's "fancy pictures" of the 1780s.

There is no certainty about which are the landscapes of the later Bath years, which coincide with the first years of the new Royal Academy. There does not seem to have been any break in style between the Bath and London periods, although direct access to the natural sources of his landscape must have been much rarer in London and he must have depended more on his old drawings and on his artificial landscape constructions with a model. He sent a single landscape to the Exhibitions of 1769 and 1770, two to that of 1771, and ten "landscapes, drawings, in imitation of oil painting" to that of 1772, and he did not further exhibit at all at the Academy until 1777. It is not quite clear what the works shown in 1772 were like. They were probably not merely varnished watercolours, but pictures such as no. 926, which appears to be mainly crayons heavily varnished, and on paper mounted on canvas. Without analysis the exact technique is inscrutable, but it seems that around 1772 Gainsborough was interested in making crayons look like oil pictures, and also trying to make oil paint imitate crayons. The background to the *Lady Margaret Fordyce* (pl. 136), which was shown at the Royal Academy in 1772, is a notable example of this, and for this reason it seems probable that a small group of landscapes, in which oil paint is used in a crayony way, should be dated around 1772. These are in particular nos. 924 and 925 (pls. 134, 135). There is some sort of tradition that Lord Camrose's large landscape (pl. 123) was shown at the

Academy for 1771 and it is probable that the landscapes with a more or less scratchy foliage date from before the London period, and also those in which trees in both spring and autumnal foliage appear on the same scene. The next certain date is the Tate Gallery *Watering Place* of 1777 (pl. 181), and an important group of landscapes has to be fitted in before then. These centre round the picture at Holloway College (pl. 115), which was seen at Stourhead in 1776. They have predominantly swinging curves and fairly solidly painted figures. Their content is strictly rustic and pastoral, and they do not exhale that faint townsman's nostalgia for the country which one can detect in the series which centres round the compositions called "The Cottage Door".

Gainsborough and de Loutherbourg

It was in 1774 that Gainsborough settled in London for the rest of his life. An influence on his art for this period, which has perhaps been underestimated, is de Loutherbourg, whose oil landscapes are unimportant, but whose experiments in lighting and scene painting fascinated Gainsborough. According to W. T. Parke[14] it was in December 1773 that Loutherbourg, who was scene-master for Garrick at Drury Lane, "first introduced his newly-invented transparent shades, so much admired afterwards in his popular Exhibition called 'The Eidophusikon', which, by shedding on them a vast body and brilliancy of colour, produced an almost enchanting effect". It is not wholly clear what this means, but it seems that Gainsborough experimented with this method in 1775, when he and other painters did some life-size figures, which were "all transparent and are lighted behind"[15] for Bach and Abel's new concert room. William Jackson also has a relevant passage[16] in his "Character of Sir J. Reynolds", saying: "Gainsborough once dealt in red shadows; and, as he was fond of referring everything to nature, or, where nature was not to be had, to something substituted for it, he contrived a lamp with the sides painted with vermilion, which illuminated the shadows of his figures, and made them like the splendid impositions of Rubens."

When Loutherbourg produced his Eidophusikon in 1781, which was a sort of extension, with moving scenes, of this principle, Gainsborough repeatedly visited it and helped to manipulate the scenes; and soon afterwards he made a small peepshow for himself, with little glass pictures (pls. 261–268), which were illuminated from behind. During the whole of his London period Gainsborough seems to have been to some extent preoccupied with heightening his style by artificial effects of this sort—both in portraits and in landscapes. It was an attempt at introducing something which it is difficult not to describe as "glamour".

Portraits of the earlier London years (1774-1781)

Gainsborough had quarrelled with the Royal Academy at the time of the 1772 exhibition and he had sent nothing during his last two years at Bath. He did not in fact exhibit there again until 1777, and his abstention may perhaps have been trying to make an apparent virtue of necessity. It is likely that a weighty reason for his leaving Bath was that the springs of patronage were drying up—as Wright of Derby was to find when he moved to Bath after Gainsborough's departure: and he does not seem to have found it altogether easy to establish his position as a portrait painter among the greater number of rivals that was to be found in London. In fact he probably waited until he could send a really remarkable contribution to the Academy, in 1777, before exhibiting in public again. We know of remarkably few portraits certainly painted during the years 1774–1777 and the only full-length is the *Lord Folkestone*, of 1776, painted for the great room of the Royal Society of Arts, which was merely a posthumous enlarge-ment from a half length by Hudson. It is unlikely that Gainsborough would have undertaken such an unsatisfactory kind of commission if he had been well employed in the portrait way. The *Hon. William Fitzwilliam* of 1775 (pl. 160), the *Paul Cobb Methuen* (pl. 167) and *Thomas Pennant* (pl. 196), both of 1776, are the only certainly dated portraits beyond some of his musical friends, such as J. C. Bach and the Linleys. These are admirable examples but make no advance on the work he was doing at Bath: and the number of portraits which one can tentatively place in these years is remarkably small—of full-lengths only *Mrs Lowndes-Stone* and *Lady Brisco* (pl. 165). But by 1777 he had started to receive commissions from the Royal Family, who were temperamentally averse to the grandiose manner of Reynolds; and it was probably this royal patronage which effectively established his position as a portrait painter in Lon-don. With it he could afford to exhibit at the Academy once more and, in 1777, he showed the full-lengths of the *Duke* and *Duchess of Cumberland* (pls. 182, 183), as well as the astonishing *Mrs Graham* (pl. 173) and the portrait of one of his closest musical friends, *C. F. Abel* (pl. 171). In all these there is a heightened romantic feeling, a deliber-ate search for "glamour", which, in the *Mrs Graham*, once the first feeling of astonish-ment at its fabulous dexterity has worn off, seems to fall into excess. These portraits are in a style of remarkable formal elegance which almost overshadows the painter's concern for likeness. Up to the end of his life, on the relatively few occasions when he had a sitter with a pronounced individuality (such as *Mark Beaufoy* (pl. 231) or *Nathaniel Cholmley* (pl. 234), Gainsborough's gifts of giving a likeness are unimpaired: but his portraits become increasingly essays in poetic moods, which often verge perilously on the eccentric. The last important full-lengths in which the figures are still solidly planted on the earth, and in which the rival tendencies towards personality and pattern are in perfect control, are the *George III* and *Queen Charlotte* shown at the Academy of 1781. The latter must rank as one of the most splendid of all royal portraits (pl. 185).

The portraits of the 1780s

During the last six years of his life, when Gainsborough was in his fifties, his art enters a new phase, which is both highly creative and experimental. Perhaps all artists who are, to the extent that Gainsborough was, largely self-taught, develop an awareness of their true powers rather late, unless some fortunate accident helps them on. Probably his genuine impatience with what he calls "face painting" delayed for him the discovery that the portrait could be used as an imaginative vehicle for conveying artistic ideas very different from the mere establishment of a good likeness. Perhaps a painter can also only so temper his portraits when he has reached a position of eminence in his profession, which enables him to some extent to pick and choose his sitters. I do not mean that *all* Gainsborough's late portraits have this special quality, only that a sufficient number of the important full-lengths of these years form a consistent group, which, if we are to do them justice, must be judged by quite different standards from those we use for judging his earlier portraits, and even for judging eighteenth-century portraits in general. Gainsborough was a most sensitive and intelligent artist and we must give him the credit for this by assuming that he had some specific artistic purpose in mind in these works. In recent years "professional criticism" (as opposed to "popular judgment") has been inclined to slight these late works, because they were the first of Gainborough's pictures which appealed to "millionaire taste", and because one supposed that this taste was always bad and was manipulated by the machinations of the art-trade! It should also be remembered that, for a whole generation of art historians—until, in fact, *The Morning Walk* was generously lent for public exhibition and finally acquired for the nation in 1954—these pictures were very difficult to see. Only the less felicitous, such as the *Lord Sandwich* at Greenwich or the *Baillie Family*, have been normally available for public inspection, and one or two of them have neither been exhibited or reproduced.

This group of pictures includes especially the following full-length portraits:

R.A. 1782	*Madame Baccelli* (pl. 235).
R.A. 1782	*Master Nicholls* (pl. 241).
R.A. 1783	*Duke of Northumberland* (pl. 242).
1783/86	*Lord Rodney* (pl. 280).
1784	*Mrs John Douglas* (pl. 237).
1784	*The Three Princesses* (colour plate): now cut down.
1785	*The Morning Walk* (pl. 274).
1785/86	*Lady Sheffield.*
1787	*Lady Bate Dudley* (pl. 278).
1788	*12th Duke of Norfolk.*
1788	*Lady Petre* (pl. 276).

Certain experimental portraits in which more than a single figure is involved (sometimes a horse or hounds rather than other figures make up the group) belong to this series, but they are more evidence of Gainsborough's ambitions than of his success—*T. W. Coke*, *Sir Peter Burrell* (pl. 279), *Sir Francis Sykes*, *The Marsham children*, and the very curious *Sloper family*, which was cut into three or four pieces by the art trade, because it was altogether too bizarre! It is significant that these last five pictures all date from the last three years of Gainsborough's life, and that William Jackson records that Gainsborough said, on his death bed, that he was sorry to leave life just as he was *beginning* to do something with his art.

There are two points especially worth noticing about the group of eleven portraits I have picked out (there are some eighteen more full-lengths from these years, which I have omitted only because they seem to me less successful). Few of the sitters have decided individual character (*Lord Rodney* alone excepted), and the pose and stance of the figures is of a different character from Gainsborough's earlier conventions. The rather insipid cross-legged ease of many of his earlier figures has vanished and there is often movement or action: but, whether in movement or repose, we are reminded, in these late paintings, of a much older European figure tradition. Gainsborough has, I think, been deliberately taking a leaf from Reynolds's book. He has learned to elevate his portrait style by borrowing from the traditional European repertory of the history painter. Mr Steegman pointed out some years ago[17] that the 1784 Gainsborough of *Captain Berkeley* was a deliberate quotation, perhaps at the sitter's instigation, of Reynolds's earlier Keppel (though not an altogether happy one); and the *Lord Rodney*, on which Gainsborough was at work at the same time, is another experiment in the dramatic and historical vein. It is much more in the theatrical tradition than Reynolds, with its cascade of fleur-de-lysed drapery suggesting the sitter's recent defeat of the French fleet; but it is a new experiment in the field of historical action portraiture parallel with what Copley was doing at the same time.

The *Baccelli*, a life-size figure captured in the movement of the dance, is an experiment of even greater boldness. Gainsborough seems to have been deliberately trying to move in directions which especially suited his own technical methods and were unattainable to Reynolds's more ponderous studio procedure. It is here that one can best see the reward of the virtue Reynolds praises in Gainsborough, "his manner of forming all the parts of his picture together; the whole going on at the same time, in the same manner as nature creates her works". It is the "movement of the pencil" in the exquisite handling of the draperies which carries on the movement of the dance throughout the whole figure. It is because we have been prone to judge such a picture as a portrait in the conventional sense, instead of as the solution of a quite different artistic problem, that it has met with less approval than it deserves.

The *Master Nicholls* and the *12th Duke of Norfolk* are the most deliberate attempts at doing Van Dyck over again—and thus belonging to the European tradition. The *Morning Walk* and the *Lady Sheffield* perhaps owe as much to Watteau as to Van Dyck. At the time he was painting them he was also engaged upon the picture known as *The Mall* (pl. 243), in which small-scale female figures of considerable elegance are walking forward in a woodland glade. These figures were studied from a home-made doll and Gainsborough's friend Bate-Dudley specifically refers to the picture, while it was being painted, as "in the manner of Watteau". Just as we shall find that the Fancy Pictures

Portrait of John Purling [566] *Leger Galleries, 13 Old Bond Street, London, W.1. By Courtesy of The Connoisseur*

of the 1780s are the small figures from his earlier landscapes enlarged to the scale of life and studied over again from the model, so these late "portraits" (as we call them), *The Morning Walk* and *Lady Sheffield* are the Watteauesque figures from *The Mall*, enlarged to the scale of life, and studied from suitable models. His sitters were of sufficiently un-formed character, of sufficient promise of loveliness—and perhaps of melancholy—for this translation, and we can only judge these pictures justly by ranging them with the fancy pictures and neglecting the names of the sitters, which happen to have survived.

The two latest of Gainsborough's portraits of ladies, the *Lady Bate Dudley* and the *Lady Petre*, carry this style a step further. At first sight one is inclined to consider them romantic to the point of being bizarre. Their portrait content (in accordance, perhaps, with the sitters' characters) is no more positive than a lingering fragrance. The figure and the trees have an equal value in the design: they blend into one another in an accord which is emphasized by the artist's handling of the paint. The shadows in the flesh tones of *Lady Bate Dudley* are the green of the foliage which supports and justifies her sylph-like existence. Considering these pictures as works of art we must abandon all preconceptions about portraiture and judge them as if they were *Nympheas* by Monet.

Although in these last years Gainsborough had discovered a way of translating his sitters into works of abstract art, his genuine capacity as a portrait painter was not diminished on the rare occasions that he had a chance of using it. Judged purely by the standards of portraiture the *Mrs Siddons* (pl. 250) of 1785 is perhaps his masterpiece. A serious critique of a picture of the English school by a foreigner of equal learning and taste is so rare, and the judgment so perceptive, that I will quote what Thoré-Burger[18] said of the picture, when he saw it at the Manchester Exhibition of 1857: "The great tragic actress, who interpreted the passions with such energy and such feeling, and who felt them so strongly herself, is better portrayed in this simple half length, in her day dress, than in allegorical portraits as the Tragic Muse or in character parts. This portrait is so original, so individual, as a poetic expression of character, as a deliberate selection of pose, as bold colour and free handling, that it is like the work of no other painter. It is useless to search for parallels, for there are none. Veronese a little—but no, it is a quite personal creation. This is genius."

The Landscapes of the London period

If we are correct in supposing that Gainsborough had fewer portrait commissions than usual during his first two years in London (1775/76), it would be natural to suppose that he had more leisure for painting landscapes. That this was so we cannot say with any certainty, for we are very ill provided with dated examples until the time of the Royal Academy of 1781, when Gainsborough for the first time showed some seapieces. The only certain (or nearly certain) examples are *The Watering Place* (pl. 181) which was at the Academy of 1777, and the Huntington version of *The Cottage Door*, which was probably at the Academy of 1780 (pl. 203). It is perhaps likely that the "Cottage Door" theme, with its suggestion of what the townsman longs for about the rural scene, may have preoccupied Gainsborough during these years and that the various versions of it, which seem to culminate in the Huntington picture, were painted during these years. The figures which inhabit these pictures have a slightly rarified quality of beauty, a sort of less modish Watteau quality, about them than those of the Bath-period landscapes. They appear also in the lovely river landscape at Philadelphia (pl. 122), which has something about it of the feeling of a "day in the country". But it may well be that this picture, in which there lingers something of the ambiguity about spring and autumn foliage, really dates from the last years at Bath.

The Watering Place, the first picture he was to show on his return to the Academy in 1777, is the turning point towards a different style. It is much more classically composed than the earlier pictures and more consciously attempts to vie with Claude as a design. Horace Walpole, in manuscript notes to one of his copies of the Academy catalogue,[19] considered it in the style of Rubens and makes the remarkable statement that it was "by far the finest landscape ever painted in England, equal to the great masters". It was certainly also the most popular and provoked the greatest number of copies and imitations. But it is good evidence for the fact that the great British collectors were not prepared to buy landscapes by British painters, that it was still in Gainsborough's possession at his death and did not find a purchaser until the sale of 1797. It was no doubt this fact, more than any dissatisfaction with himself, which led Gainsborough to change so restlessly his landscape style during the next ten years. In 1778 he showed two landscapes which were companions, and the landscape at Bowood (pl. 125) certainly is composed in a manner which suggests that it was meant to be seen with a companion piece—as nearly all of Vernet's landscapes, which were so much sought after by British patrons, were designed. It is possibly of this landscape that Mrs Thrale remarked[20]: "The subject [is] cattle driven down to drink, & the first cow expresses something of surprize as if an otter lurked under the bank. It is a *naked* looking landscape—done to divert Abel the Musician by representing *his* Country Bohemia in no favourable light . . .". This suggests that it was normal to think of Gainsborough's poetical landscapes with their more or less ideal inhabitants as representing some other country than England, for Bohemia (whose connotations have come down in the world since the eighteenth century) more or less meant "Arcadia" at this time.

The landscape shown in 1779 is unidentifiable, but two of the five which Gainsborough showed in 1780 are (probably) the Huntington *The Cottage Door* and (certainly) a picture now largely destroyed but known from an early coloured aquatint, which shows a sort of translation into contemporary terms of the "Et in Arcadia ego" theme: a peasant and a girl are spelling out an inscription in a ruined churchyard. Some lines from Gray's *Elegy* were printed under the aquatint and the mood of Thomson's *Seasons* is also apparent in the picture, but it is unlikely that Gainsborough, who "detested reading", had any such literary parallel in mind—rather that this mood was in the air and he was sensitive to it.

It is not until the last three years at which Gainsborough was represented at the Academy (1781/83) that we have a certain number of identifiable landscapes. This very important group consists of the following:

R.A. 1781   *Cattle crossing a bridge* (pl. 220).
R.A. 1781   *Fishermen dragging nets* (pl. 226).
R.A. 1781   *Seapiece* (pl. 224 or 225).
R.A. 1782   *The Woodcutter's Return* (pl. 227).
R.A. 1783   *View at the mouth of the Thames* (pl. 244).
R.A. 1783   *Rocky landscape* (pl. 257 or 258).

In both cases of uncertainty the alternatives are pictures of nearly identical character, so that the precise identification is not material to a discussion of their style. This half-dozen landscapes shows remarkable variety and versatility—for four different landscape styles are involved.

The *Cattle crossing a bridge* is perhaps the most rococo, the most ornamental, of all Gainsborough's landscape compositions: it is also the only important one painted as an oval composition, though the canvas is square-cornered, and it was not painted for any specific place, as the artist is reputed to have exchanged it for a violin. The subject content, with pastoral lovers, is the same as in his early pictures. The ruined gateway (surely an artificial ruin?) is a new element which appears in several pictures at this date and is perhaps a concession to contemporary taste. The slowly swinging curves of the composition, which ultimately derive from Rubens, and their inclusion in the oval suggests a possible influence from French prints, and this picture is perhaps closer to Fragonard in mood than any other of Gainsborough's. It marks, however, rather the end of his first mature style: it carries that about as far as it can go, and a soft evening light bathes the picture in a warm, romantic glow. It must have seemed almost too light and ethereal to go with the eclectic classicism of the prevailing Adam style, and one can see why Gainsborough looked around for something different.

The second style that he experimented with in 1781 is the seascape. Bate-Dudley reported in the *Morning Herald* (1 May 1781) that these were Gainsborough's "first attempts in this line"—although he had, of course, painted some estuary scenes in his Suffolk years. The "sea-view", in calm or storm, was still the staple of Vernet's art, but the only sea-painting tradition which existed in England was that of the van de Veldes, which had been carried on in the same style by Monamy, Samuel Scott and Brooking, and had a strongly literal bias, with an accent on the shipping. Gainsborough, who had modelled his woodland style on Ruisdael, may have taken a hint from Ruisdael's shore scenes, but these pictures of 1781 and 1783 are almost wholly original. They stand to his inland landscapes as the piscatory stands to the pastoral genre in poetry—and they are distinctly poetical. Yet there is a stronger accent of naturalism in these than there is in the pastoral landscapes. For a new type of picture Gainsborough has had to look more intensely at nature herself than he had been used to do of late years, and the effect of wind and fresh air in the *Bargaining for fish* (pl. 225) makes it one of the masterpieces of a new genre, which was to be taken up at first palely by Morland, and then with increasing impressiveness by Turner and Bonington. Compared with Vernet's often airless or over-serene prospects (although *Fishermen dragging nets* is a favourite Vernet theme) these paintings of Gainsborough are almost revolutionary. Unfortunately they seem to have been painted fifteen or twenty years too early, before the taste of collectors was ripe for them. One can hardly otherwise account for the fact that he painted only a bare half-dozen such pictures, all presumably in the space of about three years.

The third style exhibited by this group appears in *The Woodcutter's Return* of 1782 (pl. 227). Here figures and landscape do not differ in kind from his earlier style, but the experiments in lighting, clearly under the inspiration of de Loutherbourg's effects, are remarkable and novel. The sun has just set and there is an intense rosy-lemon afterglow. Inside the cottage is a blazing fire, which competes through the diamond windowpanes with the evening light (or perhaps it is the dying sun reflected in the glass, for it is a warm evening). This ingenious and theatrical light effect is clearly one of the points of the picture and we can see Gainsborough striving after similar impressions in a number of later landscapes and also in several of the fancy pictures, which begin to appear in the 1780s.

The fourth style of these years appears in the *Rocky landscape* of 1783, which was either the picture at Sutton Place or that at Philadelphia. Both are experiments in a scene of relatively savage grandeur (what the eighteenth century was prone to call "sublime" scenery) which consciously rival the works of Salvator Rosa and Gaspard Poussin. This landscape is unfit for the gentle pastoral figures of his earlier style, although its inhabitants are only relatively tough. For these too Gainsborough had to look at nature again, and, after the Academy Exhibition (after, that is, his first Salvatorial invention), he visited the Cumberland Lakes in the summer of 1783. He wrote playfully to his friend Pearce (Whitley, p. 210) that he was visiting the Lakes "to show that your Grays and Dr Brownes are tawdry fan-painters. I purpose to mount all the Lakes at the next Exhibition in the great stile . . .". And a group of pictures, such as the one now in the Diploma Gallery of the Royal Academy, show the result of this visit. But Gainsborough in fact had a row with the Academy in 1784 over the placing of the portrait of the *Three eldest Princesses* and never exhibited there again. The more subdued light of his own house, and the possibility of placing his canvases at the height at which he wished them to be seen, probably affected both the tone and style of his subsequent works.

It was pretty certainly about 1783 that Gainsborough designed his show-box,[21] the surviving transparencies for which have now found a permanent home in the Victoria and Albert Museum. This was another direct result of his interest in de Loutherbourg's Eidophusikon, and enabled him to experiment more directly with rival lights than

he had done in *The Woodcutter's Return*. An eye-witness relates[22]: "We may add, of our own knowledge, that Gainsborough in his latter years, was in the habit of sketching designs for the show-box exhibition, from which these transparencies are selected, whilst his intimate friends, who in an evening stroll, calling upon him, sat and sipped their tea. His acquaintance with de Loutherbourg . . . first led him to these amusing experiments." These transparencies were shown in a box with a lighted candle placed behind them, and, in one of them (pl. 262), there is the effect of a lighted cottage soon after nightfall. A great many of the late landscape drawings seem to have been ideas for compositions of this sort, and it seems probable that a number of the small (often, even, tiny) landscapes of this period owe their existence to his obsession with the show-box. It may well be that the glass transparencies which survive are only the remnant of a much larger number, and two of those now in the Victoria and Albert Museum look as if they were replacements by some painter of the Norwich school to make up the number to a dozen. The light from the candles was diffused and varied by a coloured silk screen, placed between the light and the glass, so that remarkable and flickering effects of light must have been produced. It was these evanescent nuances that the artist aimed at in his later works, and this show-box may be considered as a more elaborate alternative to his model landscapes of moss and sticks, etc.

Three paintings of a more or less landscape character appeared in Gainsborough's first private exhibition in the late summer of 1784. One of these (pl. 259) was no doubt the fruit of his visit to the Lakes; but the other two were a new departure—which also was never repeated. These are the pictures now known by the relatively modern titles of *The Mall* (pl. 243) and *Charity relieving distress* (pl. 229). *The Mall* (although the artist appears to have wished to deny it) is in the manner of Watteau, but it is very much brought up to date. Jackson relates that the figures were studied from a doll of the artist's making, and there is a distinct air of a stage-setting. There is also something of social commentary about the scene: as Bate-Dudley remarks, in his account of this exhibition: "Looks of characteristic significance appear to be mutually exchanged by some of the group in passing." Without doubt Gainsborough was branching out into new fields, which were being explored by artists such as Wheatley and the engravers during these years. These pictures are a sort of English equivalent of the contemporary French "modern moral subject". In spite of their considerable charm they are slightly foreign to the heart of Gainsborough's genius: they almost suggest he was turning a serious fellow, and, by his own standards, the figures take up too much of the attention and distract from the landscape.

The next certain information we have about Gainsborough's landscapes is Bate's rather full description of seven which were exhibited in the artist's house in 1786 (Whitley, pp. 255-6). These were all small (the largest about 22×28 in.) and some were said to be "almost minute". The largest was pretty certainly no. 998, but it is a curious fact that none of the others can be identified with even reasonable probability. It seems likely, however, that a group of small landscape compositions (such as pl. 269),

[*33*]

The Market Cart [1002].
London, The Tate Gallery

which have an air of kinship with the transparencies of the show-box, date from about this period. These are perhaps distractions of a leisure hour rather than serious works. Gainsborough's chief creative energies during this period was going into his fancy pictures, and we can see how he regarded these as an extension of his landscape compositions from Mrs Scudamore's *Landscape* of 1786 in which the figures of the *Girl with pigs* and the *Housemaid* are included (pl. 246). It is not altogether easy to guess whether the landscape invention provoked the fancy picture, or whether it was the other way about.

There remain three landscapes of particular importance from these last years which must be considered. The earliest of these is the second version of *The Harvest Waggon* (pl. 270) painted in the winter of 1784/5 and now at Toronto. This is the single example we know of Gainsborough taking up again not merely a theme of one of his earlier compositions, but the actual design, and remodelling it on different and more advanced lines. It is idle to dispute whether one version is "better" than the other, for both are masterpieces, and it is perhaps only the affectionate pride of custody which leads me to prefer the Birmingham version (pl. 99). Not much less than twenty years divides the two pictures and there is no doubt that the Toronto composition is more elaborate and more evolved. The Rubens *Deposition*, which was the direct model for the earlier composition, is now only a faint echo. The straight diagonal lines, which so strongly accent the picture at Birmingham, have given way to a tortuous mass of rolling curves. In the earlier picture, the figure group, though slightly deployed in depth by artful chiaroscuro, remains a more or less frieze-like arrangement before a landscape backdrop: in the later picture the landscape is the essential thing: it curls and twists round a corner into the far distance, and the figure group is used to help the eye perform this task. Figures and landscape are fused into a single unit, as we have seen they were in some of the late full-length portraits of ladies. The elaborate artistry in picture-making of Ruisdael is probably at the bottom of it, but the result is far more rococo than anything Ruisdael ever produced. The lesson of the comparison of the two pictures is that, much more than has generally been realized, Gainsborough in his later years was turning to the study of the old masters. He was really beginning, as he said on his death-bed, to learn something about his art. He had, in fact, achieved a degree of mastery which made him ready to experiment in a new and personal interpretation of landscape painting. For that is what we find in his two last landscape compositions.

These two last landscapes, *The Market Cart* (pl. 286 and colour plate) and *A peasant smoking at his cottage door* (pl. 285), painted as companions, are among the largest and certainly among the most important of his works. They are painted with a Rubens-like breadth of handling and they seem to introduce us into a new world, a world which leads directly on to Constable, as none of the earlier landscapes seemed to do. They lack the insistent ornamental and decorative accents of the earlier compositions, and they interpret the native British scene with a new solemnity and authority. That Gainsborough should have died at this moment of enhanced vision is something of a tragedy.

Gainsborough's Fancy Pictures

The term "fancy-pictures" must have been a standard studio expression in the eighteenth century: Reynolds uses it in his Fourteenth Discourse with specific reference to the pictures by Gainsborough which now come under discussion. The genre perhaps originated with Giorgione, was picked up again a century later by Caravaggio and his imitators, and has not since then entirely died out. It was probably introduced into British painting by Philippe Mercier towards the end of the 1730s, and it was exploited, more on the level of popular art than among serious painters, during Gainsborough's early years of study in London in the 1740s. Reynolds exhibited a picture of this character in most years at the Royal Academy, although his earliest (R.A. 1769) had the slightly pretentious title of *Hope nursing Love*. It was probably only regarded as a serious genre at this time when the figure was on the scale of life. In both Gainsborough's and Reynolds's fancy pictures, contrary to what one would expect from the name, a specific model was always involved, and what makes Gainsborough's especially remarkable is that these figures seem close-ups of the small figures which had previously appeared in his landscapes. Their poetic character is exactly the same: they are almost the rustic inhabitants of an ideal Arcadia suddenly come to life and sitting for their portraits. Gainsborough himself set especial store by them and expected for them prices much higher than he received for either his landscapes or his portraits. His early posthumous reputation was largely founded upon them, for we find Hazlitt, in 1814,[23] at the time of the first retrospective exhibition of Gainsborough's works, speaking "of the fancy pictures, on which Gainsborough's fame chiefly rests . . .". It is only in the present century that they have been relatively forgotten, from the fact that few of them have been easy to inspect. In the last ten years, however, two of the finest have passed to the Museums of New York and Boston.

Although the sequence of fully characteristic fancy pictures does not begin until 1781, there were indications even during the early Suffolk years that the genre was in Gainsborough's mind. The lovely *Shepherd Boy* at Toledo (pl. 34) and Mrs Standring's *Peasant with a donkey* (pl. 35) are small-scale popular anticipations of the later pictures; and the unfinished *Girl with a penny* (Cat. no. 813), which one assumes to have been a study from one of his daughters, if it had been completed, would certainly have ranked as a fancy picture. This can hardly be later than 1760, but the idea does not seem to have germinated fully in Gainsborough's mind until he saw the picture of the *Good Shepherd*, which was then famous as a Murillo in the collection of the Duchess of Bridgewater (although it is in fact only a copy after Murillo by Grimoux). He made a copy after this in 1780, allegedly from memory (Cat. no. 1025), and its similarity of mood with the *Shepherd Boy* (now known only from the engravings) which he exhibited at the Royal Academy in 1781 is so close that Murillo must be assumed as the direct source of his inspiration. This was clearly recognized by Hazlitt. The fancy pictures are also clear evidence of that increasing interest in, and study of, the old masters which has already been noticed. Murillo seems in fact to have been (perhaps after Van Dyck) Gainsborough's favourite painter. He painted a copy of another Murillo and, in 1787, bought the *S. John* (now in the National Gallery in London as the work of a follower of Murillo) for five hundred guineas.

In 1782 Gainsborough exhibited the *Girl with pigs* (pl. 245) which was not only bought (which is surprising) by Sir Joshua Reynolds, but of which Reynolds wrote at the time to Lord Ossory: "It is by far the best picture he ever painted, or perhaps ever will." This remains an unexpected judgment, but one worth exploring. I suspect that what delighted Reynolds about it was that it had something of the air of an old master, or at least of a witty variation on an historical theme, such as he liked his own pictures to be. It is a sort of "Prodigal Son" with the gender transposed, and, if it were conceivable that Gainsborough could have seen Murillo's series of scenes from the story of the Prodigal Son (in which the handling of paint is closer to his own than in any other series of Murillos), one could have spoken of another direct derivation from Murillo. The girl also is seated in a classic pose, which the eighteenth century associated with melancholy or meditation, which contributes to the "old master" air. Yet the picture has the look of real life, since all of it was studied directly from nature, and we know that the piglings were actually visitors to Gainsborough's studio. We may in fact to some degree assent to Reynolds's judgment, and it helps to indicate that we are on the right track in assessing Gainsborough's fancy pictures in this way.

The *Shepherd boys with dogs fighting* at Kenwood, which appeared at the Royal Academy in 1783, is perhaps an exercise in the manner of Snyders, another painter for whom Gainsborough expressed his admiration. In writing of this picture to the Treasurer of the Royal Academy (Whitley, p. 204), Gainsborough makes the curious remark: "I sent my Fighting Dogs to divert you. I believe next exhibition I shall make the boys fighting and the dogs looking on; you know my cunning way of avoiding great subjects in painting. . . ." This is perhaps evidence that the idea of "great subjects" was in his mind and that he was doing his best to paint pictures of the same sort without historic subject matter. He never painted the boys fighting, but he did, in these last years, paint another composition which is a rococo variation on Snyders —the *Greyhounds coursing a fox* (pl. 289). This too is an old master brought up to date.

In the spring of 1785 Gainsborough painted his masterpiece in this genre, the *Cottage Girl with dog and pitcher* (pl. 273), which he sold almost immediately for two hundred guineas. It looked at last as if Gainsborough had found a kind of picture, other than portrait, which he liked to invent and which pleased the collecting class. The relation to Murillo here is obvious, in the colour and handling as well as in the subject, yet it is impossible to consider this picture without thinking of Greuze as well. We know from a letter of 1789 from Mrs Lock to Fanny Burney[24] that engravings after Greuze found their way almost immediately into the London printshops. Greuze's *La cruche cassée*, which is the closest parallel, did in fact appear at a sale in Paris in 1785. The element

Mountain Landscape with Peasants Crossing Bridge [1008] *Washington. National Gallery of Art.*
By Courtesy of Apollo Magazine

of piquancy and sophistication about the Greuze figure, which makes it somewhat distasteful to modern eyes, is agreeably lacking in Gainsborough, but the genre is very much the same. Just as, in the 1750s, Gainsborough had produced an English variation on the French pastoral, so, in the 1780s, he was producing an English variation of the French fancy picture.

The *Woodgatherers* (pl. 281) of 1787 is only less remarkable than the Beit *Cottage Girl* because it has darkened to some extent owing to the excessive fondness for bitumen which Gainsborough sometimes shows in his latest works. It is a strangely noble invention, with what one can only call a Raphaelesque grace about the group of figures, which surely derive from some Renaissance source. In this picture also Gainsborough has combined that interest in ingenious lighting effects, which has been mentioned in relation to the later landscapes. It is the moment of the last ray of sunset, and the sun has disappeared behind the hill at the left. Its last rays fall on the right cheek of the seated red-haired boy and suggest that this effect was painted with the aid of the lantern with its sides painted vermilion to which Jackson makes reference. The same end of sunset effect was intended in the *Girl with a cat* (pl. 282), but so little of the original surface of this picture survives that one can only guess at its artistic intention. Now that the *Woodgatherers* has found a home in the Metropolitan Museum in New York, where it can be readily compared with a variety of masterpieces in other styles, its remarkable originality becomes clear. There is no picture in the least like it in mood or style, and its formal virtues enable it to take its place in any company.

More startling, though of less classic felicity, is the *Haymaker and sleeping girl* (pl. 277) at Boston. This picture is not completely finished and is painted with a greater breadth and boldness of handling than Gainsborough ever showed before. The girl has flame-coloured hair, which helps to give the picture a very high key of colour, and her head is painted in a style which looks backwards to Rubens and forward to Renoir, and with a mastery which compares not unfavourably with either. In invention it is Boucher done over again in the style of Rubens, but with an English accent and more than a side-glance at Correggio.

These last two pictures, which have only recently become available to public inspection, are so different in style from that Gainsborough whom the art trade has taught us to admire, and so novel within the canon of British eighteenth-century painting, that they have not yet made their full impact on either art-historians or on public taste. Yet they are splendid compositions in the style of the old masters, as no other of Gainsborough's pictures are, and, taken in conjunction with his last two major landscapes, they show how fertile and experimental his mind was at the very end of his life. He was even, at that moment, attempting pictures which had a subject content. The *Musidora* at the Tate Gallery, which has been shown to derive, in the figure composition, from a statuette of Adriaen de Vries, is nearer to a subject picture than the others which appeared in Macklin's *Poets' Gallery*, and the unfinished *Diana and Actaeon* (pl. 288) at Buckingham Palace is actually a picture with a historical subject. It shows that such

subjects, treated in the spirit of the French rococo, were by no means above Gainsborough's powers.

Pictures of animals

Although the single portraits of pet animals by Gainsborough amount to no more than
a handful, the number of dogs which diversify his human portraits is surprisingly large,
and many of them are more memorable than their masters. Gainsborough no doubt
found them more sympathetic and easier to understand, but their inclusion is also a
deliberate element in that search for informality, in that attempt to paint the private,
rather than the public, face, which is the secret of the charm of many of his best portraits.
Here Gainsborough falls into a tradition which was not unknown to the High Renaissance. The Pontormo at Frankfurt, the Lotto *Man and his wife* once at Gatchina, and
several of Titian's portraits employ the same device of echoing the character and
softening the formality of the portrait by the addition of pet dogs. Reynolds, in his
George Selwyn at Dalmeny, achieves the same result, but most of Reynolds's dogs,
like those of Hudson before him, have only an ornamental and not an intimate relation
to the portrait. The more solemn feelings of the age were against this sort of informality,
as one can deduce from the action of the Royal Society at Edinburgh, which declined
the portrait of the *Third Duke of Buccleuch* (pl. 120), although it had been painted as a
gift to the Society, because the dog was thought to be inappropriate. But it is only the
pet animals, those who help to soften the mask of formality, which arouse Gainsborough's sympathy and interest. The chargers who occasionally appear in his full-
length portraits are rarely interesting.

Drawings

A full study of Gainsborough's drawing would demand another book. Dr Woodall in
1939 catalogued nearly five hundred landscape drawings, but many more have turned
up since: the figure drawings have never been seriously studied, although they are very
much fewer in number. He exhibited "A Book of Drawings" at the Royal Academy
of 1770, and he gave away occasional drawings to friends or amateur pupils, but Bate-
Dudley reported, at the time of the Gainsborough sale in 1789, that he could never
be prevailed upon in his lifetime to sell any of his drawings.

The drawings of Gainsborough's Suffolk years seem mainly to have been intended
strictly for study or for use in paintings. They are described by Thicknesse as "a great
many sketches of Trees, Rocks, Shepherds, Plough-men, and pastoral scenes, drawn on
slips of paper, or old dirty letters, which he called *his riding School*". That is, they were
the means he used to teach himself to draw landscape and to compose pictures. They
are scrappy, and never aim at composition drawings for their own sake: to this period

also belongs such a drawing as that in the Whitworth Art Gallery at Manchester, which is a copy of a composition by Ruisdael. When he moved to Bath he seems to have made a number of drawings of local tree-growth and picturesque fragments of the local scenery, perhaps under the influence, as I have suggested, of the elder Uvedale Price—but from a relatively early date, probably from about the middle 1760s, the great bulk of his landscape drawings take on the character of landscape compositions, done out of his head and with no strict topographical content. Many were no doubt made of an evening with the help of his table model of cork, glass, twigs, etc.: and, after the beginning of the 1780s, many of them may have had as their general intention a suitable composition for the show-box. Although a considerable number of these drawings are closely related to oil paintings, I doubt if they were primarily considered as studies for oil paintings. They are compositions in their own right, an enormous repertory of possible landscape compositions, some of which he converted almost unchanged into paintings. There are, of course, a number of studies for figure groups which were done as preliminary drawings in order to get the exact arrangement of the figures right: and there are a number of figure studies apparently made from the dressed doll which served as the model for the picture of *The Mall*. From his later years there are very few studies made to help in the arrangement of his portraits. The elaborate process of a series of preliminary drawings was as alien to Gainsborough's practice as it was to Reynolds, but, unlike Reynolds, Gainsborough was a born draughtsman, with a love of line and the play of the crayon. He was first a draughtsman and then a painter, for his painting technique was as close to drawing as he could make it, whereas Reynolds was never a draughtsman at all. Yet Gainsborough's drawings are never necessary preliminaries to his oil paintings: he could do the same thing just as easily directly in paint, and often did so; and it is for this reason that it is not necessary to study the drawings in detail to understand his development as a painter—as it is, for instance, with Alan Ramsay. He also made certain occasional experiments in soft-ground etching.

Unknown, except to his intimate friends, during his lifetime, Gainsborough's landscape drawings form a most remarkable repertory of picturesque motives, which had a great influence after his death. This was partly due to the series of sixty plates admirably engraved by W. F. Wells and J. Laporte of a very fine group of them, which were published by Boydell as *A Collection of Prints illustrative of English Scenery*.

The problem of copies and repetitions

It has already been mentioned that sometimes one or two additional copies would be ordered from the painter of portraits at the same time as the original was commissioned. These do not present much of a problem, nor do the occasional copies made by later hands of portraits for what one might call "family use". Rather few of Gainsborough's sitters were so famous that copies of his portraits would be in demand outside the families of their sitters: but, when they were, as was the case of Pitt or Lord Mulgrave, a very large number of copies exist, very few of which are likely to deceive a careful scrutiny. Certain copies made by Dupont may be deceptive, but the problem of Dupont requires a section to itself.

It is with copies or part-copies or alleged "studies" of the landscapes that a serious problem arises. There is an undated letter from Gainsborough to a Mr Humphrey (perhaps William Humphrey (1722–87) who was six times mayor of Sudbury during Gainsborough's lifetime) in the collection of the Pennsylvania Historical Society, refusing to lend some of his landscapes to copy, since he found that such copies affected the sales of his pictures. This is the only documentary evidence I know that there was any inclination to copy Gainsborough's landscapes in his own lifetime—and it is a little surprising, since there was so little inclination on anyone's part to buy them. He himself did a few repetitions (usually with slight variations) of three or four of his most important designs—notably of the composition with milkmaids, but, in general, his mind was so fertile of landscape inventions that he would have had little inclination to repeat himself. On the other hand there is hardly an important landscape, even from the Suffolk period, of which one or more seemingly quite early versions do not exist—and the number of versions of designs like *The Watering Place* and *The Market Cart* is quite bewildering. In the case of some of the early designs, which were engraved in the 1760s for Panton Betew, the copies were probably made from the engravings, and Ibbetson and perhaps the young Morland may be responsible for some of them. The versions of the later compositions usually pass as originals and their pedigrees are often inextricably confused with those of the genuine original. Many are obvious, but some are clever, copies and I suspect that there must have been a great vogue for making such copies about the time of the retrospective Gainsborough Exhibition of 1814. I have passed over all such versions as I believe to be copies in silence in the catalogue, but it may be useful to mention one or two pictures in public collections in which the copy-original relationship may be observed. There is an accomplished copy at Leicester (E. E. Cook bequest) of the large early landscape at São Paolo (pl. 46): an attentive study of the painting of the sandy lane, the tufts of grass, and the foliage of the trees will show the difference between original and copy. An even cleverer copy is that at Worcester, Mass. (T. J. Ellis bequest) of the original which is no. 846 in the catalogue. The nearly grisaille copy of the Birmingham *The Harvest Waggon*, which is in the Metropolitan Museum, New York, is fairly deceptive in the photograph but does not stand up for a moment under autopsy: and the Victoria and Albert Museum version of *Horses watering at a fountain* is a copy of a kind which is fairly common. When such pictures are obscured by dirty varnish it is often exceedingly difficult to feel certain in what category to place them.

The small versions made for engravings (even although sometimes no engraving was made) of the fancy pictures are another problem. The small *Woodgatherers* in the Tate Gallery, for instance, has never been doubted, but comparison with the big picture in New York makes it clear to me that it is only a reduction, presumably by Dupont, and not an original Gainsborough—and I believe the same to be true of all the other small reductions of these pictures.

Gainsborough Dupont (1754–1796)

Gainsborough's nephew, Gainsborough Dupont, who lived in his house from childhood, was apprenticed to him in 1772, was his assistant in later years, and scraped mezzotints of a number of his later works, was his only close and direct follower and imitator. It was hoped by Bate-Dudley that he would succeed to his uncle's practice, as he did to his studio properties. His qualities as an artist have never been properly assessed and his name is usually only found attached (quite wrongly) to pictures so feeble that the most sanguine owner cannot believe they are by Gainsborough. His single heads, at his best, are in fact almost impossible to distinguish from the average run of his uncle's later portraits, as is attested by the portraits at Southill of *D. Jennings* and *T. Phillips*, which are signed (or at least inscribed in a contemporary hand) "Dupont pinxt. 1789". The Baltimore *Robert Adair*, which I have catalogued as a Gainsborough, may even be the picture of a Mr Adair which Dupont is known to have painted (Whitley, p. 339): and the *Mrs Hatchett* in the Frick Collection has never been doubted as a Gainsborough although it is quite clearly signed *G.D.* This picture has that attenuation of the oval of the face and of the bust, that slight added treacliness of the painting of the hair, which we come to learn as the earmarks of Dupont's style. They appear in the *Queen Caroline*, a free version of the Vanderbank at Goodwood, which was delivered by Gainsborough in 1784 to Lord Sandwich for Huntingdon Town Hall with a letter which I would certainly interpret as meaning that it was the work of Dupont,[25] whose earliest known work it would thus be. Between 1790 and 1795 Dupont exhibited at the Royal Academy a number of portraits which can be identified with greater or lesser certainty, together with a *Cottage Girl* and one or two landscapes. The following portraits provide a skeleton list of pretty certain works against which attributions to Dupont should be judged.

R.A. 1790   *Portrait of Gainsborough* (formerly Lord Annaly). (This was correctly labelled as by Dupont when I first saw it, but has now entered the market as a Gainsborough.)

R.A. 1793   *William Mainwaring* (full-length). At the Middlesex Guildhall.

R.A. 1793   *A lady and her children.* Probably the picture called "The Sheridan family" in Lord Joicey's sale 26/vii/1946 (42).

R.A. 1794   *George III* (full-length). At Windsor Castle.

R.A. 1794   *A young gentleman in the character of a shepherd's boy.* Presumably the picture in Dupont's own sale in 1797. Coll.: Hon. John Hare.

R.A. 1794   *Miss Ormsby* (full-length). Coll.: Lord Harlech: cf. *Burl. Mag.* Sept. 1946.

R.A. 1794   *Mr Quick in the character of Spado.* At the Garrick Club.

R.A. 1795   *Mr Lewis*. Coll.: Lord Glenconner.
1794/6   The big group and the Pitt formerly at Trinity House, London, but destroyed during the last war.

A number of other portraits can be grouped with these and several landscapes with genre scenes, which can be recognized from the 1797 Dupont sale, although they now pass as by Gainsborough, complete an adequate documentation of Dupont. As his uncle's eye and guidance become more a thing of the past, Dupont's mannerisms increase and he hardly has the positive qualities to stand as an independent painter on his own feet. But there need be no longer any excuse for ascribing to him the rubbish that passes under his name, and the possibility that he executed a number of the portraits which generally pass as late works by Gainsborough is considerable.

Gainsborough's influence on the next generation

The emergence of the young Lawrence in the years immediately following Gainsborough's death directed fashionable portraiture into new channels, and, although Hoppner is said always to have had an unfinished Gainsborough portrait in his studio as an example (and at one time owned the *Blue Boy*), he modelled his style in the main on Reynolds. As a portrait painter Gainsborough had no influence to speak of. But as a painter of landscapes and fancy pictures he only really begins to come into his own after his death. His interests in the picturesque in landscape and in the ideal peasant of the sort who entered the British poetic consciousness with the poetry of Wordsworth in the 1790s, enabled the new generation to look at his pictures with that sympathetic understanding which had been lacking in his lifetime. Richard Westall's *Girl going to fetch water* and *A Girl at a cottage door* (both in the possession of the National Trust at Attingham Park), which were shown at the Royal Academy of 1796, are in the direct line of descent from Gainsborough's fancy pictures; and there are many imitations by lesser painters. Thomas Barker of Bath, a somewhat Protean painter, whose work remains to be properly studied, exhibited a fancy picture of a girl in 1797 and painted a series of Woodmen (the most important is at Raby Castle) which derive from Gainsborough's *Woodman in a storm*. Both he and his brother, Benjamin Barker, produced a series of landscapes in deliberate imitation of Gainsborough's earlier style, many of which have passed in recent years as by Gainsborough himself. But the most important spiritual descendent of Gainsborough's landscape style is John Constable. Although many other elements went to form Constable's mature manner—not least among them Jacob Ruisdael and Rubens, who had played such a large part in Gainsborough's own formation—Gainsborough counts for a good deal in Constable's feeling for English landscape. Among the lecture notes which are all that survive of the lectures Constable delivered on landscape painting in the 1830s is a paragraph which is perhaps the most eloquent tribute by a great painter on Gainsborough. "The landscape of Gainsborough", says Constable, "is soothing, tender, and affecting. The stillness of noon, the depths of twilight, and the dews and pearls of the morning, are all to be found on the canvases of this most benevolent and kind-hearted man. On looking at them, we find tears in our eyes, and know not what brings them. The lonely haunts of the solitary shepherd—the return of the rustic with his bill and bundle of wood—the darksome lane or dell—the sweet little cottage girl at the spring with her pitcher—were the things he delighted to paint, and which he painted with an exquisite refinement, yet not a refinement beyond nature. . . ."

Gainsborough's place in British and in European painting

Sir Joshua Reynolds, in his Fourteenth Discourse, stated precisely the exact position of Gainsborough within the British School. "If ever", he says, "this nation should produce genius sufficient to acquire us the honourable distinction of an English School, the name of Gainsborough will be transmitted to posterity, in the history of the Art, among the very first of that rising name." This may seem to certain enthusiasts a very moderate and guarded statement, but a cooler view may judge it to be perfectly correct and to display the astonishing balance and historical detachment of Reynolds. Much painting had been done in England, even by native British artists, before the middle of the eighteenth century, but a native tradition, both original and monumental and capable of forming a background of native style to be handed down from one generation to another, is not found in portraiture before Hogarth's *Captain Coram* of 1740, or in landscape before the Richard Wilsons of the 1750s and the Gainsborough landscapes of the early 1760s. Had Reynolds and Gainsborough not been succeeded by Lawrence and Turner and Constable, we should not have had what a European could call an "English School": Reynolds and Gainsborough would have seemed simply eccentric outcrops of English genius, as one considers Hilliard in the sixteenth, or Dobson in the seventeenth, century. It is because their art was formative of the art of later generations that Hogarth, Reynolds, Wilson and Gainsborough are the real founders of an English school, and Gainsborough, I·think, is only a real founder in his landscapes and in his fancy pieces. It is for this reason that the landscapes and fancy pieces are, proportionately to their total number, so much more fully illustrated in this book than the portraits. The portraits are occasionally splendid and breathtaking, but they founded no tradition, as those of Reynolds did. They depend so much on the brightness and alertness of the painter's individual vision of his sitter. They find their only real successor in Goya, as Roger Fry[26] once pointed out—and Goya was a painter of something of the same unevenness. The relieving of a head seen in full light against a luminous sky of the same tone is a trick which Goya sometimes adopts, and occasional portraits by Goya (such as the *Man in a brown coat* at Boston) are astonishingly like Gainsborough in colour, handling, and even in the characterization of the sitter. It is has been suggested that Goya may have seen mezzotints after Gainsborough, but it is more probable that we merely have to deal with two very strong individualists who sometimes arrived at the same results independently.

In natural gifts, in artistic intuitions, and in sustained lyrical feeling it might be reasonably contended that Gainsborough surpassed any other British painter. One is sometimes led to wonder what he might have achieved had he imbibed the studio training which was the natural lot of Tiepolo or of Fragonard. In the field of pastoral landscape there is sometimes an astonishing similarity between Gainsborough and Fragonard, whose *La rentrée du troupeau* (Coll.: Marquise d'Harcourt) is almost a blend of the Gainsborough at Ryecote (pl. 220) with one of the earlier Woburn pictures (pls. 39, 41). Yet it may be that the most valuable and essential quality of English painting has owed more than we like to admit to that tinge of amateurishness which comes from the lack of a strong Academic tradition. It is the freshness of Gainsborough's perception of form, of colour, of character, and of the rhythms of landscape that makes his pictures, when they have not been overcleaned, a constant delight today. His excellences lie entirely in the realm of feeling rather than of reason, and it has always been difficult to judge him with detachment against an age which was predominantly intellectual. Gainsborough's whole work and career were the exact opposite to everything which Reynolds, in his earlier Discourses, had preached to the young students of the Royal Academy, and it is the strongest evidence of his artistic power—as it is of Reynolds's critical detachment—that the President should have made his remarkable appreciation of Gainsborough's art after his death.

Dr Ralph Schomberg [604] *Reproduced by Courtesy of the Trustees, The National Gallery, London*

NOTES

1   Published by Sydney E. Harrison in *The Connoisseur*, LXII (Jan. 1922, pp. 3 ff., and Feb. 1922, pp. 87 ff.).

2   The letters belong to the Royal Academy of Arts. They are printed in an appendix to Whitley, pp. 379 ff.

3   William Jackson, of Exeter, *The Four Ages, together with Essays on various Subjects*, 1798. The essay on "The character of Gainsborough" is on pp. 147–161, and there is more information about Gainsborough in the "Character of Sir Joshua Reynolds" and in "On Gentlemen artists", p. 229.

4   *A Sketch of the Life and Paintings of Thomas Gainsborough Esq.*, by Philip Thicknesse. Printed for the author . . . 1788.

5   August 4, 1788. It is conveniently reprinted on pp. 36 ff. of *Anecdotes of Painting in England* . . . collected by Horace Walpole and now digested and published . . . by Frederick W. Hilles and Philip B. Daghlian. Volume 5. Yale University Press, 1937.

6   Reprinted as in note 5, pp. 34 f.

7   Letter dated "May 22'nd 1788". It appeared in a sale of autographs, etc., formerly the property of Lord Wantage, Sotheby's, 27 Nov. 1945, 10t. 458.

8   In *Antiques*, New York, Oct. 1956, p. 363.

9   A detailed summary of what is known about the Vauxhall decorations, together with a list and chronology of the paintings, is given by Lawrence Gowing in *Burl. Mag.* XCV (Jan. 1953), pp. 4 ff.

10   Gowing, *op. cit.*, p. 11 (no. 6 and note 27). Fig. 6 shows the detail of a figure which may well have been painted by Gainsborough.

11   I quote from Whitley, p. 358: he puts the date as about 1762, but the letter was probably written to the Lord Hardwicke whom Gainsborough had painted as Lord Royston in 1763, and who succeeded to the title in 1764.

12   *The Four Ages*, 1798, p. 167 n.

13   Cf. Walter Heil, *Art in America*, XXI (Mar. 1933), and *The Pacific Art Review*, Summer 1941. Some of Dr Heil's detailed arguments need correcting from the fact that *The Charterhouse*, which used to be misleadingly labelled 1746, was not in fact painted until 1748.

14   W. T. Parke, *Musical Memoirs*, 1830, vol. i, pp. 2–3. Parke puts the date as December 1775, but *The Christmas Tale* was in fact produced in December 1773.

15   Earl of Malmesbury, *A series of letters of the I'st Earl of Malmesbury, his family and friends*, 1870, I, p. 287.

16 William Jackson, *The Four Ages*, 1798, p. 167.

17 *Burlington Magazine*, Apr. 1942, pp. 98–9.

18 W. Bürger, *Trésors d'art exposés à Manchester*, 1857, p. 388.

19 Quoted by Algernon Graves, *The Royal Academy Exhibitors*, III, 1905, p. 191. The evidence that this picture was the Tate *Watering Place* is in Whitley, *Artists and their friends . . .*, II, 1928, p. 378.

20 *Thraliana*, ed. K. C. Balderston, II, 1942, p. 1082 n.

21 The only proper publication of this is in the *Illustrated London News*, 20 Jan. 1934, pp. 80–81. Until after his death in 1955 these transparencies were built into the door jambs of Mr Ernest Cook's nearly inaccessible house at Bath.

22 Anonymous writer in the *Somerset House Gazette*, 1824, ii, p. 8, on the occasion of the public exhibition of three of these pictures.

23 In the *Champion* for 31 July 1814.

24 Duchess of Sermoneta, *The Locks of Norbury*, 1940, p. 45.

25 Published by J. F. Kerslake in the *Connoisseur*, June 1955, p. 237. Lord Sandwich published Gainsborough's rather jesting and ambiguous letter in *The Times* for 27 Jan. 1955.

26 Roger Fry, *Reflections on British Painting*, 1934, p. 64. Fry's whole section on Gainsborough (whom he rather reluctantly admired, since he disliked British painting) is a most valuable appreciation from the point of view of the practising artist.

BIBLIOGRAPHY

THERE are chapters or sections on Gainsborough in all general books on British painting, as well as a number of short popular biographies which add nothing to the facts about him. I list below only those books or articles of some serious documentary or interpretative value. A long list of bibliographical references (up to 1920) can be found in G. Pauli's article on Gainsborough in the thirteenth volume of Thieme-Becker's *Allgemeines Lexikon der Bildenden Künstler,* but few of these will repay examination. Articles dealing usefully with specific pictures are quoted in the catalogue and are not repeated here.

Armstrong, (Sir) Walter. *T. Gainsborough* (Portfolio Series), London, 1894.

> This is Armstrong's first essay on Gainsborough and is chiefly useful from the fact that certain pictures are illustrated in it which are not to be found elsewhere.

Armstrong, (Sir) Walter. *Gainsborough and his place in English art*, London, 1898.

> This folio volume contains an extensive catalogue, compiled in what would appear today to be a somewhat uncritical manner. It is better to use the revised octavo reprint of 1904, in which the catalogue has been enlarged and a number of its errors corrected.

Baker, C. H. Collins (and M. R. James). *British Painting*, London, 1933.

> This is the best general history of British painting and includes a valuable chapter on Gainsborough.

Baker, C. H. Collins. *Catalogue of British Paintings in the Henry E. Huntington Library and Art Gallery*, San Marino, California, 1936.

> Very detailed entries on the largest group of important Gainsboroughs in the United States.

Catalogues of Exhibitions

The catalogues of the following exhibitions, devoted wholly or in very large part to Gainsborough's works, contain information of value:

(1) The Grosvenor Gallery, London, 1885 (notes by F. G. Stephens).
(2) Ipswich 1927 (notes by P. M. Turner).
(3) Messrs Agnew's, 43 Old Bond Street, London, 1928.
(4) Art Museum, Cincinnati, 1931 (notes by W. H. Siple).
(5) 45 Park Lane (Sir Philip Sassoon's), London, 1936 (notes by E. K. Waterhouse). There is an album of plates also.
(6) Arts Council of Great Britain, 1949 (notes by M. Woodall).
(7) Victoria Art Gallery, Bath, 1951 (notes by M. Woodall).
(8) Tate Gallery, London, 1953 (notes by E. K. Waterhouse).

A Collection of Prints illustrative of English scenery from the drawings and sketches of Thos. Gainsborough, R.A. Engraved by W. F. Wells and J. Laporte. London, n.d. (the watermark on the paper is 1821).

> These lithographs, some of them in colour,

greatly contributed to extending a knowledge of Gainsborough's landscape style.

Cunningham, Allan. *The lives of the most eminent British Painters*, London, 1829. (The edition generally used is that revised and annotated by Mrs Charles Heaton, 3 vols., London, 1879.)

Several legends owe their origin to this work, but it is valuable as collecting together the general information about Gainsborough available in the early nineteenth century.

Davies, Martin. *The National Gallery Catalogues: The British School*, London, 1946.

Much more than a catalogue of the Gainsboroughs in this portion of the National Collections: it is a mine of useful information.

Edwards, Edward. *Anecdotes of Painters . . .*, London, 1808.

A rather disappointing biography, but Edwards (b. 1738) presumably knew Gainsborough and ranks as a contemporary source.

Fulcher, George Williams. *Life of Thomas Gainsborough, R.A.*, London, 1856.

Fulcher was a printer at Sudbury and the biography contains some valuable material from East Anglian sources. The book includes the first catalogue of Gainsborough's work, but it was uncritically compiled from correspondence rather than from autopsy. A second edition, with a slightly enlarged catalogue, is also dated 1856 on the title-page, but may be rather later.

Gower, Lord Ronald. *Thomas Gainsborough*, London, 1903.

The text is little more than a compilation, but there are some illustrations not to be found elsewhere.

Graves, Algernon. *The Society of Artists of Great Britain (1760–91): The Free Society of Artists (1761–83)*, London, 1907.

Lists all Gainsborough's contributions to these Exhibitions, and incorporates Horace Walpole's notes on the identity of some of the sitters.

Graves, Algernon. *The Royal Academy of Arts: A complete dictionary of contributors . . .*, 8 vols., London, 1905/6.

This does the same for the Royal Academy Exhibitions as the last for the Society of Arts, etc.

Graves, Algernon. *Arts Sales*, 3 vols., London, 1918/21.

Far from complete and often inaccurate, but the most useful accumulation of sale references to Gainsborough up to 1910.

Greig, J. (and M. Menpes). *Thomas Gainsborough*, London, 1909.

This book has some gaudy colour plates and an enormous list of pictures at the end "not in Armstrong": most of them have nothing to do with Gainsborough.

Greig, James, in the *Morning Post* for 11 October 1921.

This is the first publication of the date and place of Gainsborough's marriage.

Harrison, Sydney E. "New light on a Gainsborough mystery", in the *Connoisseur*, LXII (Jan. 1922), pp. 3 ff.; (Feb. 1922), pp. 87 ff.; and (April 1922), p. 227.

The Unwin correspondence is published here. The bulk of it is now in the British Museum (Add. MS. 48964), *see*: K. W. Gransden in the *British Museum Quarterly*, XX (1956), pp. 59–60.

Horne, Henry Percy. *An illustrated catalogue of engraved portraits and fancy subjects painted by Thomas Gainsborough* (and by George Romney).

This deals with engravings made up to 1820 and contains information not available elsewhere. There is no comparable work for the landscape engravings.

Jackson, William (of Exeter). *The Four Ages*, together with Essays on various subjects, London, 1798.

Jackson was a close friend of Gainsborough's: on pp. 147–61 is his *Character of Gainsborough*. There is also matter about Gainsborough in his *Character of Sir J. Reynolds*, p. 167 ff.

Lane, Richard. *Studies and figures selected from the sketch books of the late Thomas Gainsborough...* executed in lithography, 2 parts, London, 1825.

Millar, Oliver. *Thomas Gainsborough*, London, 1949.

Reynolds, Sir Joshua. *The Fourteenth Discourse:* delivered 10 December 1788.

> Published in all editions of Reynolds's *Discourses*. This is largely an obituary appreciation of Gainsborough's art and is perhaps the best as well as the earliest.

Spielmann, M. H. "A note on Gainsborough and Gainsborough Dupont", in *Walpole Society*, V (1915/17), pp. 91 ff.

> The 1797 Gainsborough (and Dupont) sale is published here, with prices and buyers' names: also the lists of pictures ascribed to Gainsborough in the Dupont sales of 1874 and 1892. (For the 1789 sale by private treaty at Schomberg House, see the reprint of the sale catalogue in *Burl. Mag.* LXXIV (May 1944), pp. 107 ff., and the further comments in vol. LXXVI (March 1945), pp. 76 ff., where a list of purchasers is given.)

Thicknesse, Philip. *A Sketch of the Life and Paintings of Thomas Gainsborough, Esq.*, London, 1788.

> Brought out hurriedly, immediately after the painter's death, by his eccentric friend and patron, Thicknesse. In spite of its author's unreliability, it remains a valuable source.

Thornbury, Walter. *The Life of J. M. W. Turner, R.A.*, 2 vols., London, 1862.

> In vol. 2, pp. 59 ff., are valuable reminiscences of Gainsborough by Mr Trimmer, who was son-in-law of Gainsborough's early friend, Joshua Kirby.

Waterhouse, E. K. "Gainsborough in Park Lane", in the *Connoisseur*, March 1936, pp. 123 ff.

Waterhouse, E. K. "Gainsborough's Fancy Pictures", in the *Burlington Magazine*, June 1946.

Waterhouse, E. K. "Preliminary check list of Portraits by Thomas Gainsborough", in *Walpole Society*, XXXIII (1953).

> This includes school repetitions and early copies, which are not listed in the present book, and also a good many references to pictures which I have been unable to check.

Whitley, William T. *Thomas Gainsborough*, London, 1915.

> The standard biography, which is not likely to be superseded. Little material from contemporary newspapers has escaped the author (but he does not give his references). It is strictly biographical and is hardly concerned with the painter's style, or his works other than those mentioned in contemporary sources.

Whitley, William T. *Artists and their friends in England 1700–1799*, 2 vols., London, 1928.

> Whitley included in this book all the further information he had gleaned on Gainsborough since the appearance of his biography in 1915.

Whitley, William T. "The Gainsborough family portraits", in the *Studio*, LXXXVI (Aug. 1923), pp. 63 ff.

> Whitley published here for the first time the correct ages and order of priority of Gainsborough's two daughters.

Woodall, Mary. *Gainsborough's Landscape drawings*, London, 1939.

> This contains a detailed catalogue.

Woodall, Mary. *Thomas Gainsborough*, London, 1949.

Woodall, Mary. "Gainsborough's use of models" in *Antiques* (U.S.A.), October 1956, pp. 363 ff.

A volume of small mezzotints after a number of Gainsborough's portraits was published in the 1860s by Henry Graves & Co.

INTRODUCTION TO THE CATALOGUE

THE following catalogue includes all the pictures known to me which I believe to be by Gainsborough himself, either from having seen the originals or good photographs, or, in a few cases, because their history suggests that they are originals. I have left in a few pictures about which I feel uncertain, but I have left out at least as many, of those which I have not actually seen in the original, when my uncertainty was a little more pronounced. In this matter the present catalogue is totally unlike the Check List of portraits which I published in the *Walpole Society*, vol. XXXIII, in which I was at pains to include all repetitions of at least some respectable age, whether they were originals or not, as well as a number of attributions known only from old references. Many pictures from that list have now been deliberately omitted, but the only one to which I would draw particular attention is the *Orpin, Town Clerk of Bradford*, in the Tate Gallery, long believed to be one of the most unimpeachably authenticated of Gainsborough's portraits. At the Gainsborough Exhibition at the Tate Gallery in 1953, where it was hung among unquestionable Gainsboroughs of all periods, it became clear that this attribution was impossible, and I can only suppose the picture is by William Hoare, whose work at Bath, during the years that Gainsborough lived there, occasionally shows some similarity to Gainsborough.

By guessing how long it took Gainsborough to paint a picture and by doing a few sums, it would seem either that I have listed more pictures than one can reasonably suppose Gainsborough to have painted, or at least that not many more remain to be discovered. Yet hardly a month passes without a new picture emerging from obscurity which seems certainly to be by Gainsborough. His industry was certainly remarkable, especially when one recalls that one of his daughters told Farington that her father occasionally gave way to conviviality to the extent that he was unable to paint for a day or two.

Perhaps no very great number of new portraits is likely to appear, but there must be many more of the small early landscapes than those I have listed. A good many of those, for instance, from the Trimmer sale in 1860, which were almost certainly genuine, have not yet been identified, though they were probably not important. It should be remembered, however, that copies, some perhaps by Ibbetson, of these small Suffolk landscapes are numerous. Similarly, of the small landscapes which Gainsborough exhibited in Schomberg House in 1786, about half a dozen remain to be traced. The recovery of the exact pedigree of the landscapes, which are very rarely clearly described in early references, presents exceptional difficulties—especially when one or more old copies have masqueraded as the original. I cannot hope that there are not errors in some of these pedigrees, but I have examined the backs of as many pictures as possible and sought to establish their correct history from the lingering evidence of chalk and stencil, which are among the mysteries of the picture genealogist. In this pursuit I have been greatly helped by the constant kindness of Messrs Christie's, who have put up with a barrage of enquiries.

There are about thirty entries in Armstrong's catalogue about which I know nothing, and of a good many of these it looks as though Armstrong knew nothing either. All these I have omitted and some account of the way in which Fulcher's and Armstrong's catalogues were drawn up will be found in the introduction to *Walpole Society*, vol. XXXIII. It is barely possible to keep pace with the constant changes of ownership of so many pictures, but, as far as they have become known to me, I have put them in up to the summer of 1957. In some cases a date after the current owner means that that is the date at which I have verified a picture in certain possession and that I have no knowledge of any later change of ownership.

All sales are at London and at Christie's unless otherwise indicated.

PORTRAITS OF NAMED SITTERS

1. ABEL, CARL FRIEDRICH (1725–87). *San Marino (Calif.). Henry E. Huntington Library and Art Gallery.* 88 × 58 in. (Abel sale, by Greenwood, 13/xii/1787 (42): Anon. (= Queen Charlotte) sale 25/v/1819 (93) bt. Peacock: Earl of Egremont sale 21/v/1892 (80) bt. C. J. Wertheimer: Anon. sale 8/v/1897 (78) bt. in: George J. Gould, New York, 1914: bt. from Duveen, 1925.) R.A. 1777 (135). Pl. 171.

2. *The same.* "A head" in 1797 sale (16) bt. Kilpatrick.

3. *The same* (?). 49 × 39 in. (Dr Hoskins 1856: bt. *c.* 1870 by Dr W. H. Cummings: sale 17/xii/1915 (145) bt. Sulley: with Tooth, 1919: Carl P. Dannett, New York, 1923.) If of Abel, earlier than no. 1: the features do not altogether agree. Seated, full face, his viola da gamba between his knees.

4. ABERCORN, JAMES, 8TH EARL OF (1712–89). *Barons Court (N. Ireland). Duke of Abercorn.* About 90 × 58 in. Mezzotint by John Dean, inscribed: *Pinxit* 1778. Pl. 189.

5. ABINGDON, WILLOUGHBY, 4TH EARL OF (1740–99). *London. Private collection.* 82 × 57 in. (Unfinished: in 1797 sale (36) bt. Morozani: Earl of Abingdon, Wytham: bt. with Wytham by Eric Hamilton Rose: sold by Hugh Rose, 1956: with Leggatt, 1956.) Pl. 188.

6. ACTON, MRS NATHANIEL (d. 1761). *Shrubland Park. Hon. J. V. B. Saumarez.* 30 × 25 in. Later 1750s. Arts Council Exh. 1953 (17) as *Unknown lady.* Pl. 30.

7. ADAIR, (SIR) ROBERT (1763–1855). *Baltimore. Museum of Art (Jacob Epstein coll.).* 30 × 25 in. (Marquess Townshend sale 5/iii/1904 (59) bt. Colnaghi: Sir C. Townshend sale 13/vii/1923 (130) bt. Knoedler: bt. by Jacob Epstein, 1924.) Middle 1780s: formerly called a portrait of his father. Pl. 252.

8. ADNEY, MISS ELIZABETH (Mrs John Bragge: d. 1783). 28½ × 23 in. (Bt. from family by Wallis & Son: Sir J. D. Milburn sale 10/vi/1909 (108) bt. Colnaghi—*repd.*) Later 1760s: *cf.* her husband's portrait (no. 79).

9. AILESBURY, ANN ELIZABETH, COUNTESS OF (1753–1814). 61 × 39 in. (perhaps cut down). (Marquess of Ailesbury sale, Tottenham House, by Knight, Frank & Rutley, 27/viii/1946 (135).) Later 1780s.

10. ALDBOROUGH, EDWARD, 2ND EARL OF (d. 1801). 50 × 40 in. Probably 1769/70 (*cf.* Gainsborough's letter to sitter, when Hon. Mr Stratford, of 1771, at Harvard). Engraved (with Peer's robes added) by S. Einslie.

11. ALDBOROUGH, BARBARA, COUNTESS OF (1742–85). Companion to no. 10 and mentioned in letter of 1771.

12. ALFRED, H.R.H. PRINCE (1780–82). *Windsor Castle. H.M. The Queen.* Oval: 22 × 16 in. R.A. 1783 (134): painted September 1782.

13. ALSTON, GERTRUDE, LADY (1732–1807). *Paris. Louvre.* 89 × 65 in. (C. Craven, Brighton, 1862: E. B. Foster, Clewer: sold privately to Baron Gustave de Rothschild, 1874: bequeathed by Baron Robert de Rothschild, 1947.) Probably from middle 1760s. Pl. 67.

14. *The same.* 30 × 25 in. (H. Farrar sale 15/vi/1866 (87) bt. in: Mrs C. Farwell sale, Burnham, by Phillips, 5/vii/1921 (274) bt. Roe: with Knoedler, 1921/25: with J. Levy, New York, 1925: with Marie Sterner, New York, 1942.) Later Bath period.

15. AMHERST, JEFFRY, 1ST LORD (1717–97). *Amherst College, Massachusetts.* 30 × 25 in. (Bequeathed by Lady Amherst to Admiral Stroud, 1830: Mrs Gauntlett: F. J. Montague-White: bt. by George D. Pratt, Long Island, 1932: bequeathed 1935.) Probably London period.

16. *The same. London. National Portrait Gallery* (150). 30×25 in. (Bt. from Major Mair, 1862.) Repetition of no. 15.

17. AMYAND, CLAUDIUS (1718–74). 30× 25 in. (Descended in Cornewall family, Moccas, till 1946: London art trade 1946/55: Anon. sale 18/iii/1955 (102) bt. Smith.) Middle 1760s.

18. ANDREWS, ROBERT (1726–1806) AND MARY (1732?–80), HIS WIFE. *London. National Gallery.* 27½×47 in. Probably soon after marriage of sitters in 1748. Pl. 10. Colour plate.

19. ARGYLL, JOHN, 4TH DUKE OF (1694–1770). *Edinburgh. Scottish National Portrait Gallery.* 91×60½ in. (Bt. from Duke of Argyll, 1953.) S.A. 1767 (59). Engraved in mezzotint by James Watson, 1769. Pl. 95.

20. ARGYLL, JOHN, 5TH DUKE OF (1723–1806). *Inveraray Castle. Duke of Argyll.* 30×25 in. R.A. 1779 (102). Engraved in mezzotint by William Dickinson.

21. ASHTON, REV. THOMAS (1716–75). Probably 30×25 in. (Horace Walpole: (Lady Blessington) sale, 20/vi/1846 (119) bt. in: resold by Phillips 15/v/1849 (975).) Engraved in mezzotint by McArdell (d. 1765).

22. AUGUSTA SOPHIA, H.R.H. PRINCESS (1768–1840). *Windsor Castle. H.M. The Queen.* Oval: 22×16 in. Painted in September 1782: R.A. 1783 (134) with the series of the Royal family.

23. *The same* (?). *Port Sunlight. Lady Lever Art Gallery.* 28¼×23½ in. (Harland Peck sale 25/vi/1920 (59) bt. for Lord Leverhulme.) A picture of *c.* 1775/80. Bought as *Princess Augusta Sophia*, but the identification of the sitter is doubtful. *See also* CHARLOTTE AUGUSTA MATILDA.

24. AWSE, MRS. 29×24 in. (Descended in Stevens family, Winscott, Devon: bt. by de Casseres, 1936: Fattorini, Bradford: Mrs Naylor sale 13/vii/1951 (71) bt. Bellesi.) Reproduced in colour in *The Connoisseur*, Oct. 1936, p. 210, with the correspondence which shows that it was finished in September 1767 after prolonged delays.

25. AYLESFORD, HENEAGE, 3RD EARL OF (1715–77). *Voelas. Colonel J. C. Wynne-Finch.* 30×25 in. Early 1760s: companion to no. 27.

26. *The same. Packington Hall. Earl of Aylesford.* 50×40 in. In Peer's robes: probably from the middle 1770s. Lettered in error "2nd Earl of Aylesford?".

27. AYLESFORD, CHARLOTTE, COUNTESS OF (1730–1805). *Voelas. Colonel J. C. Wynne-Finch.* 30×25 in. Early 1760s: companion to no. 25.

28. *The same.* An unfinished "Dowager Lady Aylesford and child, full length" was in Mrs Gainsborough sale, 10/iv/1797 (37) bt. Calder.

29. BACCELLI, GIOVANNA (d. 1801). *Swinton Park. Countess of Swinton.* 88½×57 in. (Painted for the Duke of Dorset: at Knole till 1890, when it was sold to Lord Masham.) R.A. 1782 (230). Engraved in mezzotint by John Jones, 1784. Pl. 235.

30. *The same. Russborough (Co. Wicklow). Sir Alfred Beit, Bart.* 22×15½ in. (Sold at Foster's *c.* 1847 as *Miss Farren*: Henry Harrison sale, by Foster's, 13/v/1896 (137) bt. Wertheimer: Alfred Beit, 1896.) Small "model" for no. 29, without the tambourine bottom left.

31. BACH, JOHANN CHRISTIAN (1735–82). *Bologna. Liceo Musicale.* 29¼×24¼ in. Painted 1776 and sent to Bologna 1778 (Sanford Terry, *J. C. Bach*, 1929—repd.).

32. *The same. Messing. Lord Hillingdon.* 29¼× 24¼ in. (Anna Robson, widow of Thomas Mudge (1789–1839): her daughter, Charlotte Walcott: Anon. (= Walcott) sale 4/vii/1874 (91) bt. in: resold 3/vii/1875 (70) bt. in: bt. privately by Sir Charles Mills, later Lord Hillingdon.) Contemporary autograph repetition of no. 31. Pl. 168.

33. BAGOT, LEWIS (1740–1802). *Lilliesleaf. Mrs Arden Haworth-Booth.* 29×24 in. (Passed through the descendants of his elder brother to H. R. H. Bagot, father of the present owner.) The sitter's identity is not absolutely certain. Exh.: Birmingham 1900 (33)—repd.

34. BAILLIE, HON. MRS GEORGE (1737–99). *Mellerstain. Earl of Haddington.* 30×25 in. Probably dating from the time of her marriage (1759). Pl. 77.

35. BAILLIE FAMILY, THE. *London. Tate Gallery* (789). 98×89 in. (Descended to Alexander Baillie, Naples: bequeathed by him, 1857, to the National Gallery but retained by agreement by his nephew, M. J. Higgins, until 1868.) Intended for R.A. 1784, but not shown. The family of James Baillie of Ealing Grove.

36. BAKER, MRS PETER WILLIAM. *New York. Henry Clay Frick collection.* 87½×59 in. (Descended in the Baker family, Ranston, until bt. by H. C. Frick, 1917.) Signed and dated 1781. Pl. 236.

37. BAKER, PETER. *Ranston. Miss Selina L. Baker.* 30×25 in. Later Bath period.

38. BAKER, MRS PETER. *Ranston. Miss Selina L. Baker.* 30×25 in. Later Bath period.

38a. BALFOUR, MRS TOWNLEY (Letitia Leigh: 1746–1838) 30×25 in. Perhaps a marriage portrait (1768). (David Crichton sale 25/x/1957 lot 58 bt. Jones.)

39. BANKS, J. 49×39 in. (Anon. sale 19/vii/1946 (126) bt. Spiller.) Once a picture of the middle 1760s.

40. BARRY, LAMBE (1704–68). *London. F. B. Hart-Jackson.* 13×12 in. (S. Kilderbee sale 30/v/1829 (111) bt. Johnson: Mr Johnson, 1856. Bt. from Leggatt by Agnew, 1919: Hon. Annie Cunliffe-Lister, 1919/29: Anon. sale 28/xi/1930 (153) as Zoffany, bt. Agnew: Anon. (= Capt. N. Colville) sale, Sotheby's 9/vi/1955 (166) bt. Agnew: bt. 1956.) Not far from 1750. Pl. 32.

41. *The same. Shrubland Park. Hon. J. V. B. Saumarez.* 30×25 in. Some years later than no. 40. It has descended through the Lee-Acton family of Livermere. Pl. 33.

42. "BARRY, LIEUTENANT". 30×25 in. (Repd. in Armstrong, 1898, p. vi., but not listed in his catalogue. Probably Bath period and perhaps misnamed.)

43. BARTTELOT, WALTER (1726–64) (?), 49×39 in. (Sir W. Barttelot sale 19/vi/1911 (147) bt. Colnaghi: with Tooth, 1915: with J. W. Anderson, Detroit, 1915: with Hirschl and Adler, New York, 1957.) From middle 1760s.

44. BASSET, FRANCIS (d. 1769) (?). 30×25 in. (Anon. sale 2/viii/1928 (145) as *Lord de Dunstanville,* bt. Howard: Francis Howard sale 25/xi/1955 (77) bt. Fischmann.) From the earlier 1750s.

BASSET. *See* DUNSTANVILLE, LORD DE.

44a. *The same.* 50×40 in. (From Ston Easton, 1956, as *Lord de Dunstanville:* with S. Sabin 1957.) Early 1760's.

45. BATE-DUDLEY, REV. SIR HENRY (1745–1824). *Needwood House. Baroness Burton.* 88×59 in. (At Bradwell Rectory until sold by J. Oxley Parker to Lord Burton, 1887.) R.A. 1780 (189): engraved in mezzotint by Gainsborough Dupont. Pl. 204.

46. *The same. London. Tate Gallery* (1044). 28½×23¾ in. (Presented by the sitter's nephew, T. Birch Wolfe, 1878.) Near in date to no. 45.

47. BATE-DUDLEY, LADY. *Needwood House. Baroness Burton.* 87×57 in. (Same history as no. 45.) Painted at Bradwell in summer 1787 (Whitley, p. 290). Pl. 278.

48. BATEMAN, JOHN, 2ND VISCOUNT (d. 1802). *London. Mrs. Dorothy de Rothschild.* Oval: 20¼×15 in. Signed: *T.G.* (Sold by Lord Bateman to C. J. Wertheimer before 1908: James de Rothschild.) Probably from 1760s. Exh.: Berlin, 1908 (87)—*repd.* (in small catalogue only).

49. BATEMAN, LADY (?). 30×25 in. (Probably ex. Lord Bateman: S. B. Joel sale 31/v/1935 (6)—*repd.* bt. Asscher: with Howard Young, 1936.) Identity of sitter is obscure: once from Bath period.

50. BEAUFOY, HENRY (1750–1795). *Steeple Aston. H. M. Beaufoy.* 90×59 in. (Given by J. H. Beaufoy to F. J. Jervoise, 1833: Anon. (= F. M. E. Jervoise) sale 3/v/1884 (138) bt. Beaufoy.) Painted 1785 (Whitley, p. 234). Engraved in mezzotint by W. Ward, 1797. Pl. 217.

51. BEAUFOY, MRS HENRY (c. 1754–1826). *San Marino (Calif.). H. E. Huntington Library and Art Gallery.* 90 × 58¾ in. (Given 1833 by J. H. Beaufoy to Sir William Heathcote (d. 1881): Alfred de Rothschild, 1884: Almina, Countess of Carnarvon, 1918: bought from Duveen, 1924.) R.A. 1780 (84). Pl. 207.

52. BEAUFOY, MARK (1718–82). *Steeple Aston. H. M. Beaufoy.* 50 × 40 in. Engraved in mezzotint, with the sitter's age given as 62, by Valentine Green; which dates it 1780/81. Pl. 231.

53. BEDFORD, JOHN, 4TH DUKE OF (1710–71). *Dublin. Trinity College (Provost's Lodge).* 95 × 60 in. Signed. Presented by the sitter when Chancellor of the University, 1768. Gainsborough's receipt for 60 guineas is dated 15/xi/1768 (Woburn MSS).

54. *The same. Woburn Abbey. Duke of Bedford.* 30 × 25 in. Inscribed with the date 1764 and the basis for no. 53. A receipt at Woburn for 60 guineas, and a letter from Gainsborough of 7/i/1765 to P. Beaumont (Woburn MSS) reveals that Gainsborough painted two replicas of this at the same time.

55. *The same. Woburn Abbey. Duke of Bedford.* 50 × 40 in. Gainsborough's receipt for this for 40 guineas is dated 23/xi/1769 (Woburn MSS): *repd.* in G. Scott Thomson, *The Russells in Bloomsbury,* 1940, p. 240.

56. *The same. London. National Portrait Gallery* (755). 30 × 25 in. (Painted for the sitter's daughter, Duchess of Marlborough: bt. at the Blenheim sale, 1886.) Not much later than no. 54, but a different sitting.

57. *The same.* 30 × 25 in. (Gainsborough's receipt for 20 guineas for a picture sent to Mrs Fortescue in Dublin is dated 28/iv/1768.)

57a. *The same.* "A head" (unfinished) in 1797 sale (31) bt. Lord Malden.

58. BEDFORD, GERTRUDE, DUCHESS OF (1715–94). *Woburn Abbey. Duke of Bedford.* 30 × 25 in. Painted in the winter of 1764/5 (*The Connoisseur,* Feb. 1922, p. 88).

59. BEDINGFIELD, MRS, AND HER DAUGHTER. 50½ × 40½ in. (Descended to V. B. Crowther-Beynon (d. 1941).) From the middle 1760s: *repd.* Grafton Galls. Loan Exh. 1911 (56).

BELFAST, EARL OF. *See* DONEGALL, MARQUESS OF.

60. BELGRAVE, ROBERT, VISCOUNT (Marquess of Westminster: 1767–1845). *London. Westminster Trustees.* 30 × 25 in. Later 1780s: *repd.* Lord R. Gower, 1903, p. 110 c.

61. BELL, RALPH (1720–83). 91 × 60 in. (Descended to Reginald Bell, Thirsk Hall: bt. Agnew, 1897: with Forbes & Paterson, 1901: Norman Forbes-Robertson sale 19/v/1911 (104) bt. Gilbert.) Companion to no. 62: probably middle 1770s.

62. BELL, MRS RALPH (Anne Conyers: d. 1814). 91 × 58 in. (Descended to Reginald Bell, Thirsk Hall: bt. Agnew, 1897: with Forbes & Paterson, 1901: Norman Forbes-Robertson sale 19/v/1911 (103) bt. A. Wertheimer: A. H. Mulliken sale, New York 5/i/1933 (52) bt. Sickles—*repd.*: Mrs William Fox sale, by Gimbel's, New York, 2/xii/1942 (84).) Companion to no. 61: probably middle 1770s.

63. BENNETT, FRANCIS. *Cowdray Park. Viscount Cowdray.* 30 × 25 in. (Anon. sale 10/v/1912 (83) bt. Knoedler.) From the 1760s.

64. BENTHALL, JAMES. Oil on paper: 5 × 4 in. (Francis Benthall: H. Pfungst sale 15/vi/1917 (87) bt. Gooden & Fox: Anon. sale 6/xii/1946 (115) bt. Simmons.) Probably from the 1770s.

65. BERKELEY, HON. GEORGE CRANFIELD (1753–1818). *Berkeley Castle. Estate of the late Earl of Berkeley.* About 90 × 60 in. Painted 1784/6 (Whitley, pp. 225, 257). Engraved by H. Birche, 1793.

66. BLACKETT, SIR THOMAS (formerly WENTWORTH), 5TH BART. (1725–92). *Bywell Hall. Viscount Allendale.* 29½ × 24½ in. Earlier London period.

67. BLACKSTONE, SIR WILLIAM (1723–80). *London. Tate Gallery* (2637). 30×25 in. (Bt. by Sir Robert Peel at W. S. Blackstone sale, by Price, 1835: Peel Heirlooms sale, Robinson & Fisher, 11/v/1900 (250) bt. Agnew: George Salting bequest, 1910.) Painted in 1774 (according to J. Hall's engraving, 1775).

68. BLACKSTONE, SARAH, LADY. *Cincinnati. E. W. Edwards* (1931). 30×25 in. (Passed to Miss M. E. Rennell: sale 21/ii/1919 (118) bt. Peacock: with Agnew.) Probably companion to no. 67 and of 1774.

69. BLIGH, GENERAL THOMAS (1685–1775) (?). *New York. Mrs. W. R. Timken.* 30×25 in. (Sir J. B. Robinson sale 6/vii/1923 (8) bt. Knoedler: with Scott & Fowles, New York, 1926.) In the Robinson sale as "General Blyth". As it is probably of the 1770s and the sitter is not of great age, the present title is very doubtful.

70. BLYTH, MR. 21×16½ in. (Dupont sale, Sudbury, 29/v/1874 (107): Anon. sale 14/vi/1875 (92a) bt. Graves: Anon. (Graves) sale 5/i/1889 (148) bt. in.) "Mr Blyth of Norfolk", called "Pilgrim Blythe". Presumably an original, but not known.

BLYTH, GENERAL. *See* BLIGH.

71. BOLTON, MRS JOHN. *São Paolo (Brazil). Dr Assis Chateaubriand.* 30×25 in. (Descended to Miss A. Bolton, Brooklyn: sale 13/vii/1923 (123) bt. in: resold Kende Galls., New York, 5/vi/1940 (39a) with Knoedler's, 1940s.) About 1770.

72. BOONE, MISS. 30×25 in. (Descended to T. Colleton Garth: with Agnew 1904: Sedelmeyer sale, Paris, 16–18/v/1907 (70)—*repd.*: A. H. Mulliken sale, New York, 5/i/1933 (64) bt. J. Wheeler—*repd.*) From the 1770s.

73. BOURCHIER, CHARLES. 30×25 in. (Anon. sale 12/vii/1912 (64) bt. Agnew: Agnew sale 7/vi/1918 (22) bt. Peacock: Mrs H. H. Cowie sale 18/v/1951 (63) bt. Court.) Later Bath work.

74. BOURCHIER, JAMES, F.I.C.S. *Wellesley Hills (Mass.). Mrs John Wendell Jr.* 30×25 in.

(Descended to Arthur Bourchier: with Colnaghi & Knoedler 1909: Frank Bulkeley Smith, Worcester, Mass., 1910.) The traditional date of 1772 seems correct.
See also GENTLEMAN UNKNOWN (no. 781).

75. BOUVERIE, HON. BARTHOLOMEW (1753–1835). *Longford Castle. Earl of Radnor.* 29½×24½ in. Painted 1773/4: paid for September 1774. Pl. 157.

76. BOUVERIE, HON. EDWARD (1760–1824). *Longford Castle. Earl of Radnor.* 29½×24½ in. Inscribed 1773: paid for September 1774. Pl. 159.

77. BOUVERIE, HON. WILLIAM HENRY (1752–1806). *Longford Castle. Earl of Radnor.* 29½×24½ in. Inscribed 1773: paid for September 1774. Pl. 158.

BOWES, MISS ELIZABETH. *See* CROFT, MRS ROBERT.

78. BOWLBY, LADY MARY (d. 1813), (born BRUDENELL). *Gilston Park. F. E. S. Bowlby.* 30×25 in. (Bt. in 1850s by George Richmond: sold to Dyer: Anon. sale 6/vi/1896 (34) bt. Mrs Bowlby.) Bath period: N.P.E. 1867 (634)—*repd.*

79. BRAGGE, JOHN (1741–86). 30×25 in. (Bt. from a member of the family by Knoedler, 1909: Walter Lewisohn, New York, 1912: Anon. sale, New York, 20/ii/1930 (92) bt. Picchetto—*repd.*) Paid for (£41) March/April 1767 (Sadborow Papers 8339 f. 50 *ap.* Devizes Record Office).

BRAGGE, MRS JOHN. *See* ADNEY, MISS (no. 8).

80. BRISCO, SIR JOHN, 1ST BT. (1739–1805). 30×25 in. (Sold by Sir Musgrave Brisco, Bt.: with Agnew: Sir Philip Sassoon, Bt., 1931.) Probably early London work.

81. BRISCO, CAROLINE ALICIA, LADY (d. 1822). *Kenwood. Iveagh bequest* (5). 90×58 in. (Sold by Sir Musgrave Brisco, Bt., *c.* 1886: James Price: with Agnew: bt. by Earl of Iveagh 1889.) Marriage portrait of 1776 (date on back of canvas). Pl. 165.

82. BRISTOL, AUGUSTUS JOHN, 3RD EARL OF (1724–79). *Ickworth. National Trust.* 91½ × 60 in. (Painted for 2nd Lord Mulgrave: passed to Lady Murray: put up for sale 21/ii/1834 (83) bt. in, and, by Hoard, 9/v/1835 (106): then bt. by Marquess of Bristol, Ickworth.) S.A. 1768 (60). Engraved in mezzotint by J. Watson 1773. A 30 × 25 in. of the bust only belongs to Dennis Cohen, London. Pl. 10.

BRISTOL, COUNTESS OF. *See* UNKNOWN LADY (no. 791).

BROCKMAN, MRS JAMES DRAKE. *See* TATTON, MISS.

83. BRODREPP, RICHARD. 30 × 25 in. (Passed to Henry F. Compton: with Leger 1950.) Fairly early Bath work.

84. BROWNE, FRANCIS JOHN (d. 1833?) 30 × 25 in. (Descended in the Sheridan family, Frampton: sold 1928 to Howard Young: with Newhouse Galls., New York, 1955.) Probably from the early 1780s.

85. BROWNE, MRS (or MISS?). 30 × 25 in. (R. B. Sheridan, 1856: sold from Frampton to Howard Young, 1928.) Companion to no. 84: probably from 1780s.

86. BROWNE, JOHN (of Tunstall), with wife and child. *Houghton Hall. Marchioness of Cholmondeley.* 33 × 55½ in. (Descended to F. B. Longe, sale 27/vii/1917 (141) bt. Agnew: Viscount D'Abernon: Sir Philip Sassoon, Bt. *c.* 1930: Mrs David Gubbay 1939: Marchioness of Cholmondeley *c.* 1947.) The date is about 1754/55 on the assumption the child is their elder daughter, Anna Maria (1753–85). Pl. 11.

BROWNE, MRS HERBERT GWYNNE. *See* DOUGLAS, MRS JOHN.

87. BRUMMELL, MISS. *Kenwood. Iveagh bequest* (6). 30 × 25 in. (Descended to Mrs White, Brussels, 1880: with Colnaghi and Agnew: bt. by Earl of Iveagh, 1888.) From the early 1780s.

BRUN, MME LE. *See* LEBRUN, MME.

88. BUCCLEUCH, HENRY, 3RD DUKE OF (1746–1812). *Bowhill. Duke of Buccleuch and Queensberry.* 48½ × 38 in. The receipt is dated 21 Nov. 1770. Engraved in mezzotint by John Dixon, 1771. Pl. 120.

89. BUCCLEUCH, ELIZABETH, DUCHESS OF (1743–1827). *Boughton. Duke of Buccleuch and Queensberry.* 30 × 25 in. Painted about the time of her marriage (1767).

90. BUCKINGHAM, GEORGE, 1ST MARQUESS OF (1753–1813). *Boconnoc. G. G. Fortescue.* 50 × 40 in. Finished in the summer of 1787: engraved by J. K. Sherwin, 1788. Formerly at Dropmore.

91. BUCKINGHAMSHIRE, JOHN, 2ND EARL OF (1723–93). *Blickling Hall, National Trust.* 91 × 57 in. (Descended through his eldest daughter, Marchioness of Lothian.) Intended for R.A. 1784, but not exhibited.

92. BUCKINGHAMSHIRE, CAROLINE, COUNTESS OF (d. 1817). *Blickling Hall. National Trust.* 91 × 57 in. Companion to no. 91. Intended for R.A. 1784, but not exhibited.

93. BUCKLER, BENJAMIN (1718–80). *Oxford. All Souls College.* 30 × 25 in. Perhaps later Bath period.

94. *The same. Wimbledon. Mrs Vivian Seymer.* 30 × 25 in. (Descended to Sir Wroth A. Lethbridge, Bt.: bt. *c.* 1912 by W. H. Buckler, Oxford, father of present owner.) Repetition of no. 93.

95. BULLOCK, COLONEL JOHN (1730/1–1809). *Needwood House. Baroness Burton.* 89½ × 60 in. (H. W. Bullock sale 19/iii/1892 (755) bt. Gooden: soon afterwards bt. by Lord Burton.) Later Bath work. Pl. 139.

BULLOCK, RICHARD. *See* UNKNOWN OFFICER (no. 772).

BURGES, LADY MARGARET. *See* FORDYCE, LADY MARGARET.

96. BURNEY, CHARLES ROUSSEAU (1747–1819). *New York. Metropolitan Museum.*

30 × 25 in. (C. H. C. P. Burney sale 20/vi/1930 (128) bt. Knoedler: Mrs Edward S. Harkness, New York: bequeathed 1950.) Probably from the later 1770s.

97. BURRELL, SIR PETER (Lord Gwydyr: 1754–1820). *New York. Mrs. James B. Duke.* 98 × 72½ in. (Sold by Lord Gwydyr, Stoke Park, 1913: with Duveen 1923: James B. Duke, New York.) Painted 1787 (Whitley, p. 274). Pl. 279.

98. BURRELL, LADY PRISCILLA (1761–1828). Sitting in the autumn of 1782 (Whitley, p. 193).

99. BURROUGH, REV. HENRY (1721–73). *London. Corporation Art Gallery (Guildhall).* 30 × 25 in. (Mrs N. Burrough (d. 1830): Thomas Fenn Addison: Miss Josephine Savill: Anon. (= Savill) sale 15/vii/1893 (85) bt. Wylie: do. 14/i/1905 (86): do. 8/vii/1905 (69): do. 14/vii/1911 (39): bequeathed to Guildhall by Lord Wakefield, 1943.) Ipswich period.

100. BURROUGH, MRS HENRY (1730–98). *Los Angeles. University of Southern California.* 30 × 25 in. (Dupont sale 10/v/1873 (113) bt. Graves: Louis Huth sale 20/v/1905 (99) bt. Wallis: Mrs Robert Paterson sale, New York, 17/iii/1938 (35)—repd.: presented with Elizabeth Holmes Fisher collection, 1940.) Inscribed in a later hand with the date 1769.

101. BURROUGH, NATHANIEL (1723–94). *New York. Metropolitan Museum.* 30 × 25 in. (Passed to Thomas Fenn Addison, 1830: Miss Josephine Savill: Anon. (= Savill) sale 15/vii/1893 (84) bt. Wylie: presented by George A. Hearn, 1896.) Bath period.

102. BURROUGH, MR. 30 × 22 in. (whole-length, with dog.) (Dupont sale, Sudbury, 29/v/1874 (173): resold 4/x/1892 (177d).) Presumably an early work, and, from its pedigree, authentic: listed by Fulcher, 1856.

103. BUTCHER, ROBERT (d. 1788). *Williamstown (Mass.), Williams College.* 30 × 25 in. (Mrs Catherine Barlow sale 3/xii/1904 (125) bt. Colnaghi: Hon. Sir Evan Charteris: with Knoedler 1926: Robert Cluett, 1926: given by his family 1957.) Probably about 1765: Steward to the Duke of Bedford.

103a. *The same. Madrid, Prado.* 30 × 25 in. (Anon. sale, 25/xi/1938 (116) bt. Freeman: Lord Mackintosh, 1948: with Leggatt, 1955: bt. 1955.) Replica of No. 103.

104. BUTE, JOHN, 1ST MARQUESS OF (1744–1814). *Mountstuart House. Marquess of Bute.* Oval: 29 × 24 in. (Descended to the Crichton-Stuarts of Fairlie: came to Mountstuart in the 1930s.) Painted in the 1780s, when Lord Mountstuart: engraved in stipple by Caroline Watson.

105. BUTLER, MISS. *Birmingham. City Art Gallery (Lent by Mrs O. S. Ashcroft).* 30 × 25 in. (Bt. from Sulley c. 1902 by F. Fleischmann, father of O. S. Ashcroft.) Bath period.

106. BUTTALL, JONATHAN (d. 1805). ("THE BLUE BOY".) *San Marino. (Calif.). H. E. Huntington Library and Art Gallery.* 70 × 48 in. (Buttall sale, Greek Street, Soho, 15/xii/1796 bt. Nesbitt: Anon. (= Nesbitt) sale, by Coxe, 25/v/1802 (63) bt. Hoppner, who sold it to 1st Marquess of Westminster: bt. from Duke of Westminster through Duveen 1921.) Possibly R.A. 1770 (85)—*see* 1936 Huntington Catalogue and *Burl. Mag.*, Apr. 1940, pp. 128/9. Pl. 127.

107. BUXTON, MISS SARAH (MRS CHARLES DUMBLETON: 1757–83). *Fort Worth (Texas). Kay Kimbell.* Cut down to 43¾ × 34½ in. (Passed to Walter Dumbleton, Chichester: sold to Duveen 1918: Judge Gary sale, New York, 28/iv/1928 (34) bt. E. Jonas—repd.) Probably c. 1776/7: another fragment from the bottom left corner, of a greyhound (34 × 24¾ in.), also exists.

108. THE BYAM FAMILY. *Marlborough. Marlborough College.* 98 × 94 in. (By descent to H. C. Hony: presented by him 1955.) About 1764: the sitters are George Byam of Apse Court, his wife, Louisa Bathurst, and their daughter Sarah (born 1760): *see* R. R. Tatlock, *Apollo*, Feb. 1935, pp. 72 ff. Pl. 82.

109. CAMBRIDGE, H.R.H. ADOLPHUS FREDERICK, DUKE OF (1774–1850). *Windsor*

Castle. *H.M. The Queen.* 22¾ × 16¾ in. R.A. 1783 (134): painted September 1782. Pl. 212.

110. CAMDEN, CHARLES, 1ST EARL (1714–94). *Northbourne Court. Lord Northbourne.* 50 × 40 in. R.A. 1782 (126). Engraved in stipple by Bartolozzi 1795.

111. *The same.* Exhibited Schomberg House 1786 (Whitley, p. 266): this may have been the same as no. 110, but Fulcher (1856) lists one belonging to a Mrs. Palmer ("standing in his study . . . His hand rests on a folio").

112. CAMDEN, JOHN, 1ST MARQUESS (1759–1840). *Bayham Abbey. Marquess Camden.* 30 × 25 in. About 1786: *repd.* H. S. Eeles, *Lord Chancellor Camden,* p. 132.

113. CAMPBELL, LORD FREDERICK (1729–1816). *Inveraray Castle. Duke of Argyll.* 88 × 57½ in. Exhibited at Schomberg House 1786 (Whitley, p. 257). Engraved as half-length by Gainsborough Dupont.

114. CAMPBELL, LADY FREDERICK (Countess Ferrers: 1727–1807). *Toledo (Ohio). Museum of Art.* 30½ × 25¼ in. (Her sister, Viscountess Curzon: thence to Lord Zouche: Gerard Lee Bevan, 1912: Anon. (= Mrs G. L. Bevan) sale 11/v/1923 (90) bt. Wills: Arthur J. Secor 1925: given to Toledo 1933.) Probably from the earlier 1770s.

115. CAMPBELL, SIR JOHN (*called*). 30 × 25 in. (E. W. Beckett sale 23/v/1903 (82) bt. Colnaghi (as *Mr Ozier*): with Gimpel 1903: E. Cronier sale, Paris, 4/xii/1905 (10)—*repd.* as *Sir John Campbell*: with Wallis & Son, London: bt. 1906 by Mrs Robert Paterson, New York: sale, New York 17/iii/1938 (33)—*repd.*) Probably later Bath period: the sitter's identity is presumably unknown.

116. CAMPBELL, SAMUEL (d. 1792?). 30 × 25 in. (Descended to Rowley James, sale 24/vi/1932 (98) bt. Ellis and Smith.)

117. CAMPBELL, LORD WILLIAM (d. 1778). 30 × 25 in. (Miss Campbell Johnstone 1868: General Campbell Johnstone, 1891.) Probably Bath period: a portrait of his wife, ascribed to Gainsborough, belonged to Mrs E. J. Adams, Baltimore, 1893.

118. CANNING, GEORGE (1770–1827). *Harewood House. Earl of Harewood.* 28 × 23 in. (By descent to Earl Canning (1862): Marquess of Clanricarde till 1916.) Traditionally painted 1788.

118a. CANNING, REV. RICHARD. (Given to Rev. Henry Hubbard (d. 1778) by sitter: bt. in London sale by Michael Harvard 1955: with S. Sabin 1957.) Companion to no. 389: middle or later 1750s. Pl. 43.

119. CARLISLE, ISABELLA, COUNTESS OF (1721–95). *Castle Howard. George Howard.* 30 × 25 in. Soon after 1760: painted when *Lady Musgrave.*

120. CARR, MARY, LADY. *New York. Harry Payne Bingham Estate* 50 × 40 in. (Descended to W. Parker Hamond: sale 6/v/1893 (111) bt. Gooden: with Tooth 1894.) Bath period: wrongly repd. as *Lady Ray,* in Armstrong's Portfolio Monograph, 1894, p. 23.

CARR, MISS MARY. *See* HAMOND, MRS W. PARKER.

121. CARR, MRS. *Upton House. Viscount Bearsted.* 7½ × 6½ in. (Anon. sale 4/v/1874 (79) bt. Agnew for Kirkman D. Hodgson: R. K. Hodgson sale 21/xi/1924 (14) bt. for Lord Bearsted.) Probably from the 1780s.

122. CARTWRIGHT, THOMAS (1735/6–72). *Aynhoe Park. Hon. Mrs Cartwright.* 30 × 25 in. From the middle 1760s.

123. CASBERD, MRS. *Mersham. Mrs L. P. Irby* (d. 1957). 30 × 25 in. (Descended to W. J. Casberd-Boteler, father of owner.) From the middle 1760s.

124. CATHCART, WILLIAM, 1ST EARL (1755–1843). *London. Earl Cathcart.* (*Lent to Manchester Gallery.*) 50 × 40 in. Unfinished: painted 1784 (Whitley, p. 228). Pl. 249.

125. CHAD, GEORGE (later Sir George Chad, Bt.: 1730–1815). *New York. Henry J. Topping.* 30 × 25 in. (Bt. from family by Sulley 1912: with Knoedler 1912/17: Daniel G. Reid, New York, 1917: Mrs Reid Topping.) Companion to next: probably marriage portrait (1775).

126. CHAD, MRS GEORGE (d. 1786). *New York. Daniel Topping.* 30 × 25 in. (Same history as no. 125.) Companion to no. 125: *c.* 1775.

127. CHAFY, REV. JOHN (d. 1782). *In possession of the family* (1948). 30 × 25 in. Early 1750s: small whole-length, in a landscape, playing on a 'cello.

128. "CHAMPIAN" (*or* CHAMPAIN), MARQUIS. "A head" in 1797 sale (2): unfinished: bt. Walton.

129. CHAMPION, MRS ALEXANDER (d. 1818). 30 × 25 in. (Passed, via Miss Frances Conway, to Cobbe family, near Dublin: sold 1913: Mrs Daniel C. Jackling, San Francisco, 1933: André de Coppet, New York, 1939/54: with Newhouse Galls., New York, 1955.) From the middle 1770s.

130. CHARLOTTE, QUEEN (1744–1818). *Windsor Castle. H.M. The Queen.* 94 × 62½ in. R.A. 1781 (168). Until 1950 at Buckingham Palace. Engraved in mezzotint by Gainsborough Dupont. Pl. 185.

131. *The same. London. H.R.H. Princess Alice, Countess of Athlone.* 23½ × 15½ in. (Bequeathed by Duchess of Gloucester to Duke of Cambridge 1857: sale 11/vi/1904 (87) bt. A. Wertheimer—*repd.*: bt. from Colnaghi by (Sir) Max Michaelis 1906: presented by him.) Traditionally the "model" for no. 130, but it is doubtful if Gainsborough did such models, and it may prove to be Dupont's "engraver's copy".

132. *The same. Windsor Castle. H.M. The Queen.* Oval: 22 × 16 in. R.A. 1783 (134): painted September 1782.

133. *The same. New York. Metropolitan Museum* (*Bache collection*). 23¼ × 17½ in. (Duke of Waldeck-Pyrmont, Schloss Arolsen: Leopold Hirsch, London: with Duveen: Jules S. Bache, New York; bequeathed 1943.) An original repetition of no. 132.

134. CHARLOTTE AUGUSTA MATILDA. H.R.H. PRINCESS (1766–1828). *Windsor Castle. H.M. The Queen.* Oval: 22 × 16 in. R.A. 1783 (134): painted September 1782.

135. *The same* (with her two sisters). *Buckingham Palace. H.M. The Queen.* Cut down to 51 × 70½ in.: (originally 100 × 70½ in.). Painted for R.A. 1784, but not exhibited. Engraved by Gainsborough Dupont, 1783, before it was cut down.

136. CHARLTON, DR RICE (1710–89). *Bath. Holburne of Menstrie Museum.* 90 × 60 in. (Anon. (= Charlton family) sale 25/iii/1893 (378) bt. in: with Agnew 1904: E. M. Hodgkins sale 29/vi/1934 (27) bt. Bethel: Ernest E. Cook, Bath: bequeathed through N.A.C.F., 1955.) S.A. 1766 (51). Pl. 87.

137. CHARLTON, ROBERT AND SUSANNAH (Mrs H. F. Yeatman). *Richmond (Va.). Museum of Fine Arts.* 57 × 46 in. (Descended to G. W. Charlton and Mrs Fleming: bt. Agnew, 1904: W. Lockett Agnew, 1904/6: with Sulley, 1906: with Sedelmeyer, 1913: S. B. Joel sale 31/v/1935 (5) bt. Vicars for Eckstein: Sir Bernard Eckstein sale, Sotheby's, 8/xii/1948 (73) bt. Bellesi: Mr and Mrs Adolph Dill Williams, Richmond, Va.: bequeathed, 1952.) Later Bath work. Pl. 149.

138. CHESTERFIELD, PHILIP, 4TH EARL OF (1694–1773). *Chevening. Earl Stanhope.* 30 × 25 in. Inscribed 1769: painted for 2nd Earl Stanhope. Pl. 119.

139. CHESTERFIELD, PHILIP, 5TH EARL OF (1755–1815). *London. Sir John Leigh, Bart.* 86 × 61 in. (Passed to Countess of Carnarvon 1871: Earl of Carnarvon sale 22/v/1925 (109) bt. for Sir J. Leigh.) R.A. 1778 (112).

140. *The same. Loch Fea (Ireland). Major J. E. Shirley.* 30 × 25 in. Bust from same sitting as no. 139.

141. CHESTERFIELD, ANNE, COUNTESS OF (d. 1798) *London. Sir John Leigh, Bt.* 86 × 61 in. (Passed to Countess of Carnarvon, 1871: Earl of Carnarvon sale 22/v/1925 (108) bt. for Sir J. Leigh.) R.A. 1778 (113): companion to no. 139.

142. *The same. Southwick Park. Mrs E. S. Borthwick-Norton.* 30 × 25 in. (By descent through the Thistlethwayte family.) Bust from same sitting as no. 141.

143. *The same. Loch Fea (Ireland). Major J. E. Shirley.* 30×25 in. Similar to no. 142: companion to no. 140.

144. CHETWYND, RICHARD, 5TH VIS-COUNT (1757–1821). 30×25 in. (Biggs sale 13/v/1870 (53) bt. Toovey: bt. from S. E. Letts by Agnew, 1906: Mrs Bevan 1906: with Vicars in 1920s.) Early London work.

145. CHOLMLEY, NATHANIEL (1721–91). *Whitwell. Hon. Mrs. I. M. H. Strickland.* 49½×39 in. (At Howsham Hall until 1948.) Dated 1785 on the back. Pl. 234.

146. CHOLMLEY, MISS. *See* MULGRAVE, LADY.

147. CHRISTIE, JAMES (1730–1803). *Malibu (California). J. Paul Getty Museum.* 49½×39½ in. (J. A. Christie sale 20/v/1927 (29) bt. Agnew: with Knoedler: bt. by J. P. Getty, 1937.) R.A. 1778 (117). Pl. 194.

148. CLANWILLIAM, THEODOSIA, COUN-TESS OF (1744–1817). 49½×39½ in. (Earl of Darnley sale 1/v/1925 (18) bt. Tooth: with Duveen, 1933 and 1957.) A marriage portrait, inscribed with the date, 1765.

CLARE, LORD. *See* NUGENT, EARL.

CLARENCE, H.R.H., WILLIAM, DUKE OF. *See* WILLIAM IV.

149. CLARGES, LOUISA, LADY (1760–1809). *Narborough (formerly) Mrs Stella Hotblack (1955).* 50×40 in. (Presumably in 1797 sale (22) bt. Crofts. Anon. (?= Clarges, sale 29/vi/1878 (84) bt. Bacon: James Price sale 15/vi/1895 (78) bt. Agnew: J. Ruston sale 21/v/1898 (21) bt. Agnew: Sir Charles Tennant: Edmund Davis by 1905: Sir E. Davis sale 7/vii/1939 (120) bt. in: resold 15/v/1942 (119) bt. Leggatt.) Possibly begun about the time of her marriage, 1777: never finished.

150. CLARGES, MISS MARY (Mrs Narbone Vincent) (?). 29×24 in. (F. Austen, Capel Manor: with Knoedler, 1927: Sulley and others sale 1/vi/1934 (32) bt. Wells—*repd.*) Probably late Bath period.

151. CLARGES, MISS. *Richmond (Va.). Virginia Museum of Fine Arts.* 29×24 in. (Anon. (?= Clarges) sale 29/vi/1878 (86) bt. Bacon: William Lee, 1882: E. L. Raphael by 1893: Raphael sale 20/v/1927 (11) bt. Tooth: bequeathed to Richmond by Mr and Mrs Adolph Dill Williams, 1952.) Probably from the 1770s. Pl. 176.

152. CLAYTON, SIR ROBERT, BT. (1740?–99). *Liverpool. Walker Art Gallery.* 49×39 in. (Sir H. Clayton sale 23/vi/1950 (34) bt. Agnew: with Tooth: presented to Liverpool, 1951.) The date 1769, probably correct, is on the back. Pl. 103.

153. CLIFFORD, LADY. "A head"—in 1797 sale (18) bt. Whitefoord.

154. CLIVE, ROBERT, LORD (1725–74). Engraved in mezzotint by J. McArdell (d. 1765).

155. CLIVE, LADY. "A head"—in 1797 sale (32) bt. Hodson. Presumably all that was completed of a whole length for which she was sitting in 1787 (Whitley, p. 271). An Inventory of 1771 of Lord Clive's pictures, at Powis Castle, includes "Gainsborough. The Family Piece", which is untraceable today.

156. COGHLAN, MISS. 30×25 in. Engraved in mezzotint by J. R. Smith, 1770: a variant engraved 1772.

157. COKE, THOMAS WILLIAM (Earl of Leicester: 1754–1842). *Holkham Hall. Earl of Leicester.* 95½×67 in. Possibly begun 1778 (a date inscribed on the picture): finished 1786 (Whitley, p. 267).

158. COKE, MR (?). 49½×39½ in. (Roger Coke sale 22/vii/1938 (64) bt. Freeman.) From the 1760s. Later called "Mr Coke of Brookhill", but there is a vague tradition the sitter was a Byng who married a Coke.

159. COLLINS, MRS. 30×25 in. (Lord Saye and Sele sale 8/vi/1928 (105) bt. Franks: *repd.* with Howard Young, New York, 1934.) Later Bath period.

160. COLLIQUE, HENRY. 30 × 25 in. (Passed to Miss Hatchett-Jackson: sale 20/vii/1934 (18) bt. Gooden & Fox: with Gooden & Fox, 1953.) London work, or by Dupont.

COLLIQUE, MISS. *See* HATCHETT, MRS CHARLES.

161. COLMAN, GEORGE (1732–94). *London. National Portrait Gallery* (59). 28½ × 23¼ in. (Bt. by Charles Webb, 1836: bt. by N.P.G. 1859.) Often engraved: the earliest is dated 1785.

162. COLTMAN, JOHN. 30 × 25 in. (Bt. from Miss Coltman, Bristol, by Newhouse Galleries, 1931.) Dated 1763 on the back.

163. CONWAY, FIELD-MARSHAL HENRY SEYMOUR (1721–95). *Inveraray Castle. Duke of Argyll.* 91 × 60½ (enlarged to 111 × 64 in.). R.A. 1780 (14). Engraved in mezzotint by Dupont, 1780. A repetition which may also prove to be an original is in the Royal Court House, Jersey.

164. CORNEWALL, RT. HON. CHARLES WOLFRAN (1735–89). 89 × 58 in. (Sir Geoffrey Cornewall, Bt., sale at Moccas Court by Russell, Baldwin & Bright, 17/vii/1946 (328) bt. in.) Painted 1785/6 (Whitley, pp. 237 and 257).

165. CORNEWALL, FREDERICK (1706–88). *Greenbank (Chester). E. Peter Jones.* 50 × 40 in. (Cornewall sale 8/vii/1905 (124) bt. Gooden & Fox: Anon. sale 10/v/1912 (72) bt. Agnew: Red Cross sale 20/iv/1918 (1915) (as *Thomas Cornewall*) bt. Gooden for E. Peter Jones.) Earlier 1760s.

166. CORNEWALL, THOMAS (1741–96). 50 × 40 in. (Cornewall sale 8/vii/1905 (123) bt. Colnaghi: Thatcher M. Adams sale, New York, 15/i/1920 (150) bt. Seaman.) Earlier 1760s.

167. CORNWALLIS, CHARLES, 1ST MARQUESS (1738–1805). *Buckingham Palace. H.M. The Queen.* 29½ × 24½ in. Painted for the Prince of Wales: the bill seems to date it 1781 (*Burl. Mag.,* Nov. 1946, p. 276.)

168. *The same. London. National Portrait Gallery* (281). 29½ × 24½ in. (Painted for Lord Rawdon (Marquess of Hastings): his heirs' sale, by Philips, 26/ii/1869 (215) bt. Graves for N.P.G.) R.A. 1783 (45).

COTTON, LADY. *See* ROWLEY, MISS PHILADELPHIA.

COURTOWN, EARL OF. *See* STOPFORD, LORD.

169. COWARD, THOMAS (d. 1773?). *Birmingham. City Art Gallery.* 50 × 40 in. (Descended to B. P. Smyth-Pigott, sale, Sotheby's, 13/x/1954 (166) bt. Agnew: bt. by Birmingham, 1955.) Early 1760s. The sitter's identity (within the Coward family) is not quite certain. Pl. 58.

170. COYTE, GEORGE. *Philadelphia. J. G. Johnson collection* (833). 29 × 24 in. (George Coyte, 1888: sold before 1898.) Reputed to be R.A. 1780 (147).

171. CRADOCK, ANNA FRANCISCA, MRS JOSEPH (d. 1816). *Merevale Hall. Sir W. F. S. Dugdale, Bart.* 30 × 25 in. Early Bath period.

CREUZE, MRS JOHN. *See* GOSSET, MISS ELIZABETH ANN.

CROCKET, CHARLES. *See under* GROUPS (no. 747).

172. CROFT, MRS ROBERT (1761–1841). *Steventon Manor. Capt. Bernard Hutton Croft* (1933). 30 × 25 in. Probably the *Mrs Crofts* shown at Schomberg House in 1784 (Whitley, p. 228).

173. CROSDILL, JOHN (1751–1825). R.A. 1780 (356). The picture has not been traced: the sitter was well known as a 'cellist.

174. CRUTTENDEN, SARAH (b. 1754) AND ELIZABETH (1753–1816). 44 × 58 in. (Elizabeth became Mrs Purvis: passed to A. K. Kennedy-Purvis: with Duveen, 1931/57.) From the later Bath period.

175. CUMBERLAND, H.R.H. ERNEST AUGUSTUS, DUKE OF (1771–1851). *Windsor Castle. H.M. The Queen.* 22 × 16 in. R.A. 1783 (134). Painted September 1782.

176. CUMBERLAND, H.R.H. HENRY FREDERICK, DUKE OF (1745–90). *Buckingham Palace. H.M. The Queen.* 93¾ × 56 in. R.A. 1777 (131). Pl. 183.

177. *The same. Buckingham Palace. H.M. The Queen.* 30 × 25 in. (reduced from 54 × 40 in.). (Unfinished: in 1797 sale (25) bt. Hammond, probably for the Prince of Wales: at Carlton House by 1816.) Only the lay-in for the head: the sittings were in 1783/4 (Whitley, pp. 210 and 227.)

178. *The same* (with the Duchess of Cumberland and Lady Elizabeth Luttrell). *Windsor Castle. H.M. The Queen.* Oval: 63¾ × 47½ in. (Exhibited for sale at Schomberg House, 1789 (70): Mrs Gainsborough sale 2/vi/1792 (74) perhaps bought for Queen Charlotte: at Carlton House 1816.) About 1785/8.

179. CUMBERLAND, ANNE, DUCHESS OF (1743–1808). *Dublin. National Gallery of Ireland* (795). 30 × 25 in. (Descended to Lady Wilmot Horton: sold from Catton Hall, 1912: bequeathed by Sir Hugh Lane, 1915.) Painted when Mrs Christopher Horton: it is inscribed with the date 1766.

180. *The same. Buckingham Palace. H.M. The Queen.* 93¾ × 56 in. R.A. 1777 (132). Pl. 182.

181. *The same. Windsor Castle. H.M. The Queen.* 48½ × 38½ in. (In 1797 sale (24) bt. Hammond for Prince of Wales.) Unfinished: painted 1783/4 (Whitley, pp. 210 and 227).

182. *The same* (?). *San Marino (Calif.). Henry E. Huntington Library and Art Gallery.* 36 × 28 in. (Probably a gift to Miss Sarah Lawley, sister of Lord Wenlock: sold by Lord Wenlock to C. J. Wertheimer, 1909: bt. from Scott and Fowles, 1909: possibly R.A. 1779 (99). See 1936 Huntington Catalogue by C. H. Collins Baker, pp. 44/6 for full details of the problems.

183. CUNLIFFE, MISS MARY (d. 1804?). 29 × 24 in. (Sir Foster Cunliffe sale, Sotheby's, 1/ii/1950 (114) bt. Hon. Mrs Macmillan.) The face seems to be Gainsborough of about 1760 and the rest to be the work of a drapery painter.

DALRYMPLE, GRACE. *See* ELLIOTT, MRS.

DANZI, FRANCESCA. *See* LE BRUN, MME.

184. DARNLEY, JOHN, 4TH EARL OF (1767–1831). *Washington. National Gallery (Widener collection).* 30 × 25 in. (Earls of Darnley till c. 1905: with Agnew: P. A. B. Widener, Elkins Park, Pa.: presented by J. E. Widener, 1942.) Painted 1785 (Whitley, p. 238).

185. DARTMOUTH, WILLIAM, 2ND EARL OF (1731–1801). *Patshull. Earl of Dartmouth.* 49 × 39 in. The receipt is dated 25/v/1769. There is also at Patshull a crayon portrait somehow connected with it.

186. DARTMOUTH, FRANCES CATHERINE, COUNTESS OF (c. 1733–1805). *Patshull. Earl of Dartmouth.* 49 × 39 in. The receipt is dated 25/v/1769. Companion to no. 185.

187. *The same. Patshull. Earl of Dartmouth.* 30 × 25 in. Presumably 1771: *cf.* Gainsborough's letter of 1771 (Whitley, pp. 73/4). There is also a small crayon at Patshull connected with nos. 186 and 187. Pl. 142.

188. DASHWOOD-PEYTON, FRANCES, LADY (d. 1808). 30 × 25 in. (Descended to Col. E. A. Bulwer: Anon. (= Bulwer) sale 10/v/1912 (45) bt. Agnew: Agnew sale 7/vi/1918 (21) bt. Tooth—*repd.* W. Wood, Boston.) Probably about the date of her marriage (1771).

189. DAVENPORT, WILLIAM YELVERTON (1750–1832). *Oyster Bay (L.I.). Mrs W. R. Coe.* 50 × 40 in. (Descended to Mrs Leicester-Warren, born Davenport, 1890: with Knoedler: with John Levy, New York: Mrs B. F. Jones, Pittsburg, by 1925: sale New York 4/xii/1941 (23).) From the 1780s.

190. DAVENPORT, MRS WILLIAM (Martha Talbot). *Castlehill (Ayr.). L. H. Wilson.* 30 × 25 in. (Miss Talbot sale 22/iii/1918 (126) bt. Blaker: with Ehrich, New York, 1920: Anon. sale 18/vii/1924 (67) bt. Colnaghi: with Croal Thompson 1929.) Bath period.

191. DAVY, ELEAZER (1725–1803). 29 × 24 in. (Passed to H. Barlee, sale 1/iii/1873 (75) bt.

Graves and sold to M. Colnaghi: Col. W. Hankey: bt. Sedelmeyer, 1899 and sold to D. H. King, 1899: King sale New York 31/iii/1905 (54); Anon. sale 14/vi/1907 (103) bt. Agnew: W. A. Coats: J. A. Coats sale 12/iv/1935 (75) bt. Tooth—*repd.*: Private collection, New York.) For the identification of the sitter see W. Roberts in *The Times* 8/vii/1907, where the date of 1774 is suggested, but it may be earlier.

192. DEHANEY, MR, MRS AND DAUGHTER. *London (in store). Princess Labia.* 94×58 in. (Anon. (=J. C. Traill) sale 29/v/1880 (117) bt. in: resold 27/v/1882 (128) bt. in: with Lesser 1885: Sir Julian Goldsmid sale 13/vi/1896 (66) bt. Tooth—*repd.*: Sir J. B. Robinson sale 6/vii/1923 (5) bt. in—*repd.*: thence to his daughter.) Bath period.

193. DERBY, EDWARD, 12TH EARL OF (1752–1834). *Knowsley. Earl of Derby.* 50×40 in. Engraved in mezzotint by George Keating, 1785.

194. DEVONSHIRE, GEORGIANA, DUCHESS OF (1757–1806). *Washington. National Gallery.* 92½×57½ in. (Painted for her mother, Countess Spencer: bt. from Althorp by Duveen, 1924: Hon. Andrew Mellon bequest, 1937.) Probably R.A. 1783 (78)—*see* Whitley, pp. 150 ff and 198 ff. Pl. 206.

195. *The same. New York. Mrs Mabel S. Ingalls.* Cut down (? from full-length) to 50×40 in. (Sold by Mrs Maginnis to J. Bentley, 1841: Wynn Ellis sale 6/v/1876 (63) bt. Agnew: stolen 6/v/1876 and recovered in Chicago 28/iii/1901: J. Pierpont Morgan, 1901: thence to his daughter, Mrs Satterlee.) Probably the remains of a very late work, perhaps belonging to Charles Boothby-Skrymshire in 1788 (*cf.* Whitley, p. 199). For its history as "The Stolen Duchess" see the Morgan Catalogue.
See also SPENCER, LADY GEORGIANA.

DILLON, LADY. *See* ERNE, LADY (and LADY DILLON).

196. DITCHER, DR. PHILIP (d. 1781). *London. Major-General Peck* (1933). 50×40 in. Probably mainly painted before 1774 but only finished in 1779 (Whitley, pp. 159/60). The sitter's daughter married the Rev. Kenrick Peck.

197. DIXON, MRS. Shown at Schomberg House, 1784 (Whitley, p. 228). Probably a half-length.

198. DODD, DR WILLIAM (1729–77). 30×25 in. (Bt. at Dodd sale 1777 by Earl of Fife: Anon. (=Rev. W. Green) sale 2/iv/1870 (156) bt. in and sold to Graves: Sir Joseph Hawley, 1873: W. Thorburn, 1898: R. W. Hudson sale 8/vii/1910 (127) bt. Dowdeswell.) Painted 1773 (Whitley, p. 98).

199. DONEGALL, ARTHUR, 1ST MARQUESS OF (1739–99) (?). *Upton House. Lord Templemore.* 91½×60 in. Within a year or two of 1770. For the problem of the identification of the sitter in this and nos. 200/1, *see* Walpole Society, XXXIII (1953), pp. 29/30.

200. *The same. Upton House. Lord Templemore.* 91½×60 in. Soon after 1780. See note to no. 199.

201. DONEGAL, ANNE, MARCHIONESS OF (d. 1780). *Upton House. Lord Templemore.* 91½×60 in. Middle 1760s. See note to no. 199.

202. DONNITHORNE, JAMES. *Woodbastwick Hall. Colonel H. J. Cator.* 80×61 in. (Descended to Arthur Mohun Harris: sale 14/vi/1907 (108) bt. for J. Cator.) Early 1760s. Pl. 71.

203. DORSET, JOHN FREDERICK, 3RD DUKE OF (1745–99). *Knole. Lord Sackville.* 30×25 in. Intended for R.A. 1782, but not shown. A receipt at Knole, dated 1784, indicates that a second version existed. Pl. 251.

204. DOUGLAS, ARCHIBALD, LORD (1748–1827). *Abercairny. Col. J. W. S. Drummond-Moray.* 50×40 in. Painted for the Duke of Queensberry, 1775, but refused and left unfinished: bt. by Lord Douglas from Mrs Gainsborough, 1797. Companion to no. 205.

205. DOUGLAS, LADY LUCY (1751–80). *The Hirsel. Earl of Home.* 50×40 in. Painted 1775 as companion to no. 204 (*q.v.*) and also refused and unfinished. Completed by George Richmond.

206. DOUGLAS, MRS JOHN (Mrs Gwynne Browne: 1746–1811). *Waddesdon Manor. National Trust.* 92½ × 57½ in. (Descended to Mrs P. S. Pierrepont (d. 1872): Baron Ferdinand de Rothschild *c.* 1873: Miss Alice de Rothschild: James de Rothschild.) Exhibited at Schomberg House, 1784. Pl. 237.

207. DOWNE, JOHN CHRISTOPHER, 5TH VISCOUNT (1764–1832). *Cincinnati. Art Museum.* 29 × 24 in. (Passed to Col. R. H. Brooke-Hunt: with Agnew *c.* 1907: with Scott and Fowles, New York: bequeathed 1928 by Mrs Mary M. Emery.) About 1781.

208. DRAPER, SIR WILLIAM (1721–87). *San Francisco. De Young Memorial Museum* (lent by Miss Elsa Schilling). 50 × 40 in. (Passed to 1st Lord Lurgan: the Misses Shirley: with John Levy, New York: E. D. Levinson by 1933: bt. by J. Weitzner 1956 from Levinson estate.) Probably the end of the 1760s.

209. DRAPER, LADY (d. 1778). 30 × 25 in. (Passed to the Drummonds of Stanmore: with Agnew, 1919: C. W. Cargill, Stanmore: Sulley sale 1/vi/1934 (6) bt. in—*repd.*: resold 3/v/1936 (36) bt. Hughes.) Probably later 1760s.

210. DRUMMOND, GEORGE (1758–89). *Oxford. Ashmolean Museum.* 90 × 58 in. (Painted for Alderman Harley: passed to Lady Rodney: bt. from Lord Rodney by Lord Burton *c.* 1887: Baroness Burton sale 4/v/1951 (46) bt. Gooden & Fox for Ernest Cook: bequeathed through the N.A.C.F. 1955.) Probably close to 1780: companion to no. 211. Pl. 218.

211. DRUMMOND, MRS GEORGE (Martha Harley: 1756–88). *Montreal. Art Gallery.* 90 × 58 in. (Same as no. 210: Baroness Burton sale 4/v/1951 (47) bt. Agnew: bt. by Montreal, 1951.) Companion to no. 210 (*q.v.*). Pl. 219.

212. *The same. London (in store). Princess Labia.* 49½ × 39½ in. (Painted for Alderman Harley and passed to Lord Rodney (*cf.* no. 210): bt. by Lord Revelstoke *c.* 1888: Revelstoke sale 3/vi/1893 (40) bt. Agnew: Mrs. Frederick Ames, Boston, 1898: Sir Joseph B. Robinson sale 6/vii/1923 (4)

bt. in—*repd.*: passed to his daughter.) Perhaps painted just before her marriage in 1779.

213. DRUMMOND, HON. HENRY (d. 1795). *Albury Park. Helen, Duchess of Northumberland.* 30 × 25 in. Probably *c.* 1775/80. Companion to no. 214.

214. DRUMMOND, HON. MRS HENRY (Elizabeth Compton: 1734–1819). *Albury Park. Helen, Duchess of Northumberland.* 30 × 25 in. Companion to no. 213 (*q.v.*): their grandson was father of Louisa, Duchess of Northumberland.

215. DUGDALE, MRS RICHARD (1733–1819). *Merevale Hall. Sir W. F. S. Dugdale, Bt.* 30 × 25 in. Early Bath period.

DUMBLETON, MRS CHARLES. *See* BUXTON, MISS SARAH.

DUNCOMBE, HON. ANNE. *See* RADNOR, COUNTESS OF.

216. DUNCOMBE, HON. FRANCES (Mrs Bowater: 1757–1827). *Longford Castle. Earl of Radnor.* 29½ × 24½ in. Inscribed with the date 1773: paid for September, 1774. Pl. 162.

217. *The same. New York. Frick Collection.* 91 × 60 in. (Passed with Old Dalby Hall to the Rev. G. W. Sawyer: sold at the house, 1871: with Graves: Earl of Chesterfield, 1871: Baron Lionel de Rothschild, 1873: with C. J. Wertheimer, 1907: bt. by H. C. Frick, 1911.) Probably about 1777.

218. DUNDONALD, ISABELLA, COUNTESS OF (d. 1808). *Rye (N.Y.) E. F. Price.* 30 × 25 in. (Descended to Rev. J. M. St Clere Raymond: sale, at Belchamp Hall, by G. Coote & Son, 29/v/1894 (79) bt. Sir Walter Greene, Bt.: Sir Raymond Greene, 1920; with Scott & Fowles, New York.) Later Bath period.

219. DUNSTANVILLE, FRANCIS, LORD DE (1757–1835). *Washington. Corcoran Gallery of Art.* 49½ × 39½ in. (Sold by A. F. Basset to A. Wertheimer, 1907: with Agnew, 1908: bequeathed by Senator W. A. Clark, 1925.) Probably about 1786: companion to no. 220. *See also* BASSET, F.

220. DUNSTANVILLE, FRANCES SUSAN-NA, LADY DE (d. 1823). *Washington. Corcoran Gallery of Art.* 49½ × 39½ in. (The same history as no. 219.) Painted 1786 as *Lady Basset* (Whitley, p. 265).

221. DUPONT, GAINSBOROUGH (*c.* 1755–97). *London. National Gallery* (6242). 17½ × 14½ in. (Passed to Richard Lane: bt. from him by George Richmond before 1856: Richmond sale 1/v/1897 (10) bt. Agnew: bt. from Colnaghi by Sir Edgar Vincent (later Viscount D'Abernon), 1897; bequeathed by Viscountess D'Abernon, 1954.) Presumably an unfinished picture of the earlier 1770s. Pl. 152.

222. *The same.* 25 × 20 in. (Passed to Mrs S. E. Browne by 1856: bequeathed by Miss Emily Sarah Browne to Mansfield College, Oxford, 1906: Anon. (= Mansfield College) sale 29/i/1954 (128) bt. Bellesi.) A few years later than no. 221.

223. DUPONT, PHILIP. *Cambridge. Fitzwilliam Museum.* 30 × 24½ in. (R. G. Dupont sale, at Sudbury, 29/v/1874 (126) bt. Chance: presented by C. Fairfax Murray, 1911.) Suffolk period.

224. DUPONT, PHILIP. 30 × 25 in. (R. G. Dupont sale, at Sudbury, 29/v/1874 (131) bt. M. Colnaghi: sold by Graves to Louis Huth, 1875: Huth sale 20/v/1905 (100) bt. Colnaghi: with F. Gurlitt, Berlin, 1906: Marcus Kappel, Berlin: with Knoedler, 1914: W. H. Sage sale, New York, 15/xi/1932 (32)—*repd.*: Friedenberg, etc., sale, New York, 4/v/1950 (99).) Presumably Bath period and probably a different sitter from no. 223.

225. DUPUIS, MRS RICHARD (Rebecca Mary Kilderbee: d. 1827). 30 × 25 in. (Descended to Admiral Spencer de Horsey: sale 14/vi/1929 (42) bt. Savile Gallery—*repd.*: with Agnew, 1948.) From the 1780s.

226. DURBIN, SIR JOHN (1734–1814). 30 × 25 in. (Anon. (= Durbin) sale 9/vii/1926 (49) bt. Leger: with Ehrich, New York, 1933.) About 1762.

226a. DURBIN (Eliza Collett, wife of Sir John: 1737–62). *Clevedon Court. Sir Arthur Elton, Bt.* 30 × 25 in. About 1762.

DYMOKE, MISS ELIZABETH. *See* WYNNE MRS ROBERT.

227. EARDLEY, MARIA MAROW, LADY (1743–94). *Havana (Cuba). Hon. Oscar B. Cintas.* 84 × 58 in. (Given by Sir Sampson Gideon (Lord Eardley) to Viscount Gage *c.* 1777: sold to J. P. Morgan *c.* 1890: sold through Knoedler, 1943.) Probably about the time of her marriage (1766). Pl. 94.

228. *The same* (with her daughter, Maria Marow). *Balcarres. Earl of Crawford and Balcarres.* 91 × 60 in. (Passed to the daughter, Lady Saye and Sele (1767–1834): sold to Sir Robert Loyd-Lindsay (later Lord Wantage), 1884: passed to Lord Crawford, 1920.) R.A. 1770 (83). Pl. 126.

229. EDEN, SIR JOHN, 4TH BART. (1740–1812). *Windlestone. Sir Timothy Eden, Bt.* 29½ × 24½ in. Probably about 1767 and companion to no. 230.

230. EDEN, DOROTHEA, LADY (d. 1792). 30 × 25 in. *New York. Estate of A. W. Ericson.* (Descended to Mrs Eden Kaye Greville, 1885: James Price, 1887: Sir Julian Goldsmid sale 13/vi/1896 (65) bt. Agnew: C. J. Wertheimer, 1904: Mrs Simpson, New York, 1915: A. W. Ericson, New York, 1931.) Probably early 1770s.

231. EDGAR, MISS ELIZABETH (1733–91). 29 × 24 in. (Sold by Mrs Mileson Gery Edgar *c.* 1898.) Presumably an original of the 1750s.

232. EDGAR, MISS KATHERINE (1740–1810). *London (in store). Princess Labia.* 29 × 24 in. (Bt. from Mrs Mileson Gery Edgar by Donaldson *c.* 1898: Sir Joseph B. Robinson sale 6/vii/1923 (9) bt. in.) From the later 1750s.

233. EDGAR, MISS. *Ipswich. Christchurch Mansion Museum* (*Loan since* 1947). 48½ × 39½ in. (Bt. from Martin Colnaghi by Donaldson: Sir George Donaldson sale, Hove, by Puttick & Simpson, 7/vii/1925 (264) bt. in: Mrs Mott sale 12/vii/1946 (62) bt. in.) About 1760: it is very doubtful if the sitter is really one of the Miss Edgars.

234. EDGAR, ROBERT (1741–78). 30×25 in. (Mrs Mileson Gery Edgar, Ipswich: sold *c.* 1897 to Lawrie: Anon. (=R. W. Hudson) sale 8/vii/1910 (128) bt. Sulley.) Presumably a late Ipswich work. A crayon of Mrs Robert Edgar, ascribed to Gainsborough, is listed in *Aedes Edgarorum*, 1868.

235. EGERTON, MRS SCROOPE (Anne Lindsay). *Montreal. Richard F. Angus.* 30×25 in. (Descended to Rev. Edward Salter (d. *c.* 1845): A. W. H. Block, Surbiton: Anon. sale 23/vii/1892 (138) bt. Gooden: R. B. Angus, Montreal, by 1912.) Said to have been painted 1768. Pl. 106.

236. EGREMONT, ALICIA MARIA, COUNTESS OF (1729–94). *Petworth. John Wyndham.* 93×57 in. Probably middle or later 1760s.

237. ELD, JOHN (1704–96). *Boston. Museum of Fine Arts.* 93×59 in. (Painted for the Staffordshire General Infirmary: sale 10/v/1912 (49) bt. Knoedler: bt. by Boston, 1912.) Traditionally painted in 1772. Pl. 147.

238. ELIZABETH, H.R.H. PRINCESS (1770–1840). *Windsor Castle. H.M. The Queen.* 22¾×16¼ in. R.A. 1783 (134): painted September 1782. *See also* CHARLOTTE AUGUSTA MATILDA. PRINCESS ETC.

239. ELLIOTT, MRS (Grace Dalrymple: 1758?–1823). *New York. Metropolitan Museum.* 92½×60½ in. (Painted for Marquess of Cholmondeley: sold to W. K. Vanderbilt, New York, *c.* 1880s: bequeathed, 1920.) R.A. 1778 (114): engraved in mezzotint by J. Dean, 1779. Pl. 184.

240. *The same. New York. Frick Collection.* 29½×25 in. (Passed to the sitter's daughter, who married Lord Charles Bentinck: bt. from Duke of Portland by Duveen, 1930: bt. for Frick collection, 1946.) Probably R.A. 1782 (184). Pl. 211.

240a. ELTON, ISAAC. 30×25 in. (With Howard Young, New York, 1926.) Bath period.

241. ERNE, LADY (1758/9–1842) AND LADY DILLON (1757–82). 39×45½ in. (Passed to Marquess of Normanby: Sir Charles Tennant, by

1885: Lord Glenconner: with Howard Young, New York, 1931.) Probably about 1776, when both sitters married.

242. ERNST, JOHANN AUGUST. *Petworth, John Wyndham.* 30×25 in. Later Bath period.

243. ESSEX, GEORGE, 5TH EARL OF (1757–1839). Sitting in 1785 (Whitley, p. 243).

244. EVANS, MISS. *Buffalo. Albright Art Gallery.* 50×40 in. (Sir C. Willoughby: Miss Gabb, 1873: Anon. (=Graves) sale 10/v/1873 (93) bt. Agnew: James Price: with Alfred de Rothschild: J. Pierpont Morgan by 1895: bt. by Buffalo, 1945.) Probably by Dupont *c.* 1790.

245. EYRE, SAMUEL (d. 1794). 30×25 in. (Mrs Warre Cornish sale, Sotheby's, 12/xii/1934 (125) bt. H. M. Clarke: Anon. sale, Robinson & Fisher, 24/xi/1938 (153) bt. Freeman: Capt. H. L. Butler, 1938.) Early Bath period.

246. FAGNANI, MARIA (Marchioness of Hertford: 1769–1856). Painted for George Selwyn, 1775 (Castle Howard MSS.).

247. FANE, HENRY (d. 1777). 30×25 in. (Sir Miles Stapleton sale 26/iii/1926 (10) bt. Leggatt: with Croal Thompson: Viscount D'Abernon, 1927: Viscountess D'Abernon sale 18/iii/1955 (40) bt. Agnew.) Bath period: probably 1760s.

248. *The same. Wormsley. F. W. Fane* (1934). 30×25 in. Probably a repetition of no. 247.

249. FANE, HON. MRS HENRY (1758–1838). *San Marino (Calif.). Henry E. Huntington Library and Art Gallery.* 35½×27½ in. (Passed to Lady Michel: sale 12/v/1888 (22) bt. Davis: E. L. Raphael (1889–1925): bt. from Duveen, 1926.) R.A. 1782 (44). Pl. 248.

250. *The same. London. Oscar Yerburgh.* 35½×27½ in. (R. J. Fane sale 9/vii/1887 (147) bt. Agnew: Daniel Thwaites 1888: thence to his daughter, Mrs Yerburgh.) Exhibited at Schomberg House, 1786: "in the habit of Rubens' wife". Pl. 247.

FERRERS, LADY. *See* CAMPBELL, LADY FREDERICK.

251. FINCH, LADY CHARLOTTE (1758/9–1808). *Packington Hall. Earl of Aylesford.* 30 × 25 in. About 1763.

252. FISCHER, JOHANN CHRISTIAN (1733–1800). *Buckingham Palace. H.M. The Queen.* 89½ × 58¾ in. (Earl of Abingdon sale, at Wytham Abbey, 1802: Blackden sale 3/vi/1803 (32) bt. Morland: presented to the Prince Regent by the Duke of Cumberland, 1809.) R.A. 1780 (222). Pl. 216.

FISCHER, MRS J. C. *See* GAINSBOROUGH, MARY.

253. FISHER, MRS (*called*). *Cambridge (Mass.). Henry S. Williams.* 30 × 25 in. (With Sulley: with Agnew, 1927: with Contini, Rome, 1928: with Knoedler, 1929–48: bt. 1948.) From the 1760s: Exh. Vienna, 1927 (60)—*repd.*

254. FITZHERBERT, MRS (1756–1837). *San Francisco. California Palace of the Legion of Honour.* 29 × 24 in. (Sent to sitter by William IV, 1830: Hon. Mrs Dawson Damer, 1837: Lord Fortescue, 1848: sold to A. Sanderson *c.* 1895: with J. H. Dunn: with Knoedler, 1912: J. Horace Harding sale, New York, 1/iii/1941 (60) bt. Knoedler: presented by H. K. S. Williams, 1941.) Delivered unfinished to Prince of Wales, 1784.

255. FITZPATRICK, LADY MARY (d. 1778). *London. Earl of Ilchester.* 30 × 25 in. Painted in the winter of 1764/5 (*The Connoisseur*, Feb. 1922, p. 88) for the Duke of Bedford.

256. FITZPATRICK, MISS. *Cincinnati. Art Museum.* 30 × 25 in. (Maurice Butler, Dublin: with Agnew: Donald G. Geddes, New York: with John Levy: Harry S. Leyman, Cincinnati, 1931: given, 1943.) Bath period.

257. FITZWILLIAM, HON. WILLIAM (1712–97). *Cambridge. Fitzwilliam Museum.* 29½ × 24½ in. Painted 1775 (inscribed on back). Pl. 160.

258. FLETCHER, COL. THOMAS (d. 1780). *Sandy. Heirs of Sir P. Malcolm Stewart, Bt.* 30 × 25 in. (With French Gallery *c.* 1909: S. Mitchell sale

24/xi/1933 (125) bt. Spink: Stewart sale, 18/x/1960 (18) bt. Leggatt. Later Bath period.

259. FLETCHER, MRS THOMAS (Mrs Mylne: 1749–1852). 30 × 25 in. (K. D. Maclachlan sale, Robinson & Fisher, 27/vi/1912 (171) bt. Wallis—*repd.*) Probably companion to no. 258.

260. FLUDYER, CAROLINE, LADY (d. 1803). 30 × 25 in. (Passed to Col. Pechell: with Leger, 1929: Leger sale, New York, 2/iii/1933 (81) bt. Ehrich—*repd.*) Later Bath period.

261. FOLKESTONE, JACOB, 1ST VISCOUNT (1694–1761). *London. Royal Society of Arts.* 93 × 57½ in. Posthumous portrait, based on a Hudson: painted 1776.

262. FOLKESTONE, ELIZABETH, VISCOUNTESS (1711–82). *Liverpool. "Sudley" Art Collection.* 49 × 39 in. (Descended in Bouverie-Pusey family: bt. in 1880s by George Holt, Liverpool: bequeathed to City of Liverpool by Miss E. G. Holt, 1945.) Perhaps also about 1776 (*cf.* no. 261.) Pl. 166.

263. FOOTE, SAMUEL (1720–77). 30 × 25 in. (Possibly Smyth-Pigott sale, at Brockley Hall, Somerset, 10/x/1849 (7): Lord Taunton: E. A. V. Stanley: bt. by Buttery, 1923: with Tooth: Col. H. C. Cox sale, Toronto, by F. Waddington, May 1949 bt. Hahn.) Bath period.
See also under GENTLEMAN UNKNOWN (no. 777).

FORD, MISS ANNE. *See* THICKNESSE, MRS PHILIP.

264. FORDYCE, ALEXANDER (d. 1789). *Balcarres House. Earl of Crawford and Balcarres.* 30 × 25 in. Probably 1770/71. Pl. 143.

265. FORDYCE, LADY MARGARET (d. 1814). *Dalmeny. Earl of Rosebery.* 30 × 25 in. (Descended to Lady Stuart de Rothesay: Louisa, Marchioness of Waterford: bt. by Earl of Rosebery *c.* 1890.) Probably *c.* 1776. Pl. 174.

266. *The same. Balcarres House. Earl of Crawford and Balcarres.* 94 × 59½ in. R.A. 1772 (94). Pl. 136.

FOX, LADY MARY. *See* FITZPATRICK, LADY MARY.

267. FRANCO, RAPHAEL (d. 1781). 60 × 56 in. (Earl of Egremont sale 21/v/1892 (81) bt. A. Wertheimer: with Lawrie, 1898: Anon. (= R. W. Hudson) sale 8/vii/1910 (125) bt. Duke, U.S.A.) Apparently dated 1780.

268. FRANCO, MRS. A full-length: shown at Schomberg House, 1786 (Whitley, p. 266).

269. FRANKS, MISS ISABELLA (b. 1766?). *Needwood House. Baroness Burton.* 47¾ × 39 in. (Descended to W. Honywood: bt. by Lord Burton *c.* 1886.) About 1770/72. Pl. 118.

270. FRERE, TOBIAS (d. 1763). 30 × 25½ in. (Bt. from Wallis by D. T. Watson, Pittsburgh, 1897: Watson sale, New York, 16/iv/1917 (148) —repd.) Early Bath work.

271. FRERE, MRS CHARLOTTE. *Port Sunlight. Lady Lever Art Gallery.* 30 × 25 in. (J. Orrock sale 4/vi/1904 (93) bt. A. Smith.) Early Bath work.

272. GAGE, WILLIAM, 2ND VISCOUNT (1718–91). *Firle Place. Viscount Gage.* 91½ × 59 in. (Exchanged by sitter, after 1777, with Lord Eardley: thence by descent to David Fremantle: returned to Firle, 1952.) R.A. 1777 (134). Pl. 172.

273. GAINSBOROUGH, HUMPHREY (1718–76). *Hatherleigh. Mrs G. E. R. Prior* (1948). 30 × 25 in. (Painted for Thomas Hall of Harpsden: his descendants' sales 8/v/1897 (34) bt. in: 12/iii/1898 (70) bt. Martin Colnaghi: A. J. Forbes-Leith (Lord Leith of Fyvie), 1904.) Probably later Bath period.

274. *The same.* 24 × 20 in. (Descended from the painter to Richard Lane: sold 1841 to William Sharpe: W. S. Sharpe sale 26/vii/1957 (117) bt. Betts.) A finished study for no. 273.

275. GAINSBOROUGH, JOHN (1711–85). *Dublin. National Gallery of Ireland.* 29 × 23 in. (Descended from the painter to Richard Lane: sold 1841 to W. Sharpe: Sharpe sale 8/v/1897 (11) bt. C. F. Murray: presented by Sir Hugh Lane, 1914.) Probably early 1750s. Pl. 4.

276. *The same. Niagara Falls. Harry Oakes* (1929). 30 × 25 in. (Baroness Lucas sale 26/v/1922 (73) bt. C. Partridge: bt. from Dyer, 1929.) Probably Bath period.

277. *The same.* 24 × 19 in. (R. Gainsborough Dupont sale, Sudbury, 29/v/1874 (124) bt. Hogarth: G. M. Butterworth, Saffron Walden, 1886.) Not known, but presumably an original.

278. GAINSBOROUGH, MRS JOHN (d. 1769). For miniatures said to be of Gainsborough's mother, see no. 796. The portrait formerly in Francis Howard's possession has proved to be of a different sitter and is signed *F. Kyte pinx./1741.*

279. GAINSBOROUGH, MISS MARGARET (1752–1820). *Upton House. Viscount Bearsted.* 13¾ × 12 in. (Bt. *c.* 1875 by Robert Lofft, Bury St Edmunds: Mrs Herbert Bell, Epsom: sold to Knoedler, 1930: bt. before 1947.) About 1756.

280. *The same. London. National Gallery* (1482). 30 × 25 in. (Probably given by the sitter to Henry Briggs: Miss Clarke, 1859: passed to family of Richard J. Lane, by whom presented, 1896.) Probably early 1770s. Pl. 153.

281. *The same. London. Estate of the late Adolph Hirsch.* 30 × 26½ in. (Passed from sitter to Rev. W. Green: bt. thence, 1876, by John Heugh: sale 10/v/1878 (238) bt. Agnew: Sir Robert Loder sale 29/v/1908 (527) bt. A. Wertheimer: Adolph Hirsch, 1914.) Unfinished: its companion (no. 289) is dated 1777. Hitherto wrongly called Mrs Fischer.

282. GAINSBOROUGH, MARGARET *or* MARY. *Sandy. Heirs of Sir P. Malcolm Stewart, Bt.* 50 × 40 in. (Empson sales 4/iv/1840 (16) bt. in: 21/xi/1840 (38) bt. in. 27/iv/1844 (15) bt. Harman: bt. from Leggatt by Sir P. M. Stewart.) Early 1760s: she is shown with a dog.

283. *The same. Chetwode Manor. Mrs Louis Fleischmann.* 29 × 25 in. (Anon. sale 16/vii/1909 (119) bt. Peile: bt. from Sir Hugh Lane by L. Fleischmann.) Perhaps very late Ipswich work: she is shown gleaning. It may have been part of a double portrait mentioned in the *Somerset House*

Gazette, 1824, and once the property of G. Strutt. *See also under* LADY UNKNOWN (no. 787).

284. GAINSBOROUGH, MARGARET AND MARY (together). *London. Victoria and Albert Museum.* 16×24½ in. (Passed from Margaret Gainsborough to John Jackson, R.A. (d. 1831): bt. jointly by Macready (sale 1873) and John Forster, and divided into two: reunited by Forster and bequeathed to V. and A., 1876.) About 1758. Pl. 50.

285. *The same. London. National Gallery* (1811). 44¾×41¼ in. (Rev. James Hingeston (d. 1777): Owen Roe, Ipswich, 1856: bt. by Henry Vernon *c.* 1870 and bequeathed to N.G., 1900.) Probably very late Ipswich work: unfinished. Pl. 52.

286. *The same. London. National Gallery* (3812). 29¾×24¾ in. (Descended from Gainsborough's sister, Susanna, to Rev. E. R. Gardiner, who bequeathed it to Mrs E. N. Harward: sale 11/v/1923 (101) bt. Knoedler: bt. 1923.) A little later than no. 285: also unfinished. Pl. 51.

287. *The same. Worcester* (*Mass.*). *Art Museum.* 49½×39½ in. (Sir Thomas Baring (d. 1848): Bryant, 1856: J. W. Brett sale 9/iv/1864 (735) bt. Myers: H. Wilkinson sale 21/vi/1888 (131) bt. Collette: Anon. sale 6/xii/1902 (81) bt. C. J. Wertheimer: Wertheimer sale 10/v/1912 (61) bt. Agnew: Sir Edgar Vincent (Viscount D'Abernon) 1913: bt. from Duveen 1917.) About 1763/4. Pl. 90.

288. *The same. Southill. Simon Whitbread.* 91×59 in. Probably early 1770s and acquired for Southill *c.* 1789.

289. GAINSBOROUGH, MARY (Mrs J. C. Fischer: 1748–1826). *London. National Gallery* (5638). 30×26½ in. (Descended to Rev. W. Green: bt. 1876 by John Heugh: sale 10/v/1878 (237) bt. Agnew: John Corbett sale 18/vi/1904 (111) bt. Carfax: Alfred Beit, 1906: bequeathed by Sir Otto Beit, Bt.: received, 1945.) Dated 1777: unfinished and companion to no. 281. Pl. 175.

290. GAINSBOROUGH, THOMAS (1727–88). *Houghton. Marchioness of Cholmondeley.* 23×19½ in.

(Passed to Richard Lane: bt. in at sale 26/ii/1831 (50) and sold to George Richmond in 1850s: Richmond sale 1/v/1897 (11) bt. Agnew: C. Fairfax Murray sale, Paris, 15/vi/1914 (14) bt. in: bt. by Sir Philip Sassoon, Bt., 1914.) Dated on back 1754. Pl. 8.

291. *The same. Northwick Park. E. G. Spencer-Churchill.* 29¾×24½ in. (Passed to Richard Lane and bt. in at sale 26/ii/1831 (51): bt. from Dunsford by Lord Northwick, 1832.) Some years later than no. 290. Pl. 6.

292. *The same. London. Royal Academy.* 29½×24 in. (Presented by Miss Margaret Gainsborough, 1808.) Not quite finished: probably the picture he was painting for Abel, when he died in 1787. Pl. 208.

293. *The same. London. Courtauld Institute.* 30×25 in. (Passed to Richard Lane: bt. in at sale 7/vii/1838 (171): sold to W. Sharpe, 1841: bt. from Sharpe family 1921 by Samuel Courtauld.) Replica of no. 292, completed by Dupont.

294. *The same. Holkham. Earl of Leicester.* 30×25 in. Probably about 1786.

295. *The same. London. Hugh L. Agnew.* 29×17 in. (T. Hakewill sale 23/ii/1895 (49) bt. Agnew: Sir William Agnew.) Finished study of no. 294.

296. GAINSBOROUGH, THOMAS (with wife and daughter). *Houghton. Marchioness of Cholmondeley.* 35½×27 in. (Descended from Gainsborough's sister, Susanna, to Rev. E. R. Gardiner, who bequeathed it to Mrs E. N. Harward: sale 11/v/1923 (103) bt. Knoedler: bt. by Sir Philip Sassoon, Bt., 1927.) About 1751/2. Colour Plate. *See also* no. 752.

297. GAINSBOROUGH, MRS THOMAS (1728–98). 30×25 in. (Passed to Richard Lane: sold to W. Sharpe, 1841: Sharpe sale 8/v/1897 (12) bt. Coureau: M. Gagnier, Brussels, 1924.) From the middle or later 1750s. Pl. 7.

298. *The same.* 28×23½ in. (Descended to Rev. W. Green: bt. 1876 by John Heugh: sale 10/v/1878 (236) bt. Agnew: Sir Robert Loder sale 29/v/1908 (528) bt. A. Wertheimer: with Brummer, Paris,

1912.) Unfinished: companion to nos. 281 and 289, the latter dated 1777.

299. *The same. London. Courtauld Institute.* 29¼ × 24¼ in. (Passed to Richard Lane: bt. in at sale 7/vii/1838 (172) and sold to W. Sharpe, 1841: bt. from Sharpe family by Samuel Courtauld, 1921.) Probably from the end of the 1770s. Pl. 209. *See also under* LADY UNKNOWN (no. 794).

300. GARDINER, EDWARD. *Bournemouth. Miss Gainsborough Gardiner.* 24 × 20 in. Probably late Ipswich period. The picture is destined for the Tate Gallery.

301. GARDINER, SUSAN (d. 1818). 24 × 21½ in. (Bequeathed by Rev. E. R. Gardiner to Mrs E. N. Harward: sale 11/v/1923 (105) bt. Knoedler: P. McFadden, New York, 1923.) Probably late Ipswich period.

GARLAND, MRS. *See* TALBOT, MISS INDIANA.

302. GARNETT, JOHN. D.D. (1709–82). 30 × 25 in. (Major Blois Brooke, Ufford Place: sold *c.* 1932. Anon. sale Sotheby's 14/xi/1962 (156).) Engraved in mezzotint by McArdell, when consecrated Bishop of Clogher, 1758.

303. GARNIER, GEORGE CHARLES (1739–1819). 42¼ × 36 in. (J. Carpenter Garnier sale 27/vii/1928 (135) bt. Colnaghi: with Colnaghi, 1955: Anon. sale 20/vii/1956 (71) bt. Klein.) Probably about 1766.

304. GARRICK, DAVID (1717–79). *Destroyed by fire at Stratford on Avon Town Hall, 1946.* 92¼ × 60 in. S.A. 1766 (50). Rehandled for the commission for the 1769 Shakespeare Commemoration at Stratford. Pl. 86.

305. *The same. Swinton Park. Countess of Swinton.* 30 × 25 in. (Albany Wallis (d. 1800): passed to Sir Belford H. Wilson: Anon. (= B. W. Wilson) sale 16/vi/1900 (105) bt. Agnew: Lord Masham.) R.A. 1770 (86 *or* 87).

306. *The same. Tockenham Manor. Major G. J. Buxton.* 30 × 25 in. (Passed by descent from James Clutterbuck.) Original repetition of no. 305

307. *The same. London. Mrs Oscar Ashcroft.* 30 × 25 in. (Presumably painted for Dr R. Schomberg: E. C. Schomberg sale 7/v/1904 (120) bt. Martin: F. Fleischmann, father of O. S. Ashcroft.) Original repetition of no. 305.

308. GARRICK, MRS DAVID (1724–1822). Oval: 28½ × 23½ in. (Probably Frances, Lady Rivers (d. 1860): Dr Hodges, 1868: Anon. sale 1/vi/1911 (125) bt. Hanson Walker: Sir T. Glen Coats sale 2/vii/1920 (11) bt. Hotham: Anon. sale 29/vii/1948 (13) bt. Bier.) Probably from the 1770s.

309. GEORGE III (1738–1820). *Windsor Castle. H.M. The Queen.* 94 × 62½ in. R.A. 1781 (146). Formerly at Buckingham Palace.

310. *The same. Windsor Castle. H.M. The Queen.* 22 × 16 in. R.A. 1783 (134): painted September 1782.

GEORGE IV. *See* WALES, GEORGE, PRINCE OF.

311. GIARDINI, FELICE DE (1716–96). *Knole. Lord Sackville.* 30 × 25 in. (Bt. by Duke of Dorset, 1793.) Early 1760s.

312. GIARDINI, MR (?). *Old Warden. Mrs. Shuttleworth.* 30 × 25 in. (John Chapman Walker, 1885: Major Shuttleworth, 1896.) Perhaps from the 1770s: a handsome young man, wholly unlike the elderly sitter in no. 311: perhaps another member of the Giardini family.

313. GIBBS, JOSEPH (1700?–88). *London. National Portrait Gallery* (2179). 23¼ × 19 in. (Anon. sale 20/vi/1919 (65) bt. Wheeler: G. Bullen sale 27/i/1928 (117) bt. Gooden & Fox: bt. 1928.) From the middle 1750s. Pl. 28.
See also GROUPS (no. 748).

GIDEON, LADY. *See* EARDLEY, LADY.

314. GISBORNE, JOHN. 30 × 25 in. (Anon. sale 11/vi/1920 (96) bt. Holt: Anon. sale 14/v/1926 (49) bt. Smith: Max Horwitz sale, New York, 15/xi/1945 (56).) Probably end of the 1750s.

315. GISBORNE, MRS JOHN (Anne Bateman: 1732–1800). 30 × 25 in. (Anon. sale 11/vi/1920 (95) bt. Tooth: Harold W. Hack sale,

New York, 2/xii/1938 (35)—*repd.*) Companion to no. 314: probably soon after marriage (1758).

316. GLENORCHY, WILLIELMA, LADY (1743–86). *New York. Mrs Ogden Reid.* 30×25 in. (Passed to T. G. B. Morgan-Grenville-Gavin: sale 26/v/1922 (120) bt. Leggatt.) Later Bath period.

317. GLOUCESTER, H.R.H. WILLIAM HENRY, DUKE OF (1743–1805). *Chewton Manor. Earl Waldegrave.* 91×55 in. (Mrs Gainsborough sale 10/iv/1797 (35) bt. Hammond: given to Princess Sophia of Gloucester by the Prince Regent, 1816.) Unfinished: perhaps begun 1775 (Whitley, p. 116).

318. GLOUCESTER, MARIA, DUCHESS OF (Lady Waldegrave: 1736–1807). *Los Angeles. County Museum.* 50×40 in. (Marquess of Bath sale, Sotheby's 18/xii/1940 (54) bt. Koetser: Alfred Hart, Los Angeles: presented 1951.) Painted during her widowhood as Lady Waldegrave, 1764/5.

319. *The same. Cincinnati. Institute of Fine Arts (Taft collection).* Cut down to 36¼×28½ in. (Perhaps Mrs Gainsborough sale 10/iv/1797 (27) bt. Dr Duval: Duchess of Gloucester, 1857: bequeathed to Duke of Cambridge: sale 11/vi/1904 (85) bt. Agnew: with Scott & Fowles: Charles P. Taft, Cincinnati, by 1909.) Possibly R.A. 1779 (98) as a full-length.

GODDARD, MRS WILLIAM. *See* SLOPER, MRS.

320. GOSSET, ISAAC (1713–99). *Northampton. Dr Gosset.* 30×25 in. R.A. 1780 (33).

321. GOSSET, ELIZABETH ANNE (Mrs John Creuzé: 1740–1804). *Paris. Louvre.* 30×25 in. (Mrs Gardner, 1867: Rev. I. H. Gosset: sold to Agnew *c.* 1904: bt. from Knoedler, 1928 by Marczell von Nemes and bequeathed to Louvre, 1932.) Late London work: shortly before her marriage (1788).

GOULD, SIR CHARLES. *See* MORGAN, SIR CHARLES.

GRAFTON, ELIZABETH, DUCHESS OF. *See* WROTTESLEY, MISS.

322. GRAHAM, HON. MRS THOMAS (1757–92). *Washington. National Gallery.* 35×27 in. (Descended to A. G. Maxtone-Graham: with Knoedler, 1912: Joseph E. Widener, 1912: passed to Washington, 1942.) Probably 1775: a little earlier than no. 323.

323. *The same. Edinburgh. National Gallery of Scotland.* 93×60 in. (Inherited from Lord Lynedoch by Robert Graham of Redgorton: bequeathed to Edinburgh, 1859.) R.A. 1777 (133). Pl. 173.

324. GRAVES, THOMAS, 1ST LORD (1725–1802). *London (in store). Princess Labia.* 49×39 in. (Sir Joseph B. Robinson *c.* 1900: sale 6/vii/1923 (6) bt. in: passed to his daughter.) Finished 1785 and shown at Schomberg House 1786.

325. GRAVES, WALWYN (1745–1813). *Mickleton Manor. Miss Mary Graves Hamilton.* 30×25 in. Later Bath period.

326. GREEN, SAMUEL (b. 1726). *Southill. Simon Whitbread.* 30×25 in. Dated 1781: painted for Samuel Whitbread.

327. GREGG, SIR FRANCIS (1700–88). *London. Tate Gallery.* 29½×24½ in. (Anon. sale 17/vi/1949 (35) bt. in: resold 14/x/1949 (115) bt. Agnew: bt. 1950.) Later Bath period.

328. GRIFFITH, CHRISTOPHER, Sr. (d. 1767). 30×25 in. (Inherited from Major Darby-Griffith by Lord Roundway, 1933: Lady Roundway sale, Sotheby's, 2/x/1946 (115) bt. Lumley: A. P. Good sale, Sotheby's, 15/vii/1953 (18) bt. in: resold 4/xi/1953 (59) bt. Leger.) Soon after 1760.

329. GRIFFITH, CHRISTOPHER, Jr. (1731–76). 30×25 in. (Inherited from Major Darby-Griffith by Lord Roundway, 1933: Anon. sale 23/vii/1954 (69) bt. Agnew.) Early 1760s. Companion to no. 330. A replica, in coll. J. G. Couper, Glasgow, 1937/56, was called *Robert Budd Vincent, R.N.*

330. GRIFFITH, MRS CHRISTOPHER, Jr. (1729–1801). 30×25 in. (Inherited from Major Darby-Griffith by Lord Roundway, 1933: Anon.

sale 23/vii/1954 (69) bt. Agnew.) Early 1760s:
companion to no. 329.

331. GRIGBY, JOSHUA. *London. Viscountess Kemsley.* 49×39 in. (Descended to Capt. J. Harcourt Powell: bt. from Leggatt.) Probably from middle 1760s. Pl. 102.

332. GROSVENOR, HENRIETTA, COUNTESS (d. 1828). *Eaton Hall. Estate of late Duke of Westminster.* Cut down to 39½×34½ in. S.A. 1767 (58) as a full-length.

GROSVENOR, ROBERT, EARL. *See* BELGRAVE, VISCOUNT.

333. GUILFORD, FRANCIS, 1ST EARL OF (1704–90). *Waldershare Park. Earl of Guilford.* 29½×24½ in. Receipt dated 20/v/1773 (£31/14/–). (Bodleian North MSS.) Pl. 140.

GWYDYR, LORD. *See* BURREL, SIR PETER.

334. HALLAM, MRS JOHN. 30×25 in. (Descended to Lady Lennard (née Hallam): Sir Henry Lennard sale 27/iv/1901 (46) bt. A. Wertheimer: with Agnew: Humphrey Roberts, 1901/3: bt. from Agnew by Gooden & Fox, 1903: with Wallis & Son, 1912/13.) Probably early London work.

335. HALLETT, WILLIAM (1764–1842) and wife (1763/4–1833). *London. National Gallery.* 93×70 in. (Passed to W. E. Hilliard: sold to Agnew, 1884: Sir N. M. Rothschild (Lord Rothschild), 1884: bt. from Lord Rothschild, 1954.) Painted in the autumn of 1785 (Whitley, p. 258). Pl. 274.

336. HAMILTON, DUKE OF. *Detroit. Mrs Horace Dodge.* 92×60 in. (Descended from Lady Anne Hamilton, Marchioness of Donegall, to Lord Templemore: bt. thence by Duveen, 1925: Lady Duveen, New York.) One of a series with nos. 199–201: for a discussion of the problems of identification, see Walpole Society, XXXIII (1953), pp. 29/30. It was reputed to be James, 5th Duke of Hamilton (1703–43), which is impossible. On grounds of likeness it may be Douglas, 8th Duke of Hamilton (1756–99), and a marriage portrait of 1778—although the line of descent for this and no. 337 is unexpected. Pl. 198.

337. HAMILTON, DUCHESS OF. *Detroit. Mrs Horace Dodge.* 92×60 in. (Same history as no. 336.) Companion to no. 336 (*q.v.*): it may be a marriage portrait of 1778. Pl. 199.

338. HAMILTON, ALEXANDER, 10TH DUKE OF (1767–1852). *Waddesdon Manor. National Trust.* 25¼×20¼ in. (Passed to the Duke of Somerset: sale 28/vi/1890 (25) bt. Agnew: Baron Ferdinand de Rothschild: Miss Alice de Rothschild: James de Rothschild.) Painted 1786 (Whitley, p. 266).

339. HAMILTON, LORD ARCHIBALD (1769–1827). *Waddesdon Manor. National Trust.* 25¼×20¼ in. (Same history as no. 338: 1890 sale lot 24.)

340. HAMILTON, HON. CHARLES (1727–1806). *Tyninghame. Earl of Haddington.* 30×25 in. About 1756. Pl. 27.

341. HAMILTON, HON. MRS CHARLES (1710–85). 76½×59½ in. (Passed to W. O. Brigstoke: bt. in at sales 1899, 1901, 1902, 1903: sold, Robinson & Fisher, 29/vi/1905 (75a) bt. Wall: Alfred H. Mulliken, Chicago: sale, New York, 5/i/1933 (55) bt. for Springfield: sold 1946.) Probably once from middle 1760s.

342. HAMMOND, MR. 30×25 in. (Descended in Corkran family: Sedelmeyer, 1912: Anon. (= Sedelmeyer heirs) sale, Paris, 23/xi/1927 (21): with Van Diemen and Lilienfeld, New York, 1931/3: Anon. sale, Paris, 27/v/1946.) Probably late work.

343. HAMMOND, MRS WILLIAM (1766–1829). *Cincinnati. Art Museum.* 30×25 in. (Descended in Hammond family, St. Alban's Court: with Knoedler, 1925: Miss Mary Hanna, Cincinnati: presented 1946.) Probably a marriage portrait (1785).

344. HANMER, SIR THOMAS, BT. (1747–1828). *Bettisfield Park. Sir E. Hanmer, Bt.* 36×28 in. Painted 1785: partly repainted by Sir M. A. Shee.

345. HAMOND, MARY (Mrs W. Parker Hamond, 1768–?). *Cambridge (Mass.). Bailey Aldrich.* 30×25 in. (W. P. Hamond sale 6/v/1893

(112) bt. Lawrie: D. P. Kimball, Boston, 1897.)
Painted 1776.

346. HAMPDEN, ROBERT, 1ST VISCOUNT
(1701–83). *Williamstown (Mass.). Sterling and
Francine Clark Art Institute*, 30×25 in. (Descended
to Earl of Hardwicke: sale 30/vi/1888 (53) bt.
Agnew: James Price sale 15/vi/1895 (76) bt.
Agnew—*repd.*: J. Ruston sale 4/vii/1913 (117)
bt. Colnaghi: Mr and Mrs R. Sterling Clark:
presented 1955.) An early copy is dated 1776.

HAMPDEN, VISCOUNTESS. *See* LADY UN-
KNOWN (no. 791).

347. HANHAM, LADY. "A head", unfinished
in 1797 sale (3) bt. Walton.

HARBORD, SIR HARBORD. *See* SUFFIELD,
1ST LORD.

348. HARBOROUGH, REV. ROBERT, 4TH
EARL OF (1719–99). 88×56 in. (Passed to Earl
of Lonsdale: bt. in at Lowther Castle sale 1947:
sale 7/iii/1952 (26) bt. Leggatt.) Probably late
Bath work, left unfinished and completed by a
drapery painter.

349. HARBOROUGH, ELIZABETH, COUN-
TESS OF (1739/40–97). 30×25 in. (Descended
to Lord Braye: bt. from Wallis, 1896, by David
T. Watson, Pittsburgh: sale, New York,
16/iv/1917 (146)—*repd.*) Perhaps a marriage
portrait (1767).

350. HARDWICKE, PHILIP, 2ND EARL OF
(1720–96). 50×40 in. (Descended to Lady Lucas:
sale 16/xi/1917 (44) bt. Tooth: E. R. Wood,
Toronto, 1932: sold by National Trust Company,
Toronto.) Painted 1763, when *Lord Royston*
(Whitley, pp. 41/2). Pl. 74.

351. HARLEY, ROBERT. 30×25 in. (C. P.
Scott, Chicago, 1915.)

352. HARRINGTON, CHARLES, 3RD
EARL OF (1753–1829). A half-length or head,
"in regimentals" was shown at Schomberg
House in 1784 and 1786 (Whitley, pp. 228 and
257).

353. HASTINGS, FRANCIS, 1ST MAR-
QUESS OF (1754–1826). *São Paolo (Brazil).
Art Gallery.* 90×58 in. (Descended to Viscountess
St Davids: with Leggatt, 1949: bt. 1951.) In-
tended for R.A. 1784, and shown at Schomberg
House.

354. HATCHETT, MRS CHARLES (Miss
Collique: 1769–1837). *New York. Frick collection.*
30×25 in. (Descended in family till 1890s:
Archibald Coats, 1898: bt. H. C. Frick, 1903.)
Probably a marriage portrait (1786). It is a signed
Dupont.

355. HAVERFIELD, MISS. *London. Wallace
Collection* (44). 49×39 in. (Anon. (=sitter's
family) sale 26/iii/1859 (72) bt. Marquess of
Hertford.) From the 1780s.

356. HAVILAND, THOMAS. *Stockholm. Art
Gallery* (2100). 49×39 in. (J. Haviland sale
19/vii/1875 (128) bt. Graves: C. F. Murray, 1898:
sale, Paris, 15/vi/1914 (15): bt. 1918.) From the
earlier 1760s.

357. HAYWOOD, CLARA. R.A. 1778 (apparently 30×25 in.). *See* Whitley, p. 154.
See also HEYWOOD.

358. HEATHCOTE, MASTER JOHN (1767–
1838). *Boston. Alvan T. Fuller.* 49×39 in. (Descended to J. N. Heathcote: Lord Michelham
sale, by Hampton's, 24/xi/1926 (292) bt. Duveen.)
Very late Bath period. Pl. 148.

359. HEBERDEN, MISS MARY (Mrs Jenyns).
Chestnut Hill (Pa.). Mrs S. P. Rotan. 29½×24½ in.
(Descended in the Jenyns family till *c.* 1917: with
Scott and Fowles: G. W. Elkins, Philadelphia.)
Earlier London years.

360. HENDERSON, JOHN (1746–85). *London.
National Portrait Gallery* (980). 30×25 in. (Descended to Miss Julia Carrick Moore: presented
1895.) Painted 1777 (Whitley, p. 142—but this is
doubtful). R.A. 1780 (194). Engraved in mezzotint by J. Jones, 1783.

361. *The same.* 30×25 in. (Painted for John
Ireland.) Painted 1772/3 (Whitley, p. 86):
engraved in stipple by John Jones, 1786. The
original seems lost.

HERTFORD, MARIA, MARCHIONESS OF. *See* FAGNANI, MISS

HERVEY, CAPT. AUGUSTUS. *See* BRISTOL, 3RD EARL OF.

362. HERVEY, AUGUSTUS (*c.* 1765–82). *Ickworth. National Trust.* Octagonal miniature on tin, 8¾ × 7 in. (Hon. Edmund Phipps sale 25/vi/1859 (72) bt. Marquess of Bristol.) About 1780.

363. HERVEY, JOHN AUGUSTUS, LORD (1757–96). *Ickworth. National Trust.* 87 × 59 in. Perhaps about the date of his marriage (1779). Pl. 205.

364. HEYWOOD, MRS JAMES MODY-FORD. *Newburgh. Capt. V. M. Wombwell.* 49 × 39 in. Late Bath work.

365. HEYWOOD, JAMES MODYFORD (1732–98). *Swaffham. Lord Suffield.* 50 × 40 in. (Anon. sale 29/vi/1889 (37) bt. Hamond.) Late Bath work.

366. HIBBERT, THOMAS (1744–1819). *Sunton House. Major General Hugh Hibbert.* 50 × 40 in. Probably about 1786 (*see* no. 367).

367. HIBBERT, MRS THOMAS (1760–1827). *Chantilly, Baronne Edouard de Rothschild.* 50 × 40 in. (Descended to J. N. Hibbert: bt. *c.* 1885 for Baron Alphonse de Rothschild.) Painted 1786 (Whitley, p. 266).

368. HILL, REV. HENRY (1697–1775). 29 × 24½ in. (Anon. (= Rev. M. Hill) sale 6/v/1910 (101) bt. Maude.) Late Ipswich work: companion to no. 369 but perhaps earlier.

369. HILL, MRS HENRY (1717–94). *Sandy. Heirs of Sir P. Malcolm Stewart, Bt.* 29½ × 24½ in. (Anon. (= Rev. M. Hill) sale 6/v/1910 (100) bt. Wyatt: Mrs W. H. Leslie sale 13/xii/1929 (48) bt. Tooth: bt. from Leggatt by Sir P. M. Stewart and destined for the National Trust.) Pl. 31.

HILL, JACK. *See under* FANCY PICTURES no. 816.

370. HINGESTON, REV. ROBERT (1699–1776) (?) *Bristol. Bruce Nelson.* 30 × 24 in. (Passed through Hingeston Ogier family to Edward Milles Nelson (d. 1938), Clifton.) Probably from the middle 1750s: formerly identified as Rev. James Hingeston (1733–77), which is impossible.

371. HINGESTON, MRS ROBERT (d. 1793) *Bristol. Mrs D. M. M. Bell (née Nelson).* 30 × 24 in. (Same history as no. 370). Companion to no. 370 and of same date: formerly called Mrs James Hingeston.

372. *The same. Bristol. Bruce Nelson.* 30 × 24 in. (Same history as no. 370.) From the later 1780s: from family tradition, one of Gainsborough's latest works.

373. HOBSON, MISS ELEANOR (Mrs J. Willoughby). 30 × 25 in. (With Sulley—A. Reid, Glasgow—John Levy, New York: Mrs B. F. Jones, Pittsburgh: sale, New York, 4/xii/1941 (82) bt. J. J. Gillespie.) Possibly about the date of her marriage (1778/9).

HOLLAND, LADY. *See* FITZPATRICK, LADY MARY.

374. HOLTE, SIR CHARLES, 6TH BT. (1721–82). *Birmingham. City Art Gallery.* Oval: 29½ × 24 in. (Bequeathed by Charles Holte Bracebridge, 1872.) Later Bath period.

375. HONYWOOD, LT.-GEN. PHILIP (1710–85). *Sarasota (Fla.). John and Mable Ringling Museum.* 124½ × 115½ in. (Descended in Honywood family, Marks Hall: bt. by Agnew *c.* 1897: Sir Edgar Vincent (Viscount D'Abernon) 1910: with Agnew and sold to J. Ringling, 1928.) S.A. 1765 (33): probably painted in 1764. Pl. 83.

376. HOOD, SAMUEL, 1ST VISCOUNT (1724–1816). *London. Ironmongers' Hall.* 50 × 40 in. Intended for R.A. 1784 and shown at Schomberg House. Presented by sitter in 1784, on being admitted.

377. HOOD, MR. *Manchester (Mass.). Jefferson Coolidge.* 30 × 25 in. (Bt. from Wallis & Son, 1899 by Agnew: Mrs Marion E. Knapp, 1901.) Probably from the 1760s.

378. HOPETOUN, JANE, COUNTESS OF (d. 1767). *Hopetoun House. Marquess of Linlithgow.*

50×40 in. Probably about the time of her marriage (1762). In Sir William Musgrave's 1796 list of pictures at Hopetoun is also a portrait of her husband, John, 2nd Earl of Hopetoun (1704–81) unknown today.

379. HOPETOUN, ELIZABETH, COUNTESS OF (1750–93). Sitting in 1787 (Whitley, p. 271).

380. HORNBY, REV. GEOFFREY (1750–1812). *Dalton Hall. C. W. L. Penrhyn-Hornby.* (On loan to Preston.) 30×25 in. Probably once from early 1780s.

381. HORNBY, HON. MRS GEOFFREY (d. 1833). *Dalton Hall. C. W. L. Penrhyn-Hornby.* (On loan to Bristol.) 30×25 in. From the middle 1780s.

382. HORTON, CHRISTOPHER (1741–68). *Catton Hall. Col. G. H. Anson.* 30×25 in. Probably companion to the 1766 portrait of his wife (no. 179), also formerly at Catton.

HORTON, MRS CHRISTOPHER. *See* CUMBERLAND, DUCHESS OF.

383. HOTCHKISS, CHARLES. *Budapest. Museum* (789a). 30×25 in. (Anon. sale 19/vii/1890 (119) bt. Hawkins: bt. from Shirley, Paris, 1907.) Bath period.

HOWARD, MR. *See* NORFOLK, 12TH DUKE OF.

384. HOWARD, MRS PHILIP (d. 1794). 29½×24½ in. (Descended to P. J. C. Howard: sale 31/iii/1922 (24) bt. Marshall: with Ehrich-Newhouse Galls., New York: sold 1936.) Probably later Bath period.

385. HOWARD, MRS. "A head"—unfinished: in 1797 sale (19) bt. Whitefoord.

386. HOWE, ADMIRAL, EARL (1726–99). *Penn House. Earl Howe.* 96×59 in. (Passed to the Marquess of Sligo, who sold it to Earl Howe in the 1880s.) Probably middle 1760s. Companion to no. 387.

387. HOWE, MARY, COUNTESS (1732–1800). *Kenwood. Iveagh bequest* (4). 96×60 in. (Passed to Marquess of Sligo; sold to Earl Howe

in 1880s: with Agnew: Earl of Iveagh, 1888.) Companion to no. 386: probably from middle 1760s. Pl. 88.

388. HOWLAND, MISS ISABELLA. *New York. Mrs McLane van Ingen.* 30×25 in. (Descended with the Beaumonts of Coleorton: with Colnaghi and Knoedler, 1902: H. L. Terrell, New York, 1903: Mrs H. Terrell van Ingen.) Not far from 1770. Pl. 108.

389. HUBBARD, REV. HENRY (1708–78). *Cambridge. Emmanuel College.* 30×25 in. (Given by sitter to Rev. Richard Canning: bequeathed by Rev. Richard Canning Jr., 1789.) Middle or later 1750s. Pl. 42.

390. HURD, BISHOP RICHARD (1720–1808). *Windsor Castle. H.M. The Queen.* 30×25 in. R.A. 1781 (39). Painted for Queen Charlotte.

391. *The same. Hartlebury Castle. The Bishops of Worcester.* 30×25 in. Painted 1788: different design from no. 390.

392. *The same. Cambridge. Emmanuel College* (given by the sitter). 30×25 in. An original repetition of no. 391.

HYLTON, ELEANOR, LADY. *See* JOLLIFFE, MRS. THOMAS.

393. IBBETSON, MRS. "A head"—unfinished: in 1797 sale (15) bt. Kilpatrick.

394. IMPEY, LADY (1749–1818). 29½×24½ in. (Descended to Lady Affleck: sale 7/v/1904 (112) bt. Vicars: Marquess Curzon: Viscount Scarsdale sale, 18/vii/1930 (95) bt. Smith: with J. Levy, New York, 1937: E. D. Levinson: with J. Weitzner 1957.) Presumably the picture of 1786 (Whitley, p. 259).

395. INNES, LADY (d. 1770). *New York. Frick Collection.* 39¾×28 in. (Anon. (= Innes) sale 3/vi/1876 (35) bt. in: G. Fairholme: Anon. sale 16/vi/1911 (79) bt. Colnaghi: with J. H. Dunn: bt. by H. C. Frick, 1914.) Late Ipswich work. Pl. 48.

396. IZARD, MRS RALPH (Alice de Lancey). 30×25 in. (Descended to Mrs Henry Fulton,

New York, 1878: said to have been burnt in California.) Probably from the 1770s.

IZZARD, SARAH. *See under* CAMPBELL, LORD WILLIAM.

397. JACKSON, BISHOP CHARLES (d. 1790). *Cambridge. Emmanuel College.* 30×25 in. Bath period: the sitter was Bishop of Kildare.

JACKSON, MISS ELIZABETH. *See* PLEYDELL, MRS MORTON.

398. JACKSON, WILLIAM (1730–1803). *Burleigh Court. Gerard M. Young.* 30×25 in. (Passed from the sitter's son to Sir William Young.) R.A. 1770 (86) or (87). *See Burl. Mag.* lxxx., p. 46.

399. JERSEY, WILLIAM, 3RD EARL (*c.* 1706–69). *London. Earl of Clarendon.* 30×25 in. Probably about 1760. Perhaps= "*the late Lord Jersey*" in Mrs Gainsborough sale 10/iv/1797 (9) bt. Lord Malden.

400. JERSEY, GEORGE, 4TH EARL OF (1735–1805). 30×25 in. (Earl of Jersey, Middleton: with Howard Young, New York, 1936.) This may possibly be the picture painted in 1758, when the sitter was *Lord Villiers* (Whitley, pp. 28/9).

401. JODRELL, RICHARD PAUL (1745–1831). *New York. Frick Collection.* 29×24½ in. (Sir E. R. Jodrell sale 30/vi/1888 (71) bt. Agnew: J. Ruston sale 4/vii/1913 (116) bt. Agnew: G. Harland Peck sale 25/vi/1920 (60) bt. Sulley: Mitchell Palmer, Detroit, 1931: with Duveen, 1940: bt. 1946.) From the 1770s.

403. JOHNSTON, GENERAL JAMES (1721–97). *Dublin. National Gallery of Ireland.* 89½× 57½ in. (Descended to Capt. Campbell Johnston, 1912: bequest of Sir Hugh Lane, 1918.) Probably from the middle 1760s. Pl. 96.

JOHNSTONE-PULTENEY. *See* PULTENEY.

404. JOLLIFFE, THOMAS SAMUEL (1746–1824). *Ammerdown. Lord Hylton.* 30×25 in. Companion to no. 405: perhaps *c.* 1780.

405. JOLLIFFE, MRS THOMAS SAMUEL (1756–1802). *Cleveland (Ohio). Museum of Art.* 30×25 in. (Descended to Lord Hylton: bt. by Knoedler, 1911: John L. Severance, Cleveland: bequeathed, 1942.) From the middle 1780s: companion to no. 404: it has latterly wrongly been called *Eleanor, Lady Hylton.*

KEEBLE, WILLIAM. *See under* GROUPS (no. 747).

406. KENT, H.R.H. EDWARD, DUKE OF (1767–1820). *Windsor Castle. H.M. The Queen.* 22×16 in. R.A. 1783 (134): painted September, 1782. Pl. 215.

407. KILDERBEE, SAMUEL (1725–1813). *San Francisco. De Young Memorial Museum.* 50×40 in. (Descended to Admiral Spencer de Horsey, sale 14/vi/1929 (47) as *Unknown man* by Dupont after Gainsborough, bt. Daws: A. L. Nicholson sale, New York, 18/v/1933 (34) bt. for San Francisco.) Probably about 1755. Pl. 44.

408. *The same. Ipswich. Christchurch Mansion Museum.* 28¾×23¾ in. (Anon. sale 14/xi/1919 (191) bt. Agnew: 18/ii/1921 (128) bt. in: Mrs Ernest Innes sale 13/xii/1935 (108) bt. for Ipswich.) A little later than no. 407.

409. KILDERBEE, REV. SAMUEL (d. 1830). 30×25 in. (Admiral de Horsey sale 14/vi/1929 (45) bt. Agnew.) Probably from the later Bath period.

410. KILDERBEE, MRS SAMUEL (Mary Wayth: 1723–1811.) *Ipswich Museum.* 29½×24½ in. (Admiral de Horsey sale 14/vi/1929 (43) bt. Saville Gallery.) Probably from the early 1760s. Colour plate.

411. KILMOREY, JOHN, 10TH VISCOUNT (1710–91). *London. Tate Gallery* (4777). 92×61 in. (Bt. from Earl of Kilmorey, 1934.) Probably about 1768. Pl. 116.

412. KING, MRS (*née* Spence). *Dublin. National Gallery of Ireland.* 30×25 in. (Bequeathed by Sir Hugh Lane, 1918.) Late Bath work.

413. KINLOCH, MRS DAVID. *Pittsburgh. Mrs J. Denniston Lyon.* 30×25 in. (Sold by the Kinlochs of Gourdie *c.* 1898: bt. from Lawrie by A. M. Byers, Pittsburgh, 1898: J. F. Byers.) Probably later 1770s.

414. KINNOULL, ROBERT, 9TH EARL OF (1751–1804). *Albury Park. Helen, Duchess of Northumberland.* 30×25 in. Probably from the 1770s.

415. KINNOULL, SARAH, COUNTESS OF (1760–1837). 49½×39½ in. (Painted for her father, Alderman Harley: descended to Lord Rodney: bt. by Lord Burton in 1880s: Baroness Burton sale 4/v/1951 (45) bt. Leggatt.) Probably shortly before her marriage in 1781.

416. KIRBY, JOHN (1690–1753). *Cambridge. Fitzwilliam Museum.* 30×25 in. (Passed to Rev. Kirby Trimmer: Anon. sale 12/v/1888 (61) bt. C. Fairfax Murray: presented, 1908.) Probably before 1750: companion to no. 417. Pl. 2.

417. KIRBY, MRS JOHN. *Cambridge. Fitzwilliam Museum.* 30×25 in. (Same history as no. 416.) Probably before 1750: companion to no. 416. Pl. 3.

418. KIRBY, JOHN JOSHUA (1716–94). *London. Victoria and Albert Museum* (D. 19). 16½×11½ in. (Passed to Mrs Trimmer: bequeathed by Rev. Alexander Dyce, 1869.) Probably middle 1750s. Pl. 9.

419. *The same. Cambridge. Fitzwilliam Museum.* 30×25 in. (Passed to Rev. Kirby Trimmer: Anon. sale 12/v/1888 (62) bt. C. Fairfax Murray: presented 1911.) Possibly S.A. 1764 (37) (Whitley, p. 43).

420. KIRBY, JOHN JOSHUA (and his wife). *London. National Portrait Gallery* (1421). 30×25 in. (Descended to Rev. H. Scott Trimmer: bt. in at 1860 sale: Rev. Kirby Trimmer: Anon. (=Trimmer) sale 14/iii/1903 (119) bt. in: bt. 1905.) About 1750. Pl. 16.

421. KNAPP, JEROME (1722–92). *London. Haberdashers' Company.* 91×60 in. Commissioned by a minute of the Court 16/xi/1786: painted in 1787.

422. KNATCHBULL, COL. NORTON (1711–82). *Parham Park. Hon. Clive Pearson.* 91×60 in. (Passed to Lord Brabourne: bt. thence 1918.) Later Bath work.

423. "KNIGHTON, LADY". 30×25 in. (Lord Waterpark: Anon. sale 17/vi/1905 (80) bt. Hugh Lane: with Sulley: Blakeslee sale, New York, 9/iv/1908 (111): A. H. Mulliken, Chicago: sale New York 5/i/1933 (66) bt. Ehrich.) Probably later Bath period: but no "Lady Knighton" of the period is recorded. (At one time with Sulley as *Miss Harriett Lloyd*.)

424. LAMBTON, WILLIAM HENRY (1764–97). *Lambton Castle. Earl of Durham.* 30×25 in. Late London work.

425. LANGSTON, JOHN. 92×60½ in. (Descended to the Countess of Ducie, 1895: thence to Lady Kekewich (d. 1956), the wife of Sir Jocelyn Lucas: sale 17/v/1957 (69) bt. Appleby.) Finished 1787 (Whitley, p. 290).

425a. LANGSTON, MRS JOHN. 30×25 in. (Descended with no. 425: 1957 sale (70) bt. Leggatt.) From the 1770s,

426, 427. LANGTON, MR AND MRS JOSEPH. Two full-length portraits which descended in the Gore-Langton family. They are reported to have been destroyed by enemy action in a warehouse at Bath, 1941.

428. LANSDOWNE, WILLIAM, 1ST MARQUESS OF (1737–1805). Painted 1787 and reputed to be as a present for the King of France (Whitley, p. 271). Only known from the stipple engraving by Bartolozzi.

429. LANSDOWNE, JOHN, 2ND MARQUESS OF (1765–1809). *Grimsby. Rev. G. W. Markham.* 30×25 in. (Presented by the sitter to Admiral Markham.) Painted when Lord Wycombe, 1787 (Whitley, p. 273).
See also GENTLEMAN UNKNOWN (no. 780).

430. LASCELLES, MRS EDWIN. *St. Louis (Mo.). Paul B. Jamison* (1932). 30×25 in. (With Tooth: with Newhouse, New York: bt. 1931.) Probably a picture of the Bath period.

431. LAUDERDALE, JAMES, 8TH EARL OF (1759–1839). *Cincinnati. E. W. Edwards.* 30×25 in. (Earl of Lauderdale, 1905: with Agnew: with Scott & Fowles, New York.) From the 1780s.

432. LAWRENCE. GENERAL STRINGER (1697–1775). *London. National Portrait Gallery* (777). 29½ × 24½ in. (Anon. (= Lord Haldon) sale 29/vii/1887 (172) bt. Smith: presented by Col. Henry Yule, 1888.) Late Bath work.

433. LE BRUN, MADAME (Francesca Danzi: 1756–91). *Elizabeth Bay (N.S.W.). F. Penfold Hyland* 1934. 50 × 40 in. (W. Stirling Crawfurd: his widow, Duchess of Montrose, 1894 sale (bt. in); sale 4/v/1895 (85) bt. in: Leopold Hirsch, 1900: sale 11/v/1934 (103) bt. F. Howard.) R.A. 1780 (162).

434. LEE, WILLIAM (d. 1778). *London. Mrs Geoffrey Hart* (1952). 30 × 25 in. (Mrs B. Eyre sale, Sotheby's 26/iv/1938 (116) bt.—with no. 435.) The receipt, dated 19 April 1759, is in the archives of the National Gallery, London.

435. LEE, PHILADELPHIA, MRS WILLIAM (d. 1799). 30 × 25 in. (In same lot as no. 434 in Eyre sale 1938: Lord Doverdale sale, Sotheby's, 8/xi/1950 (108) bt. Bellesi.) The receipt, dated 1759, is in the archives of the National Gallery, London.

LEICESTER, EARL OF. *See* COKE, THOMAS WILLIAM.

435a. LEIGH, JOHN (d. 1810). 30 × 25 in. (Descended through the Townley-Balfour family.) David Crichton sale 25/x/1957 lot 59 bt. Agnew.) Late Bath work.

436. LESLIE, GENERAL THE HON. ALEXANDER (1731–94). *Luffness House. Major A. J. G. Hope.* 30 × 25 in. Probably early London work.

437. LETHBRIDGE, DOROTHEA, LADY (d. 1831). 30 × 25 in. (Sir Wroth A. Lethbridge: sold *c.* 1911: with Knoedler, 1912: Mrs Katherine Deere Butterworth, Moline, Ill.: sale, New York, 20/x/1954 (32)—*repd.*) Probably a marriage portrait of 1776.

438. LEYBORNE, WILLIAM LEYBORNE. *Bristol. Art Gallery.* 50 × 40 in. (Descended to Major E. T. Buller-Leyborne-Popham: bt. 1956.) From the 1760s: previously called *Edward*

Popham, but it seems to be the companion to no. 439, and both are probably marriage portraits of 1763. Pl. 73.

439. LEYBORNE, MRS WILLIAM (Anne Popham: b. 1737). *Bristol. Art Gallery.* 50 × 40 in. (Same history as no. 438.) Probably companion to no. 438 and a marriage portrait of 1763. Pl. 72.

440. LEYCESTER, RALPH (1699–1777). *Gredington. Lord Kenyon.* 30 × 25 in. (Passed to C. L. M. Roxby: sale, Sotheby's, 14/v/1930 (98) bt. Gwynne: bt. from Agnew, 1939.) Traditionally 1763/4.

441. LEYCESTER, MRS RALPH, (1709–99). 30 × 25 in. (Passed to C. L. M. Roxby: sale, Sotheby's, 14/v/1930 (97) bt. Langman: with Agnew, 1936.) Traditionally painted 1764.

442. LEYCESTER, RALPH, Jr. (1738?–   ). 30 × 25 in. (Passed to C. L. M. Roxby: sale, Sotheby's, 14/v/1930 (99) bt. Gwynne: Ehrich sale, New York, 2/iv/1931 (74)—*repd.*) Traditionally painted 1762.

443. LIGONIER, EDWARD, 2ND VISCOUNT (1740–82). *San Marino (Calif.). Henry E. Huntington Library and Art Gallery.* 94 × 62 in. (Painted for Lord Rivers: bt. from W. Pitt-Rivers *c.* 1901, by C. J. Wertheimer: bt. 1911.) R.A. 1771 (76): painted in 1770. Pl. 130.

444. LIGONIER, PENELOPE, VISCOUNTESS (1749–1827). *San Marino (Calif.). Henry E. Huntington Library and Art Gallery.* 94½ × 62 in. (For history see no. 443.) R.A. 1771 (75): painted in 1770. Pl. 131.

LINDSAY, LADY MARGARET. *See* FORDYCE, LADY MARGARET.

445. LINLEY, SAMUEL (1760–78). *Dulwich College* (302). 29 × 24 in. (Bequeathed by William Linley, 1835.) Traditionally 1777/8.

446. LINLEY, THOMAS, Sr. (1733–95). *Dulwich College* (140). 29½ × 24½ in. (Bequeathed by William Linley, 1835.) Probably from the later 1760s. Pl. 107.

447. LINLEY, THOMAS, Jr. (1756–78). *Dulwich College* (331). 29½ × 24½ in. (Bequeathed by William Linley, 1835.) Probably about 1773/4. Pl. 155.

448. *The same. Vaduz (formerly Vienna). Prince Liechtenstein.* 30 × 25 in. (E. L. Tickell sale 3/v/1884 (152) bt. Sedelmeyer: bt. 1886.) Probably about 1777/8.

LINLEY, THOMAS AND SISTER. *See* FANCY PICTURES (no. 801).

449. LINLEY, ELIZABETH (1754–92). *Philadelphia. Pennsylvania Museum.* 30 × 25 in. (George Mowser, by 1883: Anon. (= Mowser) sale 23/v/1903 (64) bt. C. J. Wertheimer: W. L. Elkins, Philadelphia.) Probably early London work: the identification is likely but not certain. *See also* SHERIDAN, MRS.

450. LINLEY, ELIZABETH (1754–92) AND MARY (1758–87). *Dulwich College* (320). 77¾ × 60 in. (Presented by William Linley, 1831.) Probably R.A. 1772 (95). Pl. 145.

451. LITTLETON, FRANCES, LADY (d. 1781). *Catton Hall. Col. G. H. Anson.* 30 × 25 in. (Perhaps the unfinished picture in the 1797 sale (8) bt. Lord Malden.) Probably late Bath work.

452. LLOYD, HENEAGE (1743–76) AND SISTER. *Cambridge. Fitzwilliam Museum.* 25 × 31½ in. (Passed to Col. Lloyd-Anstruther: with Colnaghi, 1895–1904: given by C. Fairfax Murray, 1911.) About 1750. Pl. 15.

453. LLOYD, SIR RICHARD (1698–1761). *Cardiff. National Museum of Wales.* 30 × 25 in. (Col. Lloyd-Anstruther sale, at Hintlesham Hall, 16/vi/1909 (374) bt. Anstruther: Sir Gerald Ryan, Bt., *c.* 1915: sale, at Hintlesham Hall, 10/xii/1937 (1315); with Vicars, 1947: bt. from C. Marshall Spink, 1949.) From the later 1750s.

454. LLOYD, RICHARD SAVAGE (1730–1820) AND CECIL (1734–91). *Waldershare. Mrs Harman Hunt.* 25 × 30 in. (Col. Lloyd-Anstruther sale, at Hintlesham Hall, 16/vi/1909 (399) bt. Brooke: Brooke sale, Ufford Place, *c.* 1930: R. Eden Dixon: bequeathed 1937 to

Lord North, whose widow is the present owner.) About 1750. Pl. 14.

455. LLOYD, MISS (?). 27½ × 21½ in. (Said to be ex. Sir William Knighton and W. de Zoete: with Scott & Fowles, New York, 1931: sale, New York, 28/iii/1946 (84).) About 1750.

456. LOUTHERBOURG, PHILIP JAMES DE (1740–1812). *Dulwich College* (66). 30 × 25 in. (Bequeathed by Sir Francis Bourgeois, 1811.) R.A. 1778 (408). Pl. 197.

457. LOWNDES, HENRY (1723–99). *Dunedin (N.Z.). Art Gallery.* 29 × 24½ in. (R. F. E. Lowndes-Stone-Norton sale 8/vi/1928 (94) bt. Colnaghi: Anon. (= Colnaghi) sale, Sotheby's, 19/vi/1935 (157) bt. in: bt. 1936.) Probably shown at Schomberg House, 1784 (Whitley, p. 228).

458. LOWNDES, WILLIAM (1687/8–1775). *England. Hon. Mrs B. M. Talbot Rice.* 50 × 40 in. (Passed to Mrs Lowndes-Stone-Norton (d. 1882): Anon. sale 19/iii/1892 (729) bt. in for family.) Inscribed as painted in 1771. Pl. 141.

459. LOWNDES-STONE, MRS WILLIAM (1758?–1837). *Lisbon. Gulbenkian Foundation.* 91¾ × 60½ in. (Descended to Mrs Lowndes-Stone-Norton: bt. Alfred de Rothschild *c.* 1892: bequeathed to Countess of Carnarvon: bt. from Duveen, 1923.) Probably a marriage portrait of 1775.

460. LOWNDES, MRS. *Montreal. Estate of late Robert W. Reford.* 30 × 25 in. (Descended to Mrs More-Molyneux, *née* Lowndes-Stone: with Sulley: bt. from Agnew by R. W. Reford, 1927.) From the earlier 1770s: formerly called *Mrs Lowndes-Stone*, but a different sitter from no. 459. Pl. 163.

461. LOWTHER, REV. SIR WILLIAM, BT. (1707–88). *Lowther Castle (formerly). Earl of Lonsdale.* 30 × 25 in. Bath period: not at the moment traceable.

462. LUCY, GEORGE (d. 1786). *Charlecote Park. National Trust (Fairfax-Lucy gift).* 30 × 25 in. There were receipts, each for eight guineas and dated 27/ii/1760 and 25/iv/1760, for this and no.

463 (Mary Elizabeth Lucy, *Biography of the Lucy family*, 1862, p. 112).

463. *The same. Charlecote Park. National Trust (Private Rooms).* 30 × 25 in. (Passed to Rev. John Lucy: came to Charlecote, 1875.) *See* no. 462.

464. LYNCH, WILLIAM. *Muskegon. Hackley Art Gallery* (1912). 30 × 25 in. (Anon. sale 23/ii/1907 (125) bt. Pfungst: Anon. sale 7/vi/1912 (113) bt. Tooth.) Probably Bath period: engraved in mezzotint by S. W. Reynolds.

MAGILL, MISS THEODOSIA. *See* CLAN-WILLIAM, COUNTESS OF

MALDEN, LORD. *See* ESSEX, EARL OF.

"MANNERS, LORD ROBERT". *See* RUT-LAND, CHARLES, DUKE OF.

465. MANSFIELD, LOUISA, COUNTESS OF. Sat as *Lady Stormont* in 1782 (Whitley, p. 193).

466. MARKHAM, WILLIAM (1760–1815). 30 × 25 in. (Passed to E. G. Markham; sale 8/vii/1932 (13) bt. Spink.) From the 1780s.

467. MARLBOROUGH, CAROLINE, DUCHESS OF (1743–1811). *Woburn Abbey. Duke of Bedford.* 30 × 25 in. About 1764/5.

468. MARSH, SAMUEL. 30 × 25 in. (Anon. sale 13/vi/1913 (126): with Knoedler, New York: Mrs John S. Rovensky (Mrs W. Hayward) sale, New York, 16/i/1957 (463) *rep.*) Probably later Bath work.

469. MARSHAM, HON. HARRIOTT (1721–96.) *Birmingham University. Barber Institute.* 30 × 25 in. (Passed to Hon. Robert Marsham, 1889: Earl Sydney sale, Knight, Frank & Rutley, 7/vi/1915 (27) bt. in: H. S. Marsham-Townshend sale 12/vii/1946 (65) bt. for Barber Institute.) Probably from later 1770s. Pl. 169.

470. MARSHAM CHILDREN, THE. 94½ × 71 in. (Descended to the Earl of Romney: bt. by Baron Rothschild, 1888: sold by Lord Rothschild, 1956.) Painted in July 1787 (Whitley, p. 286).

471. MARY, H.R.H. PRINCESS (1776–1857). *Windsor Castle. H.M. The Queen.* 22 × 16 in. R.A. 1783 (134): painted in September 1782.

472. MASSEY, B. *Southill. Simon Whitbread.* 30 × 25 in. Inscribed as painted 1780.

473. MATTHEW, CAPTAIN THOMAS (1741–1820). *Boston. Museum of Fine Arts.* 29¾ × 24½ in. (Descended to R. O. Jones, Fonmon Castle: with Howard Young, New York, 1923: Robert J. Edwards, Boston: given by Hannah Marcy and Grace M. Edwards, 1925.) Unfinished: seen in Gainsborough's studio in 1772 (*Diary of John Baker*, ed. Philip C. Yorke, 1931, p. 252). Pl. 151.

474. MATTHEW, MRS THOMAS (Diana Jones: d. 1822). *Boston. Museum of Fine Arts.* 29½ × 24½ in. (Same history as no. 473.) Also seen in Gainsborough's studio in 1772. Pl. 150.

474a. MAYHEW, WILLIAM (1700–64). *Perth (W. Australia). Art Gallery.* 30 × 25 in. (Brought to W. Australia by his grandson, William Mayhew, 1867, and bequeathed to Mrs Richard Whiteford, who gave it to Perth, 1942.) Inscribed on the back: "Gainsborough de Ipswich pinxit 1757."

475. MAYNARD, VISCOUNTESS (Nancy Parsons: 1734?–1814?). 36 × 28 in. (In 1797 sale (28) bt. Col. Byde: W. Cox sale 24/vi/1852 (59) bt. for Marquess of Lansdowne: with C. J. Wertheimer *c.* 1888: Comte Boni de Castellane, Paris: C. J. Wertheimer 1904: stolen 12/ii/1907 and apparently destroyed.) Unfinished, but perhaps early London work.

476. MEARES, MRS JOHN (Henrietta Read: b. 1765). *San Marino (Calif.). Henry E. Huntington Library and Art Gallery.* 88 × 55½ in. (Passed to Henry Villebois: bt. Alfred de Rothschild, 1886: bequeathed to Countess of Carnarvon, 1918: bt. from Duveen, 1924.) Probably soon after 1780.

477. MEDLYCOTT, THOMAS JOHN. *Bermuda. Hereward T. Watlington.* 87 × 57 in. (Descended to Mrs G. A. Quentin (bt. in at sales, 1911 and 1917): C. Quentin sale 1/v/1925 (114) bt. Rankin: J. S. Rankin sale 3/xii/1937 (24) bt.

Abbey: bt. from Leger, 1951.) S.A. 1763 (42). Pl. 68.

478. MENDIP, WELBORE, 1ST LORD (1713–1802). *Oxford. Christ Church (Hall, no. 197).* 49 × 39 in. The date 1763 is on a letter: came to Christ Church, 1769. Pl. 75.

479. MENDIP, ANNA, LADY (1725–1803). 30 × 25 in. (Lord Normanton: with Agnew & Tooth, 1934/5: with Howard Young, New York: André de Coppet, New York, 1936.) Being painted late in 1787 (Whitley, p. 294).

480. MERLIN, JOSEPH (1735–1804). R.A. 1782 (43). Untraced.

481. METHUEN, PAUL (1723–95). *Corsham Court. Lord Methuen.* 50 × 40 in. Exhibited at Schomberg House, 1784: the receipted payment is dated 1786. Pl. 232.

482. METHUEN, PAUL COBB (1752–1816). *Corsham Court. Lord Methuen.* 50 × 40 in. The receipt is dated 1776 (Corsham MSS.). Pl. 167.

483. METHUEN, MRS PAUL COBB (1754–1826). *Washington. National Gallery (Widener collection).* 33 × 28 in. (perhaps cut down from 50 × 40 in.). (Bt. from a descendant by Wallis & Co., 1893: P. A. B. Widener, Philadelphia: passed to Washington, 1942.) Probably a marriage portrait of 1776 (companion to no. 482). It may have been the unfinished picture in the 1797 sale (12) bt. Whitefoord.

484. MEYRICK, MR. 30 × 25 in. (With T. Humphrey Ward: sold by Agnew to J. J. Moubray, 1901: Moubray sale 28/vi/1929 (79) bt. Colnaghi: with Knoedler: André de Coppet, New York (1933–54): with Agnew, 1955.) Probably from the later 1770s. The title of "General Meyrick" seems incorrect.

485. MIDDLETON, SURGEON GENERAL DAVID (1703–85). 29½ × 24½ in. (Marquess of Lansdowne, 1844, as *Benjamin Franklin*: sale 7/iii/1930 (41) bt. Meteyard—repd.: with Tooth: sold in U.S.A.) Perhaps from the middle 1770s.

486. MIDDLETON, JOHN CHARLES (1757–). *Bruern Abbey. Hon. Michael Astor.* 29½ × 24½ in. (Col. E. F. Hall sale 19/vi/1942 (50) bt. Tooth: bt. 1952.) Late London work.

487. MINET, DANIEL (1729–90). *Little Hadham Manor. Miss Minet.* 30 × 25 in. R.A. 1778 (409).

488. MINET, MRS REBECCA (1744–1819). *Little Hadham Manor. Miss Minet.* 30 × 25 in. (T. Minet, Athens, 1845: passed to Mrs Lewes: bt. by Lesser, 1877: with Graves: H. L. Bischoffsheim, 1885: Mrs Bischoffsheim sale 7/v/1926 (34) bt. for Miss Minet.) R.A. 1778 (407).

MOLYNEUX, VISCOUNTESS. *See* SEFTON, COUNTESS OF.

489. MONCK, MRS WILLIAM (d. 1775). 29 × 24 in. (Earl of Darnley sale 1/v/1925 (19) bt. for Sir Edward Hulton: with Agnew, 1953.) Probably from the middle 1760s.

490. MONTAGU, GEORGE, DUKE OF (1712–90). *Bowhill. Duke of Buccleuch and Queensberry.* 48 × 39 in. Recorded as lately painted in 1768 (Whitley, p. 62): an original drawing in crayons of the same sitter (10½ × 9 in.) was acquired by the British Museum, 1950. A full-length copy after this was commissioned in 1787 (Whitley, p. 290), but was probably not executed. Pl. 101.

491. MONTAGU. MARY, DUCHESS OF (1711–75). *Bowhill. Duke of Buccleuch and Queensberry.* 49½ × 39½ in. Recorded (with no. 490) as lately painted in 1768. Pl. 100.

492. *The same. Boughton. Duke of Buccleuch and Queensberry.* 29½ × 24½ in. From the same sittings as no. 491.

493. MONTAGUE, JOHN (of Avisford) (1749–1818). 29½ × 24½ in. (Bt. from family by Agnew c. 1906: with Sedelmeyer, Paris, 1911: A. R. Wilson Wood, 1912: passed to Mrs Maitland Heriot, sale 18/vi/1954 (15) bt. Leggatt.) From the earlier 1770s.

494. MONTAGU, MISS SOPHIA (Lady Thomas: 1759–1854). *New York. Walter P. Chrysler.* 30 × 25 in. (Bt. from family by Agnew *c.* 1906: Mrs Sloane (later Mrs Emily Vanderbilt White): with Knoedler, New York, 1947.) Probably late Bath work.

495. MONTGOMERIE, GEORGE (1712–66). *Vancouver. Art Gallery.* 49½ × 39½ in. (Molyneux-Montgomerie sale 23/vi/1933 (7) bt. for Vancouver.) From the later 1750s.

496. *The same.* 29 × 24 in. (Molyneux-Montgomerie sale 23/vi/1933 (9) bt. F. Howard.) A little later than no. 495.

497. MONTGOMERIE, MR (?). 29 × 24 in. (Molyneux-Montgomerie sale 23/vi/1933 (8) bt. Waters.) From the end of the 1750s.

498. MOODEY, MRS SAMUEL (1756–82) AND CHILDREN. *Dulwich College. Art Gallery* (316). 91¼ × 59½ in. (Presented by Captain George Moodey, 1835.) From the later 1770s.

499. MOORE, SIR JOHN, BART. (1718–79). 50 × 40 in. (Lord Poltimore sale, at Poltimore Park, 20/vii/1923 (881)—*repd.*) Early Bath work, with the Ribbon of the Bath added after 1770. John Baker met him in Gainsborough's studio in 1772.

500. MORGAN, SIR CHARLES (1726–1806). *London. Equitable Life Assurance Society.* 89¾ × 60 in. R.A. 1783 (27). Painted for the Society when the sitter was Sir Charles Gould.

MORTON-PLEYDELL. *See* PLEYDELL.

501. MOSTYN, BARBARA, LADY (1729–1801). *Albany (N.Y.). Institute of History and Art.* 30 × 25 in. (Descended to Mrs Mostyn, West Pennard: with Agnew, 1937: presented by Mrs David C. Hanrahan, 1947.) Early Bath work.

502. MOTT, MISS JULIET (Mrs George Smith: 1754–1838). *U.S.A. Private collection.* 29½ × 24½ in. (Passed by bequest to Mrs Charles Foxe and to Edmund Backhouse; sale 28/iv/1922 (47) bt. Knoedler: J. Horace Harding, New York: sale, New York, 1/iii/1941. Miss Lucy Aldrich, Providence, 1941.) Traditionally painted in 1766.

503. MOTT, MRS RICHARD. 29½ × 24½ in. (With Knoedler, 1924: Sulley sale 1/vi/1934 (7) bt. Nicholson: with Newhouse Galls., New York, 1934.) Once a picture of the Bath period.

504. MOUNTMORRES, HERVEY, 2ND VISCOUNT (1743?–97). 28 × 23 in. (W. Agnew, 1887: J. Price sale 15/vi/1895 (73) bt. Agnew: Mrs W. S. M. Burns, 1898.) Later Bath period.

MOUNTSTUART, LORD. *See* BUTE, MARQUESS OF.

505. MOYSEY, DR ABEL (1715–80). *Torquay. C. F. Moysey.* 50 × 40 in. Painted about 1764. Pl. 91.

506. MOYSEY, ABEL (1743–1831). *Torquay. C. F. Moysey.* 92¼ × 56¾ in. Perhaps about 1771 (*cf.* Whitley, p. 79). Pl. 137.

507. *The same. London. Tate Gallery* (678). 22¾ × 18 in. (Presented by H. G. and Rev. F. L. Moysey, 1861.) An unfinished sketch, probably *c.* 1764.

MUILMAN, PETER DARNAL. *See* GROUPS (no. 747).

508. MULGRAVE, CONSTANTINE JOHN, 2ND LORD (1744–92). *Mulgrave Castle. Marquess of Normanby.* 29½ × 24½ in. (Marquess of Normanby sale 19/vii/1890 (19) as *Capt. Charles Phipps*, bt. for Lady Laura Hampton: Anon. (=Hampton) sale, by Hurcombe, 29/vii/1930 (146b) bt. Spiller: bt. 1943.) R.A. 1772 (97).

509. *The same. Mulgrave Castle. Marquess of Normanby.* 91 × 60 in. Presumably one of two full-lengths commissioned 1785/6 (Whitley, p. 244 and 253). The execution is traditionally by Dupont.

510. *The same. Washington. Smithsonian Institution.* 91 × 60 (cut down to about 50 × 60 in.). (Presumably the picture which passed to his daughter, Lady Murray, and eventually passed from John Bulteel of Flete to H. B. Mildmay: sale 24/vi/1893 (15) bt. Sedelmeyer: Baron de Hirsch sale 6/ii/1897 (30) bt. Wallis: given by R. C. Johnson, 1920.) Presumably the other full-length of 1785/6 (*see* no. 509). It seems to have been sold by Lady

Murray in 1834 and 1835 (*cf.* Walpole Soc., XXXIII, p. 78). Its condition precludes judgment.

511. MULGRAVE, ANNE ELIZABETH, LADY (1769–88). *Paris. Pierre Groult.* 29 × 24½ in. (Bt. from Marquess of Normanby, 1880, by James Price: sale 15/vi/1895 (70) bt. Campbell: Camille Groult, Paris.) Probably about 1785.

MUSGRAVE, LADY. *See* CARLISLE, COUNTESS OF.

MYLNE, MRS. *See* FLETCHER, MRS THOMAS.

512. NASSAU, HON. RICHARD SAVAGE (1723–80). 88½ × 59½ in. (Descended through the 12th Duke of Hamilton to the Duchess of Montrose: with Ruck, 1927.) Probably later Bath work.

513. NEAVE, SIR RICHARD, BT. (1731–1814) AND LADY NEAVE (d. 1830). *Llysdulas. Sir Arundell Neave, Bt.* 87 × 59 in. From the middle 1760s, but Lady Neave's head may have been remodelled by Gainsborough at a later date.

514. NEEDHAM, HON. THOMAS (1744–73). *Ascott. National Trust (Anthony de Rothschild).* 91 × 60 in. (Acquired from Earl of Kilmorey *c.* 1927.) S.A. 1768 (59). Pl. 104.

515. NICHOLLS, MASTER ("The Pink Boy"). *Waddesdon Manor. National Trust.* 72 × 50 in. (Capt. Stokes, 1856: sale 28/v/1857 (202) bt. Grundy for John Naylor: Baron Ferdinand de Rothschild, 1898: Baroness Edmond de Rothschild, Paris: James A. de Rothschild, 1935.) R.A. 1782 (372). Pl. 241.

516. NISBET, MRS HAMILTON (1756–1834). *Edinburgh. National Gallery of Scotland* (1521). 91 × 60 in. (Bequeathed by Mrs Nisbet Hamilton Ogilvy, 1921.) Later London work.

517. NORFOLK, CHARLES, 11TH DUKE OF (1746–1815). *Arundel Castle. Duke of Norfolk.* 91½ × 60 in. Painted 1784/6, when the sitter was *Earl of Surrey.*

518. NORFOLK, BERNARD, 12TH DUKE OF (1765–1842). *Arundel Castle. Duke of Norfolk.*

88 × 54 in. Probably the *Mr Howard* being painted in 1788 (Whitley, p. 303).

519. NORTHUMBERLAND, HUGH, 1ST DUKE OF (1715–86). *London. Middlesex Guildhall.* R.A. 1783 (153). Full-length. Engraved in mezzotint by G. Dupont. The picture was placed in 1786 in the Sessions House of the County of Middlesex. Pl. 242.

520. The same. *Albury Park. Helen, Duchess of Northumberland.* 29½ × 24½ in. From the same sitting as no. 519: presumably *c.* 1783.

521. The same. *Dublin. National Gallery of Ireland.* 29½ × 24½ in. (Sir George Bisshopp sale 19/vii/1862 (87) bt. in: W. Anthony sale 4/ii/1871 (396) bt. Graves: bt. 1872.) A repetition of no. 520.

"NORTON. MRS". *See* LOWNDES-STONE, MRS WILLIAM.

522. NUGENT, ROBERT, EARL (1702–88). *Bristol. City Estates Committee.* 51 × 39 in. Painted 1760 for Bristol Corporation. Pl. 57.

523. The same. *Batheaston. Sir Guy Nugent, Bart.* 91 × 59 in. (Passed to Duke of Buckingham: sale at Stowe, 12/ix/1848 (347) bt. Sir G. Nugent: bt. in at 1929 sale.) S.A. 1761 (34). Pl. 64.

524. NUGENT, HON. EDMUND CRAGGS (1731–71). *Fredericton (New Brunswick).* 92 × 59½ in. (Given by Duchess of Buckingham to Sir George Nugent, Bt.: Nugent sale, Puttick & Simpson, 2/v/1929 (100) bt. Knoedler: Baron Thyssen, Lugano: Baroness Bentinck, *née* Thyssen: with Agnew, 1956: bt. by Lord Beaverbrook and presented to *Beaverbrook Art Gallery.*

525. NUTHALL, MR. R.A. 1771 (77): said to be a whole-length (Whitley, p. 77).

526. NUTHALL, MR. 30 × 25 in. (G. Harland Peck sale 25/vi/1920 (61) bt. Gooden & Fox: Lord Leverhulme sale, Knight, Frank & Rutley, 12/x/1925 (78)—repd.: resold, New York, 17/ii/1926 (106) bt J. Levy.) Bath period.

527. OCTAVIUS, H.R.H. PRINCE (1779–83). *Windsor Castle. H.M. The Queen.* 22 × 16 in. R.A. 1783 (134): painted in September 1782.

528. *The same. Stuttgart. Gallery (Queen Charlotte Matilda Trust).* 23¾ × 17¾ in. 1782/3: in profile to left.

529. ORD, JOHN (1729–1814) (?). *Wellesbourne. Martin S. Crabbe.* 50 × 40 in. (Lord Ravensworth sale, at Eslington Park, by Anderson & Garland, 6/xi/1951 lot 486: with Leggatt: bt. 1955.) London period: as a Master in Chancery.

530. OSWALD, GEORGE (1735–1819). 29½ × 24½ in. (J. G. Oswald, Scotstoun, 1868.) Probably late Bath work: companion to no. 531.

531. OSWALD, MRS GEORGE (1747–91). *Fort Worth (Texas). Kay Kimbell.* 29½ × 24½ in. (J. G. Oswald, Scotstoun, 1868: with Newhouse Galls., New York, 1950.) Probably late Bath work: companion to no. 530.

532. OTTLEY, RICHARD (1729–75). 29½ × 24½ in. (W. Young Ottley, 1833: Mrs Ernest Innes sale, 13/xii/1935 (105) bt. Jurgens.) Probably later Bath work.

OZIER, MR. *See "*CAMPBELL, SIR JOHN*".*

533. PALMER, JOHN (1742–1818). *Philadelphia. Pennsylvania Museum.* 29 × 24 in. (Col. Palmer sale 18/vii/1874 (56) bt. Agnew: James Price sale 15/vi/1895 (74) bt. Agnew: William L. Elkins, Philadelphia.) Probably early London work.

534. PALMER, ROBERT (1715–87). *Thurton Hall. Jocelyn Beauchamp.* 30 × 25 in. (Descended to Sir Reginald Proctor-Beauchamp, Bart.: at Langley Park till 1939.) Dated 1783 by an old inscription on the back.

PARRY. *See* BARRY, LAMBE.

534a. PATTISON, A. 30 × 25 in. (W. G. Pattison (d. 1951): with M. Harvard, 1953.) From the later 1740s.

535. PAUL, SIR ONESIPHORUS (*c.* 1705–74). *See* no. 536.

536. PAUL, LADY (1708–66). Nos. 535/6 were two whole-lengths commissioned in 1764 (Whitley, p. 43).

537. PEACOCKE, MRS WILLIAM. 30 × 25 in. (Anon. sale 25/iii/1893 (365) bt. Gooden: bt. from Dowdeswell by Sedelmeyer, 1894: Collis P. Huntington, New York, 1895: Col. C. H. Cox sale, Toronto, 1949, bt. Lewis.) Bath period.

538. PEARCE, WILLIAM (*c.* 1751–1842). *London. Mrs F. N. Ashcroft.* Oval: 25 × 21 in. (Passed to Mrs Luck: J. Rubens Powell, 1879: F. C. K. Fleischmann, 1904, father of F. N. Ashcroft.) About 1780.

539. PECHELL, SIR PAUL, 1ST BART. (1724–1800). *New York. Harry Payne Bingham* (1942). 30 × 25 in. (Anon. sale 12/vii/1912 (83) bt. Colnaghi: with Knoedler.) London period.

540. PENNANT, THOMAS (1726–98.) *Cardiff. National Museum of Wales.* 36 × 28 in. (Descended to Countess of Denbigh: Viscount Feilding sale 1/vii/1938 (46) bt. Tooth: bt. from Tooth, 1953.) Painted 1776 according to W. Ridley's engraving of 1793. Pl. 196.

541. PERRYN, SIR RICHARD (1723–1803). 50 × 40 in. R.A. 1779 (100): engraved in mezzotint by Dupont, 1779.

542. PETRE, JULIANA, LADY (1769–1833). *San Marino (Calif.). Henry E. Huntington Library and Art Gallery.* 88¾ × 57½ in. (Bt. from Lord Petre by C. J. Wertheimer *c.* 1908: bt. 1911.) Painted 1788 (Whitley, pp. 302/3). Pl. 276.

PEYTON. *See* DASHWOOD-PEYTON.

543. PHIPPS, CAPTAIN CHARLES (1753–86). *Parham Park. Hon. Clive Pearson.* 30 × 25 in. (Marquess of Normanby sale 19/vii/1890 (18) as *Lord Mulgrave,* bt. for Lily, Duchess of Marlborough (Lady William Beresford): bt. from her by Sir Berkeley Sheffield: sale 16/vii/1943 (42) bt. Gooden & Fox.) About 1785: previously always as *Lord Mulgrave.*

544. PIGOTT, REV. WADHAM (*c.* 1751–1823). *Walmer. Major and Mrs R. J. Pinto.* 30 × 25 in. (Anon. (= Smyth-Pigott) sale 19/v/1911 (86) bt. A. Wertheimer: Adolph Hirsch.) From the later 1760s.: *repd.* in *The Sphere* 30/ix/1911, p. 344.

PITT, GEORGE. *See* RIVERS, GEORGE, 1ST LORD.

545. PITT, WILLIAM (1759–1806). 50×40 in. Engraved by J. K. Sherwin, 1789. It was begun 1787 and was completed (perhaps by Dupont) for the Marquess of Buckingham (*cf.* Whitley, pp. 271, 290, and 338/9). It cannot be identified with certainty among the twenty or so Pitts ascribed to Gainsborough, but mostly by, or after, Dupont (see list in Walpole Society, XXXIII, pp. 85/6). The most likely candidate is: Anon. sale 20/v/1842 (116) bt. Seguier: Sir Robert Peel, 1846: with Kleinberger, 1898: Marquis du Chaponay, Paris: Mrs. B. F. Jones, Pittsburgh: sale, New York, 4/xii/1941 (33).

546. PLAMPIN, JOHN (*c.* 1726–1805). *London. National Gallery* (5984). 19½×23¼ in. (Possibly R. Almack, 1856: Anon. sale 12/xii/1903 (72) bt. Barling: Mrs Wallis, 1904: F. Hindley Smith, 1925: P. M. Turner, 1927: bequeathed, 1951.) From the earlier 1750s. Pl. 13.

547. PLEYDELL, EDMUND MORTON (1724–94). *U.S.A. John M. Morehead.* 50×40 in. (Passed to Col. E. M. Mansel-Pleydell: bt. Sulley, 1909: with Knoedler, New York, 1912: Daniel G. Reid, New York: Mrs Reid Topping.) From the middle 1760s: companion to no. 548.

548. PLEYDELL, MRS EDMUND MORTON (1731–1819). *Boston. Museum of Fine Arts.* 49¾×41¼ in. (Passed to Col. E. M. Mansel-Pleydell: bt. Sulley, 1909: with Blakeslee, New York: Robert Dawson Evans, Boston, 1909: bequeathed by Mrs R. D. Evans, 1917.) Companion to no. 547.

549. PLEYDELL, MRS J. MORTON (Elizabeth Jackson). 49×39 in. (Descended to Sir Harold Farquhar: sale, Sotheby's, 13/xii/1950 (2) bt. F. Sabin.) From the earlier 1760s.

550. PONSONBY, LADY ANNE (*called*). 29½×24½ in. (Passed to D. L. Allen, sale 14/vii/1911 (100) bt. Agnew: Agnew sale 7/vi/1918 (19) bt. Sulley—*repd.*) A picture of about 1770: the identification of the sitter as Lady Anne (or as Lady Charlotte) Ponsonby is impossible.

PONSONBY, LADY CATHERINE. *See* ST. ALBAN'S, DUCHESS OF.

551. PONSONBY, MRS CHAMBRÉ (d. 1773). (*Mary Barker: Lady Staples.*) *Kilcooley (Ireland). T. B. Ponsonby.* 29½×24½ in. From the later 1760s.

POPHAM, EDWARD. *See* LEYBORNE, WILLIAM LEYBORNE.

552. PORTMAN, MRS HENRY WILLIAM BERKELEY (1707–81). *Lent to Tate Gallery, London, by Viscount Portman.* 82×58 in. From the earlier 1760s. Pl. 70.

553. POWIS, LADY (or LORD). "A head" —unfinished, in 1797 sale (33) bt. Hodson. The advertisement calls it Lady Powis, the sale catalogue Lord Powis.

553a. POWIS, EDWARD (CLIVE), EARL OF (1754–1839). *Powis Castle. Earl of Powis.* 50×40 in. Full-length as a child: about 1763.

554. POYNTZ, WILLIAM (1734–1809). *Althorp. Earl Spencer.* 92½×60 in. S.A. 1762 (30): painted for the sitter's sister, Georgiana Countess Spencer. Pl. 63.

555. PRATT, MR. 29½×24½ in. (Bt. "in an inn in London" *c.* 1867 by Mr Reed: Misses Reed sale 15/xii/1922 (103) bt. Knoedler: with John Levy, New York, 1923.) London period.

556. PRICE, UVEDALE TOMKYNS (1685–1764). *Munich. Alte Pinakothek* (1476). 49×39 in. (T. Price sale 6/v/1893 (46) bt. M. Colnaghi: Arthur Kay sale 11/v/1901 (40) bt. in: bt. in art trade 1909.) About 1760. Pl. 60.

PRINCESSES, THE THREE ELDEST. *See* CHARLOTTE AUGUSTA.

557. PRINGLE, SIR JOHN, BT. (1707–82). 30×25 in. (Bt. from T. Humphrey Ward by Agnew, 1913: with Leggatt, 1913: Sir A. J. Bennett sale, New York, 16/xi/1933 (6) bt. Loring —*repd.*) Probably London work.

558. PROBY, JOHN (1695/8–1762). *Elton Hall. Sir Richard Proby, Bt.* 29×24 in. Early or middle 1750s: the sitter's identity is not quite certain.

559. PROVIS, WILLIAM (d. 1808). 29½ × 24½ in. (Anon. (= Smyth-Pigott) sale 19/v/1911 (87) bt. A. Wertheimer: with Brummer, Paris, 1919: Anon. sale 14/v/1920 (74) bt. Lewis.) Probably about the same date as no. 560 (1766): *repd.* in *The Sphere*, 30/ix/1911, p. 344.

560. PROVIS, MRS WILLIAM. *Rochester (N.Y.). University Gallery.* 29½ × 24½ in. (Anon. (= Smyth-Pigott) sale 19/v/1911 (88) bt. Colnaghi: George Eastman, Rochester.) Inscribed with the date 1766.

561. PROVIS, MRS. 30 × 25 in. *Cincinnati. Museum.* (Gerard Lee Bevan: with Knoedler *c.* 1916 and *c.* 1950: with Howard Young, N.Y: Harry S. Lyman bequest, 1954.) A picture of about 1775: a different sitter from no. 560. It has also been called *Mrs Purvis.*

562. PROWSE, THOMAS (1708–67). *Brill. A. Edgell Baxter* (1936). 30 × 25 in. Earlier 1760s.

563. PROWSE, MRS THOMAS. *Leeds. Art Gallery.* 30 × 25 in. (Sir Hill Child sale 22/vii/1938 (132) bt. Agnew: bt. 1946.) Earlier 1760s: the wife of no. 562. The identity of nos. 562/3 was established by two copies in the Mordaunt sale, 1948: a third pair have belonged to Michael Harvard, 1949/56.

564. PUGET, MRS (Catherine Hawkins). *Paris. Baronne Edouard de Rothschild.* 29 × 24 in. (Col. J. Puget sale 8/v/1897 (86) bt. C. J. Wertheimer: Baron Alphonse de Rothschild.) Being painted December 1787 (Whitley, p. 294).

565. PULTENEY, SIR WILLIAM JOHNSTONE (1729–1805). *Rossie Priory. Lord Kinnaird.* 93 × 57 in. Between 1769 and 1774, possibly R.A. 1772 (*cf.* undated letter to sitter in Morgan Library, New York). Pl. 144.

566. PURLING, JOHN (1727–1801). 30 × 25 in. (Descended to Hastings N. Middleton, 1871: Middleton sale, Sotheby's, 18/vi/1952 (47) bt. Leger.) Probably from the 1770s: illustrated *The Connoisseur*, Dec. 1954, p. 260. Colour plate.

PURVIS, MRS. *See* PROVIS, MRS. (no. 561).

567. QUIN, JAMES (1693–1766). *Dublin. National Gallery of Ireland.* 92 × 60 in. (Wiltshire sale 25/v/1867 (128) bt. Duke of Cleveland: Duke of Cleveland sale 8/iii/1902 (21) bt. Lawrie: bt. 1905.) S.A. 1763 (41). Pl. 69.

568. *The same. Buckingham Palace. H.M. The Queen.* Cut down to 25½ × 20 in. (Mrs Gainsborough sale 10/iv/1797 (17) bt. for Prince of Wales.) Unfinished head from the same sitting as no. 567.

569. RADNOR, WILLIAM, 1ST EARL OF (1725–76). *Longford Castle. Earl of Radnor.* 49 × 39 in. Dated 1770: the receipt is dated 5/i/1772. Pl. 121.

570. *The same. Longford Castle. Earl of Radnor.* 29 × 24½ in. Dated 1773: paid for 28/ix/1774. Pl. 156.

570a. RADNOR, ANNE (HALES), COUNTESS OF (1736–95). 30 × 25 in. (P. H. Pleydell-Bouverie sale, Sotheby's, 27/vi/1956 (78) bt. S. Sabin.) Dated (in a later hand) 1773.

571. RADNOR, ANNE (DUNCOMBE), COUNTESS OF (1759–1829). *Longford Castle. Earl of Radnor.* 49 × 39 in. Receipt is dated 4/vi/1778. Pl. 195.

572. *The same. Cheltenham. Miss M. E. Pleydell-Bouverie.* 30 × 25 in. One of the series of six pictures, some dated 1773, which were paid for 28/ix/1774: the others are still at Longford Castle.

573. RAMUS, MR. R.A. 1783 (273). Untraced.

574. RAMUS, THE MISSES. *Destroyed by fire at Waddesdon Manor in 1890.* 48 × 39 in. (Descended to Colonel Townely: sale 10/v/1873 (90) bt. Agnew: John Graham sale 30/iv/1887 (95) bt. for Baron Ferdinand de Rothschild.) R.A. 1779 (101).

RAWDON, FRANCIS, LORD. *See* HASTINGS, MARQUESS OF.

RAWDON, LORD (*called*). *See* UNKNOWN OFFICER (no. 772).

RAY, LADY. *See* CARR, MARY, LADY (no. 120)

574a. RAYMOND, REV. SAMUEL (1744–1826). 30 × 25 in. *Belchamp Hall. P. St. C. Raymond.* Later Bath work.

READ, MISS. *See* MEARS, MRS, *and* VILLEBOIS, MRS.

575. RICHARDS, MRS. 30 × 25 in. (John Bowman, 1880: Anon. sale 19/iii/1904 (107) bt. Rutley.) Engraved in mezzotint by J. Spilsbury, 1768.

576. RICHMOND, MARY, DUCHESS OF (1740–96). *Ascott. National Trust (Anthony de Rothschild).* 91½ × 59½ in. (Descended in Conolly family: bt. in 1870s by Baron Lionel de Rothschild: Leopold de Rothschild.) Late London work. Pl. 275.

577. RIVERS, GEORGE, 1ST LORD (1721–1803). *Hinton St. Mary. G. H. Lane-Fox-Pitt-Rivers.* 91½ × 60 in. R.A. 1769 (36). Pl. 110.

578. ROBERTS, CAPTAIN HENRY. *Floors Castle. Duke of Roxburghe.* 49 × 39 in. (Mrs Whitcomb, 1856: Anon. sale, Robinson & Fisher, 21/v/1903 (95) as *Captain Cook*: with Reid & Lefevre: John A. Holms, Glasgow, 1911: Ogden Goelet, New York: thence to late Duchess of Roxburghe.) Probably about 1780.

579. ROBINSON, MRS "PERDITA" (1758–1800). *London. Wallace Collection* (42). 90 × 58¼ in. (Sold with Mrs Robinson's effects, 1784: George, Prince of Wales by 1790: presented 1818 to Marquess of Hertford.) Painted 1781/2 (Whitley, pp. 180 ff.). Pl. 238.

580. *The same. Windsor Castle. H.M. The Queen.* 30 × 25 in. (Gainsborough Dupont sale 10/iv/1797 (7) bt. for Prince of Wales). A fairly finished study for no. 579.

581. *The same. Waddesdon Manor. National Trust.* 30 × 25 in. (Said to have passed from the sitter to the grandfather of Isaac Espinasse, the owner in 1868: sold to Knowles: Agnew before 1872: Baron Ferdinand de Rothschild: Miss Alice de Rothschild: Baroness Mathilde von Rothschild, Frankfurt: James de Rothschild.) About 1782.

582. RODES, MISS MARY (1714–89). *London. Lord O'Neil.* 49½ × 39. Early 1760s: it has descended via Lord Houghton and Lord Crewe.

583. RODNEY, GEORGE, 1ST LORD (1719–92). *Dalmeny. Earl of Rosebery.* 90½ × 58½ in. (Painted for Alderman Harley: bt. from Lord Rodney in 1880s.) Painted 1783/6: engraved in mezzotint by Gainsborough Dupont, 1788. Pl. 280.

584. RODNEY, ANNE, LADY (1759–1840). *Philadelphia. Pennsylvania Museum.* 49 × 39½ in. (Painted for Alderman Harley: bt. from Lord Rodney in 1880s by Lord Revelstoke: sale 3/vi/1893 (41) bt. Agnew: John H. McFadden, Philadelphia.) About 1779/80 and companion to the portrait of her sister, *Mrs Drummond* (no. 212).

ROMNEY, CHARLES, EARL OF. *See* MARSHAM CHILDREN.

585. ROMNEY, FRANCES, COUNTESS OF (1755–95). 30 × 25 in. (Lady E. Marsham, 1904: Douglas Wyndham Lydgytt sale, Robinson & Fisher, 27/vi/1912 (170) as *Hoppner—repd.*) Probably late London work.

586. ROSEBERY, NEIL, 3RD EARL OF (1728–1814). *Dalmeny. Earl of Rosebery.* 30 × 25 in. Bath work after 1771.

587. ROWLEY, MISS PHILADELPHIA (Lady Cotton: 1763–1855). *Lisbon. C. S. Gulbenkian Foundation.* 30 × 25 in. (Passed to Major King, 1886: Baroness Mathilde von Rothschild, Frankfurt: bt. from Rudolph von Goldschmidt-Rothschild, 1929.) From the 1780s.

ROYSTON, PHILIP, LORD. *See* HARDWICKE, EARL OF.

588. RUMBOLD, SIR THOMAS (1736–91) and his son, William Richard Rumbold (1760–86). *London. Captain C. E. A. L. Rumbold.* 93 × 60 in. Middle to later 1760s.

RUMFORD, COUNT. *See* THOMPSON, SIR BENJAMIN.

589. RUSSELL, MRS WILLIAM (1758–86). *London. Lord Moyne.* 50 × 40 in. (Passed to Joseph Smith, Shortgrove: bt. by Earl of Iveagh, 1888.) Inscribed with the date 1782.

590. RUTLAND, CHARLES, 4TH DUKE OF (1754–87). *Destroyed in New York*, 1941. 50 × 40 in. (Given to Earl of Chatham: sale 16/v/1836 (59) bt. Capt. Victor Pringle: Anon. sale 28/iii/1919 (130) bt. Bell: with Jackson Higgs, New York, 1930: Mrs Rockefeller McAlpin sale, New York, 1/xi/1935 (49) bt. J. Weitzner: destroyed when with D. Sickles, 1941.) About 1771/3. An early replica, from Viscount Canterbury's sale, 1869, is at Belvoir Castle.

591. RUTLAND, ISABELLA MARY, DUCHESS OF (1756–1831). Sitting to Gainsborough in 1782 (Whitley, p. 193).

592. SACKVILLE, GEORGE, VISCOUNT (1716–85). *Knole. Lord Sackville.* 49 × 39 in. Probably about 1783/5: the sitter was better known when Lord George Sackville.

593. ST ALBANS, CATHERINE, DUCHESS OF (1742–89). 29½ × 24½ in. (Descended in the Ponsonby family till 1916: with Reinhardt, New York: John Willys, New York, 1921: Mrs van Wie Willys sale, New York, 25/x/1945 (27): Nate B. Spingold sale, New York, 2/iii/1950 (36).) London work: unfinished.

594. ST LEGER, COLONEL JOHN HAYES (1756–1800). *Buckingham Palace. H.M. The Queen.* 97½ × 73½ in. R.A. 1782 (58): commissioned by the Prince of Wales. Pl. 239.

595. ST QUINTIN, SIR WILLIAM, 4TH BART. (1700–70). *Scampston. Mrs L'Estrange-Malone.* 49½ × 39 in. (Passed to Major Darby-Griffith, who bequeathed it to Mrs St Quintin, Scampston, 1933.) Soon after 1760. Pl. 59.

596. ST QUINTIN, SIR WILLIAM, 5TH BART. (1729–95). *Scampston. Mrs L'Estrange-Malone.* 49 × 39 in. Probably from the middle 1760s.

597. ST QUINTIN, LADY (Charlotte Fane, wife of last). *Scampston. Mrs L'Estrange-Malone.* 30 × 25 in. Labelled Rebecca St Quintin (1726–58) but it seems the same sitter as no. 597a. Early 1760s.

597a. *The same.* 30 × 25 in. (In Fane family, Brympton d'Evercy, till 1956: with S. Sabin 1957.) A little earlier than no. 597.

597b. SAMPSON, MRS. 30 × 25 in. (F. W. Adams, Cheltenham: George D. Widener, Philadelphia, 1923.) About 1786.

598. SANCHO, IGNATIUS (1729–80). *Ottawa. National Gallery of Canada.* 29 × 24 in. (Given by sitter's daughter to W. Stevenson, Norwich: H. Stevenson, 1885: bt. in at sales, 1887, 1888: Anon. sale 24/i/1903 (70) bt. Wallis: bt. by Ottawa, 1907.) Traditionally "painted at Bath in one hour and forty minutes, Nov. 29, 1768": engraved in stipple by F. Bartolozzi, 1781.

SANDBY, THOMAS (and wife). *See* UNKNOWN GROUP (no. 752).

599. SANDWICH, JOHN, 4TH EARL OF (1718–92). *Greenwich. National Maritime Museum.* 92 × 60 in. R.A. 1783 (190): commissioned as a gift to Greenwich Hospital by Sir Hugh Palliser.

600. *The same. Paris. Maurice Routhier* (1934). 29 × 24 in. (Earl of Cork: bought from Agnew, 1897, by Sedelmeyer: Marquis de Ganay, 1898: Marquise de Ganay sale, Paris, 8/v/1922 (47)—repd.) Perhaps a little earlier than no. 599.

601. SAUMAREZ, MRS. Painted in 1760—see *The Connoisseur*, Jan. 1922, pp. 5 ff.

602. "SAVOI, SIGNOR". "A head"—unfinished: in 1797 sale (20) bt. Whitefoord.

603. SAYE AND SELE, ELIZABETH, LADY (d. 1816). *Broughton Castle. Lord Saye and Sele.* 30 × 25 in. Probably a marriage portrait (1767): bt. in at sales in 1933 and 1934.

SAYE AND SELE, MARIA, LADY. *See* EARDLEY, LADY (no. 228).

604. SCHOMBERG, DR RALPH (1714–92). *London. National Gallery* (684). 91¾ × 60½ in. (Bought from J. T. Schomberg, 1862.) Late Bath work. Pl. 146. Colour plate.

SCRIMGEOUR. *See no.* 770.

SCROOPE, MRS EGERTON. *See* EGERTON, MRS SCROOPE.

605. SEBRIGHT, SIR JOHN, BART. (1725–94). *Charlton Musgrove. Sir Hugo Sebright, Bart.* 30 × 25 in. Earlier 1760s. Pl. 79.

606. SEFTON, ISABELLA, COUNTESS OF (1748–1819). *Croxteth Hall. Earl of Sefton.* 92 × 60 in. R.A. 1769 (35): painted as Viscountess Molyneux. Pl. 111.

607. SEQUEIRA, DR ISAAC HENRIQUE (1738–1816). *Madrid. Prado.* 50 × 40 in. (Anon. (= H. J. Sequeira) sale 27/iv/1901 (67) bt. Agnew: Cecil Raphael, 1904: presented by Bertram Newhouse, 1953.) Probably earlier London period.

608. SEYMOUR, LADY HORATIA (1762–1801). 28 × 24 in. (Descended to Hugh F. Seymour: with Duveen by 1930.) R.A. 1783—not catalogued (Whitley, p. 205).

609. SHEFFIELD, SOPHIA CHARLOTTE, LADY (d. 1815). *Waddesdon Manor. National Trust.* 89½ × 58¾ in. (Bt. from the family for Baron Ferdinand de Rothschild, 1886: Miss Alice de Rothschild: James de Rothschild.) Painted 1785/6 (Whitley, pp. 238 and 257).

SHELBURNE, LORD. *See* LANSDOWNE, 1ST MARQUESS OF.

610. SHELLEY, JOHN (1729–90). 30 × 25 in. (Sir John Shelley-Rolls sale, at Avington Park, 25/vii/1951 (1007)—*repd.*) Probably from the 1760s.

611. SHERIDAN, RICHARD BRINSLEY (1751–1816). *Pittsburgh. Miss Helen C. Frick.* 27½ × 23½ in. (Sir Robert Peel: Edward R. Bacon, New York, 1919: W. R. Bacon: H. C. Frick.) London work.

612. SHERIDAN, THOMAS (1775–1817). *Piqua (Ohio). A. L. Flesh* (1945). 18 × 12 in. (In Sheridan family till *c.* 1928: with John Levy, New York: Leo Flesh, 1931.) Late London work.

613. SHERIDAN, MRS R. B. (1754–92). *Washington. National Gallery (Mellon collection).* 85 × 58¾ in. (Descended in the family of Bouverie of Delapré Abbey until 1871: Baron Lionel de Rothschild, 1872: bt. from Lord Rothschild, by Hon. Andrew W. Mellon, 1936: Mellon bequest, 1937.) Probably R.A. 1783 (140), but it may have been begun as early as 1774, and Gainsborough was certainly still working on it in 1785: it remains not quite finished. G. Dupont scraped a mezzotint, but it was not published. Pl. 256.

See also LINLEY, MISS ELIZABETH, *and* LINLEY, THE MISSES.

614. SHIRLEY, HON. JOHN (d. 1768). 30 × 25 in. (Descended to Col. E. C. Shirley: with Tooth, 1953/5.) About 1765.

615. SHRIMPTON, JOHN (d. 1781). Cut down to 30 × 25 in. (originally 50 × 40 in.). (Painted for William Perrin: descended to Sir William Fitzherbert, Bart.: sale, Robinson, Fisher & Harding, 15/vi/1922 (141) bt. in—*repd.*, before cutting down: sold privately, 1922 and later cut down: Anon. sale 18/vii/1924 (71) bt. Woodhouse: with Scott & Fowles, New York, 1931: sale, New York, 28/iii/1946: with Newhouse Galls., 1947.) Perhaps late Bath work.

616. SHUCKBOROUGH, MISS SARAH (?). *Tapley Park. John Christie.* 30 × 25 in. London work.

617. SIDDONS, MRS SARAH (1755–1831). *London. National Gallery* (683). 49¾ × 39¼ in. (Descended to Mrs Mair: bt. from Major Mair, 1862.) Perhaps begun 1783: finished, 1785. Pl. 250.

618. SINGLETON, MISS ELIZABETH. *London. National Gallery* (2638). 13¾ × 11¼ in. (Bt. from Miss Snow by Colnaghi, 1903: Sir J. D. Linton, 1903: G. Salting by 1906: bequeathed, 1910.) Dated 1769 on back.

619. SKYNNER, SIR JOHN (1723–1805). *Oxford. Christ Church* (Hall). 48½ × 39½ in. One of three versions ordered 1785: of which two at least were finished 1786.

620. *The same. London. Lincoln's Inn.* 50 × 40 in. (Painted for Francis Burton: bequeathed, 1832.) *See* no. 619.

621. *The same. Holyoke (Mass.). William Skinner II.* 50 × 40 in. (Passed from J. T. Batt to Abel

Buckley: sale 4/v/1901 (60) bt. Lawrie: with Colnaghi, 1901: with Tooth, 1903: bt. from Scott & Fowles *c.* 1906 by William Skinner I.) *See* no. 619.

622. SLOPER FAMILY, THE. Originally 98 × 72 in. (Passed to Lady Erle, 1878: with Agnew, 1920.) Painted 1787/8 but never finished. This is the picture shown R.A. 1878 (241) under the wrong title of "Mrs William Goddard (posthumous) and her children". It is reproduced in its complete form in *Illustrated London News,* 11 Dec., 1920. Soon afterwards it was cut up into three bits: (1) *Mrs Sloper.* (2) *The Misses Sloper.* 50 × 40 in. *Fort Worth (Texas). Kay Kimbell.* (3) A strip of Landscape, which measured 54½ × 30½ in. (1931) and has now been reduced further to 41 × 30 in. (no. 1005).

623. SMEATON, JOHN (1724–92). *Southill. Simon Whitbread.* 30 × 25 in. Probably very late work, unfinished.

624. SMITH, JOHN (d. 1797). *London. Draper's Company.* 54 × 44 in. Painted 1787 for the Company, of which the sitter was Clerk.

625. SOPHIA, H.R.H. PRINCESS (1777–1848). *Windsor Castle. H.M. The Queen.* Oval: 22¾ × 16¾ in. R.A. 1783 (134): painted in September, 1782.

626. SPARROW, MISS. *New York. Metropolitan Museum.* 30 × 25 in. (W. Pearce sale, by Phillips, 1/v/1872 (553): Louis Huth, 1898: with Gooden & Fox, 1908: with Sir G. Donaldson: Isaac D. Fletcher, New York: bequeathed, 1917.) Probably from the later 1770s.

627. SPARROWE, JOHN (1689/90–1762). *Auckland (N.Z.). City Art Gallery.* 50 × 40 in. (Descended to Lt. Col. F. M. Bailey, Northrepps: with Agnew, 1955: bt. 1956.) From the middle 1750s.

628. SPENCER, JOHN, 1ST EARL (1734–83). *Althorp. Earl Spencer.* 30 × 25 in. About 1763. Pl. 78.

629. SPENCER, GEORGIANA, COUNTESS (1737–1814). *Althorp. Earl Spencer.* 28½ × 23½ in. Painted as a wedding present for her son, 1781. Pl. 210.

630. *The same. London. Mary, Duchess of Devonshire* (1955). 49 × 39 in. (Bequeathed to the family by an old Governess.) An unfinished trial for no. 629, with a sketch for a frame in the background.

631. SPENCER, LADY GEORGIANA (1757–1806). *Althorp. Earl Spencer.* 29 × 23¾ in. Painted in 1763. Pl. 76.
See also DEVONSHIRE, GEORGIANA, DUCHESS OF.

632. STANHOPE, CHARLES, 3RD EARL (1753–1816). *Chevening. Earl Stanhope.* Cut down from 50 × 40 to 30 × 25 in. Left unfinished at the artist's death.

633. STANLEY, JOHN (1714–86). Engraved in stipple by Mary Ann Rigg (Scott), 1781.

STAPLES, LADY. *See* PONSONBY, MRS CHAMBRÉ.

634. STEVENS, RICHARD. 30 × 25 in. (Bt. from family by de Casseres, 1936: Fattorini, Bradford: Mrs Naylor sale 3/vii/1951 (72) bt. Davidge.) Completed in April 1762 (*The Connoisseur,* Oct. 1936, p. 209.)

635. STEVENS, REV. WILLIAM (1732–1800). *Ottawa. National Gallery of Canada.* 49½ × 39½ in. (Passed to Rev. G. Corby White, 1885: Anon. sale 3/iv/1914 (95) bt. Agnew: with Agnew, 1927: bt. 1928.) R.A. 1780 (121).

636. STONE, ANDREW (1703–73). 29½ × 24½ in. (Passed to A. C. Norman, Bromley, 1892.) *Repd.:* J. Biddulph Martin, *The Grasshopper in Lombard Street,* 1892, p. 71. Late Bath work.

STONE. *See* LOWNDES-STONE.

637. STOPFORD, JAMES GEORGE, VISCOUNT (1769–1835). "A head"—unfinished: in 1797 sale (14) bt. Crofts. Perhaps shown unfinished in 1784 (Whitley, p. 228): the sitter later became 3rd Earl of Courtown.

STRATFORD, HON. EDWARD. *See* ALDBOROUGH, EARL OF.

STRATFORD, HON. MRS. *See* ALDBOROUGH, COUNTESS OF.

STRATFORD, FRANCIS (1705–62) AND WIFE. *Merevale Hall. Sir W. F. S. Dugdale, Bart.* 30 × 50 in. Early 1760s.

639. STRATFORD, MISS MARIA (1742–97). *Merevale Hall. Sir W. F. S. Dugdale, Bart.* 30 × 25 in. From the early 1760s.

640. STRATFORD, MISS SARAH. *Merevale Hall. Sir W. F. S. Dugdale, Bart.* 30 × 25 in. From the early 1760s.

STRATFORD, MISS PENELOPE BATE. *See* DUGDALE, MRS.

641. STURT, MRS HUMPHREY (d. 1807). *Crichel. Hon. Mrs Marten.* 30 × 25 in. Probably latter 1770s.

642. SUFFIELD, HARBORD, 1ST LORD (1734–1810). *Norwich. Castle Museum (on deposit).* 93 × 60½ in. R.A. 1783 (201): engraved in mezzotint by J. R. Smith, 1783: commissioned for St Andrew's Hall, Norwich.

643. SUSSEX, H.R.H. AUGUSTUS FREDERICK, DUKE OF (1773–1843). *Windsor Castle. H.M. The Queen.* 22¾ × 16¾ in. R.A. 1783 (134): painted September 1782.

644. SUSSEX, HESTER, COUNTESS OF (1728–77) AND LADY BARBARA YELVERTON (1759–81). *Needwood House. Baroness Burton.* 87¾ × 58¾ in. (Descended through Marquess of Hastings, Countess of Loudoun, and Lord Donington: bt. by Lord Burton in 1890s.) R.A. 1771 (74). Pl. 128.

645. SWINBURNE, SIR EDWARD, 5TH BART. (1733–86). *Humshaugh. Lady Swinburne.* Oval: 25 × 20¾ in. Probably about 1785.

646. SWINBURNE, SIR JOHN EDWARD, 6TH BART. (1762–1860). *Detroit. Institute of Arts.* 26¼ × 23¼ in. (At Capheaton until 1930s: with Howard Young, New York: Mrs Walter P. Chrysler: presented by Mrs Byron C. Foy, 1949.) Traditionally painted in 1785. Pl. 254.

647. SWINBURNE, EDWARD (1765–   ). *Detroit. Institute of Arts.* 27¼ × 23½ in. (Same history as no. 646.) Traditionally painted 1785. Pl. 253.

648. SYKES, SIR FRANCIS (1732–1804). *Burnt in the Pantechnicon, London, 1874.* About 120 × 144 in. Painted 1787 (Whitley, p. 283): the composition included two horses, a groom, and a dog.

649. TALBOT, JOHN (d. 1778). *Lacock Abbey. National Trust.* 29½ × 24½ in. Early 1760s.

650. TALBOT, CHARLOTTE, COUNTESS (1754–1804). *London. Duke of Devonshire.* 92 × 57½ in. The head appears to be very late Gainsborough: the rest is finished by another hand, traditionally Hoppner's.

651. TALBOT, MISS INDIANA (Mrs L. P. Garland: d. 1780). *Cowdray. Viscount Cowdray.* 35½ × 27½ in. (Anon. (= A. N. Garland) sale 6/v/1905 (91) bt. in: C. T. Garland sale 26/v/1906 (129) bt. Vicars: Sir Edmund Davis, 1913: bt. from him by Viscount Cowdray.) Unfinished: probably early London work: *c.* 1775.

652. TARLETON, COL. BANNASTRE (1754–1833). R.A. 1782 (213). An equestrian full-length in a rather unconventional pose (Whitley, p. 190). It is not certain this was ever delivered to its sitter.

653. TATTON, MISS CATHERINE ELIZABETH (Mrs J. D. Brockman). *Washington. National Gallery.* 29½ × 24½ in. (Acquired from the Brockman family by Knoedler *c.* 1908: Lord Michelham sale, by Hampton's, 24/xi/1926 (290) bt. Duveen: Hon. Andrew W. Mellon: given to Washington, 1937.) Probably painted shortly before her marriage in 1786.

654. TAYLOR, JOHN (1738–1814). *Boston. Museum of Fine Arts.* 29½ × 24½ in. (Passed to George Taylor, Swaffham, 1903: with Agnew, 1910: Holbrook Gaskell sale 11/vi/1920 (21) bt. Agnew: with Howard Young, New York: Robert J. Edwards, Boston: bequeathed, 1925.) Probably a marriage portrait (*c.* 1778): companion to no. 655.

655. TAYLOR, MRS JOHN. *Washington. National Gallery.* 29½ × 24½ in. (Passed to George Taylor, Swaffham, 1903: with Agnew, 1910: gift of Hon. Andrew W. Mellon, 1937.) Probably a marriage portrait (1778): companion to no. 654.

656. TENDUCCI, GIUSTO FERDINANDO (1736–90). *Birmingham University. Barber Institute.* 29 × 24½ in. (Samuel Archbutt: John Neeld: bt. at Sir Audley Neeld sale 9/vi/1944 (7).) Late Bath work: from comparison with the engraved Beach of Tenducci at Ammerdown, the identity of the sitter may be doubted. Pl. 154.

657. TENNANT, MAJOR WILLIAM (d. 1803). *Fyvie Castle. Sir Ian Forbes-Leith, Bart.* 52 × 42 in. (Passed to C. R. Tennant: with Agnew *c.* 1903: Lord Leith of Fyvie.) From the 1780s: companion to no. 658.

658. TENNANT, MRS WILLIAM (d. 1798). *New York. Metropolitan Museum.* 50 × 40 in. (Passed to C. R. Tennant: with Agnew *c.* 1903: J. P. Morgan, New York: Jules S. Bache by 1929: bt. 1945.) From the 1780s: companion to no. 657.

659. THICKNESSE, PHILIP (1719–92). *St Louis. City Art Gallery.* 25 × 30 in. (Col. Wollaston sale, Foster's, 8/vii/1891 (50) bt. Smith: Anon. sale 30/i/1897 (102) bt. Gooden: W. H. Fuller sale, New York, 25/ii/1898 (9): with Scott & Fowles: Mrs Chauncey Blair sale, New York, 16/i/1932 (315) bt. Sickles: bt. 1945.) From the middle of the 1750s. Pl. 12.
See also UNKNOWN OFFICER (no. 765 *note*).

660. THICKNESSE, MRS PHILIP (Miss Ford: 1732–1824). *Cincinnati. Art Museum (Emery coll.).* 77½ × 53 in. (Passed to Rev. J. W. Richards: sales 13/iii/1869 (117) bt. in: 2/iv/1870 (155) bt. Agnew: Alfred de Rothschild: with C. J. Wertheimer, 1894 and 1908: with Scott & Fowles, New York: Mrs Mary M. Emery, Cincinnati: bequeathed, 1928.) Painted at Bath, 1760 (Whitley, p. 36). Pl. 62.

661. THISTLETHWAYTE, ROBERT (d. 1802). *Lent to Aberdeen by Mrs H. F. P. Borthwick-Norton.* 99½ × 60 in. Presumably a marriage portrait of 1778. Pl. 186.

662. THISTLETHWAYTE, MRS ROBERT (1760–). *Lent to Aberdeen by Mrs H. F. P. Borthwick-Norton.* 99½ × 60 in. Presumably a marriage portrait (1778): companion to no. 661. Pl. 187.

663. THOMPSON, SIR BENJAMIN (Count Rumford: 1753–1814). *Cambridge (Mass.). Fogg Art Museum.* 29½ × 24½ in. (Miss Cox: Augustus Winterbottom, 1908: Edward Cogswell Converse, Greenwich, Conn.: Archibald A. Hutchinson: presented by Florence Ellsworth Wilson, 1922.) London work.

664. THOMPSON, SIR CHARLES (1740?–99). *London. National Gallery (4090).* 49½ × 39½ in. (With Agnew: Sir Edward Stern: bequeathed, 1933, with life interest to Lady Stern.) Painted 1774 according to the mezzotint, 1800, by R. Earlom. Pl. 161.

665. THORNTON, JOHN (1720–90). *London. Marine Society.* 92 × 61 in. Accepted as a gift from the sitter at a meeting of the General Court, 21/iii/1782: engraved in mezzotint by Valentine Green, 1782. A half-length version was in possession of the family, 1885.

666. TICKELL, RICHARD (1751–93). *Messing. Lord Hillingdon.* 29 × 24 in. (Col. Tickell sale 2/v/1874 (73) bt. Agnew for Sir Charles Mills, later Lord Hillingdon.) London work.

667. TOMKINSON, EDWARD (1773–1819) AND WILLIAM (1772–). *Cincinnati. Charles P. Taft Museum.* 83¾ × 59½ in. (Passed to Henry J. Tollemache: with Agnew *c.* 1889: Ludwig Neumann: with Agnew, 1906: with Scott & Fowles, New York: bt. 1909.) Intended for R.A. 1784, but not sent. Pl. 221.

668. TOMPION, JAMES. 28 × 23 in. (Anon. sale, Robinson & Fisher, 13/xii/1900 (106) bt. Wallis: Sir J. D. Milburn sale 10/vi/1909 (109) bt. in—repd.: resold 3/vi/1910 (67) bt. Wallis.) Probably later Bath work.

669. TORRINGTON, LUCY, VISCOUNTESS (1744–92). *Weston. Earl of Bradford.* 29 × 24½ in. From the later 1760s.

670. TOWNSHEND, CAPTAIN. A letter of 22/iv/1762 (former Scadbury MSS) from Gainsborough to "Capt. Townshend at Thomas Townshend's Esqr. Old Burlington Street" mentions a portrait of the addressee to which some alterations were being made. This could be the "Col. Townshend" 29½ × 24½ in. Sedelmeyer sale, Paris, 16/v/1907 (68): bt. from Ehrich by Martin V. Kelley, Toledo (*Art and Archaeology*, 1918, p. 151).

671. TRACY, CHARLES THOMAS, 6TH VISCOUNT (1719–92). *Dochfour. Baroness Burton.* 49 × 39½ in. (Passed to Lord Sudeley: bt. by Lord Burton in 1880s.) Early Bath work: companion to no. 672.

672. TRACY, HARRIET, VISCOUNTESS (d. 1795). 49 × 39½ in. (Passed to Lord Sudely: bt. from S. T. Gooden by E. M. Denny 1895: Denny sale 31/iii/1906 (27) bt. Vokins—*repd*.: E. J. Wythes sale 1/iii/1946 (3) bt. Spielman.) Early Bath work, companion to no. 671.

673. TREVELYAN, MISS SUSANNA (Mrs Hudson: 1737?–   ). *Wallington Hall. National Trust (Sir C. P. Trevelyan, Bart.).* 49½ × 39½ in. Dated 1761 on back: the drapery is plausibly said to have been altered by Reynolds *c.* 1777.

674. TRUMAN, SIR BENJAMIN (1711–80). *Spitalfields. Messrs Truman, Hanbury & Co.* 93 × 58½ in. (Descended to Henry Villebois: bt. at his death by the firm, 1886.) Late Bath work. Pl. 117.

675. TRUMAN-VILLEBOIS, JOHN (1773?–   ) AND HENRY (1777–1847). *New York. Mrs Carll Tucker.* 61 × 51 in. (Descended to Henry Villebois (d. 1886): with Duveen, 1923.) About 1783. Pl. 222.

676. TUDWAY, CHARLES (d. 1770). *London. Courtauld Institute (Lee collection).* 89 × 60½ in. (Sold by C. C. Tudway, Wells, c. 1912: Viscount Lee of Fareham, 1933: bequeathed, 1947.) From the middle 1760s: companion to no. 677. Pl. 85.

677. TUDWAY, MRS CHARLES. *Baltimore. Museum of Art (Jacob Epstein collection).* 89 × 60½ in.

(Sold by C. C. Tudway c. 1912: with Sedelmeyer, 1913: Sedelmeyer estate sale, Paris, 2/iv/1936 (7) bt. Knoedler: bt. by J. Epstein, Baltimore, 1939.) From the middle 1760s: companion to no. 676. Pl. 84.

678. TUDWAY, CLEMENT (d. 1815). 30 × 25 in. (Sold by C. C. Tudway, c. 1912: with Newhouse Galls., New York, 1953/5.) Probably late Bath work: companion to no. 679.

679. TUDWAY, MRS CLEMENT. *Philadelphia. Pennsylvania Museum.* 30 × 25 in. (Sold by C. C. Tudway, c. 1912: with Scott & Fowles, New York: George W. Elkins, Philadelphia.) Probably late Bath work: companion to no. 678.

680. TUGWELL, WILLIAM. *Sandford Orcas. Sir Hubert Medlycott, Bart.* 30 × 25 in. Early Bath work: companion to no. 681.

681. TUGWELL, MRS WILLIAM. *Sandford Orcas. Sir Hubert Medlycott, Bart.* 30 × 25 in. Early Bath work: companion to no. 680.

682. TUGWELL, WILLIAM, Jr. *Sandford Orcas. Sir Hubert Medlycott, Bart.* 30 × 25 in. Early Bath work.

683. TUGWELL, MR. *Sandford Orcas. Sir Hubert Medlycott, Bart.* 30 × 25 in. Early Bath work: younger brother of no. 682.

684. TURNER, SIR EDWARD, BT. (1719–66). *London. Mrs Green (née Page-Turner).* 90 × 60 in. Painted 1762: engraved in mezzotint by J. McArdell, 1763.

685. TYLER, MISS ELIZABETH (1739–1821). *London. Lord Moyne.* Cut down to 24 × 30 in. (Lord Bateman sale 27/v/1882 (121) bt. in.: Lord Iveagh, 1888.) Said to have been painted for Lord Bateman in 1775.

686. *The same.* Oval: 28¾ × 24¾ in. (Mrs E. S. Browne, 1856: Anon. (=Rev. H. Hill) sale, 30/vi/1877 (113) bt. in: Hill sale, Robinson & Fisher, 29/iii/1917 (100) bt. Arthurton: with Knoedler, 1920.) Also about 1775.

687. UNWIN, JAMES (1717–76). 29 × 24 in. (Anon. (= Unwin) sale, Sotheby's, 26/vii/1950 (173) bt. Bellesi.) Late Ipswich work.

688. UNWIN, MRS JAMES. *Montreal. A. J. Nesbitt.* 49½ × 42 in. (Anon. (= Capt. E. Unwin) sale 8/vi/1928 (98) bt. in: with A. Tooth, 1929.) Begun about 1760, but only finished in 1771: *cf. The Connoisseur*, Jan. 1922, pp. 3 ff.: Feb. pp. 87 ff.

689. UVEDALE, REV. SAMUEL (1699–1775). 13½ × 11¼ in. (Anon. sale 8/vi/1928 (64) bt. Leggatt: P. M. Turner, 1936/1950: with Gooden & Fox, 1953.) Late Bath work.

690. VERE, THOMAS. *Shrubland Park. Hon. J. V. B. Saumarez.* 30 × 25 in. Probably early 1750s: from Broke Hall, Nacton, and companion to no. 691: *repd. Burl. Mag.* Nov. 1927 with sitter unidentified.

691. VERE, MRS THOMAS. *Shrubland Park. Hon. J. V. B. Saumarez.* 30 × 25 in. Probably early 1750s: companion to no. 690.

692. VERNON, ADMIRAL EDWARD (1684–1757). *London. National Portrait Gallery* (881). 48¾ × 39¾ in. (B. B. Hunter Rodwell, 1891: Anon. sale 20/vi/1891 (135) bt. Shepherd: bt. 1891.) Probably about 1753: engraved in mezzotint by J. McArdell. Pl. 45.

693. VERNON, GEORGE, 2ND LORD (1735–1813). *Southampton. Art Gallery.* 97 × 59 in. (Lord Vernon sale 20/vi/1919 (78) bt. Leggatt: Frederick C. Stout, Ardmore, Pa., 1925: Frank D. Stout, 1955: with Leggatt, 1956: bt. 1957.) S.A. 1767 (60). There is also an engraving by R. Josey of a different bust, which may well be from an original. Pl. 97.

694. VERNON, HON. LOUISA BARBARINA (d. 1776). 30 × 25 in. (Passed to Hon. Matthew Fortescue (d. 1842): M. Fortescue Isacke: Lt. Col. Edmeades: with Knoedler: Lord Vernon, 1913.) Lithographed by E. Morton, 1835: the sitter was the first wife of no. 693. Middle 1760s.

695. VESTRIS, GIOVANNI AGOSTINO (1760–1842). *Walmer. Mr and Mrs R. J. Pinto.* 30 × 25 in. (Sir Robert Peel, 1856: Broderip sale 11/vi/1859 (83) bt. Heathcote: Louis Huth, 1885: sale 20/v/1905 (98) bt. A. Wertheimer: Adolph Hirsch.) From the middle 1780s.

696. VILLEBOIS, MRS WILLIAM (Miss Read: 1757–before 1801.) *Cowdray Park. Viscount Cowdray.* 87½ × 50½ in. (Descended to Henry Villebois (d. 1886): Alfred de Rothschild, 1886: Almina, Countess of Carnarvon, 1918: bt. *c.* 1923.) Sitting as *Miss Read*, 1777. Pl. 164. *See also* TRUMAN-VILLEBOIS.

VILLIERS, LORD. *See* JERSEY, EARL OF.

VINCENT, ROBERT BUDD. *See* GRIFFITHS, CHRISTOPHER, JR.

697. WADE, CAPTAIN WILLIAM (d. 1809). *Needwood House. Baroness Burton.* 91 × 59 in. (Presumably in 1797 sale (39) bt. Pierce: In New Assembly Rooms, Bath, till sale 18/vii/1903 (141a) bt. Lane: bt. *c.* 1903 by Lord Burton.) R.A. 1771 (78). Gainsborough later modified the background as the result of contemporary criticism (Whitley, pp. 77/8). Pl. 129. *See also* UNKNOWN MAN (no. 763).

698. WALCOT, DR WILLIAM (1719–   ). *Lent to Ministry of Works by J. C. C. Vowler, 1937.* 30 × 25 in. Dated 1767 on back of picture.

699. WALCOT, MRS WILLIAM. *Lent to Ministry of Works by J. C. C. Vowler, 1937.* 30 × 25 in. Dated 1767 on back of picture.

700. WALCOT, MR (?). *Lent to Ministry of Works by J. C. C. Vowler, 1937.* 30 × 25 in. From the 1760s.

701. WALDEGRAVE, JOHN, 3RD EARL (1718–84). *Chewton. Earl Waldegrave.* 30 × 25 in. The remains of a later Bath work.

702. WALDEGRAVE, ELIZABETH, COUNTESS (d. 1784). *Chewton. Earl Waldegrave.* Cut down to 23 × 19 in. An unfinished head from the 1760s.

WALDEGRAVE, MARIA, COUNTESS. *See* GLOUCESTER, DUCHESS OF.

WALDEGRAVE, LADY HORATIA. *See* SEYMOUR, LADY HORATIA.

703. WALES, GEORGE, PRINCE OF (George IV: 1762–1830). *Windsor Castle. H.M. The Queen.* 22¾ × 16¾ in. R.A. 1783 (134): painted September 1782 for George III with the series of Royal family portraits. All other authentic portraits were done for the sitter and are documented in a bill (probably from the end of 1784: Windsor MSS, Georgian Papers 26791) published *Burl. Mag.*, Nov. 1946, p. 276, where numbers have been added to which reference is given below. Pl. 213.

704. *The same. Havana. Oscar B. Cintas.* 30 × 25 in. (Given to Colonel (later Viscount) Lake, 1781: Sam Mendel sale 24/iv/1875 (441) bt. Graham: W. B. Beaumont, 1885: with Sedelmeyer, 1911 (*Eleventh Series*, no. 89—*repd.*): Lord Michelham: with Duveen: Mrs H. K. McTwombly, New York: with Knoedler, 1940s.) Painted 1781 (Bill no. 1).

705. *The same. Middleton Park. Mrs A. C. J. Wall.* 28 × 22 in. (Presented *c.* 1781 to Lord Lothian: Marquess of Lothian till *c.* 1935: bt. from F. Partridge by A. C. J. Wall.) Presumably also 1781 (Bill no. 2): similar to no. 704.

706. *The same.* 30 × 25 in. Bill. no. 3, presumably of same design as no. 704. This was "sent abroad by particular orders" and has not been traced.

707. *The same. Waddesdon Manor. National Trust.* 90 × 82 in. (Given by the sitter to Colonel St Leger: bt. from Misses St Leger by Agnew, 1882: Baron Ferdinand de Rothschild: Miss Alice de Rothschild: James de Rothschild.) R.A. 1782 (77): engraved in mezzotint by J. R. Smith, 1783. No. 5 in Windsor Bill. Pl. 240.

708. *The same. Aske. Marquess of Zetland.* 90 × 82 in. No. 6 of the Windsor Bill as a copy of no. 707 and "delivered by order to Sir Thomas Dundas".

709. *The same.* "The head and sketch of part of the body": given by the sitter to Lord Heathfield, 1/xii/1801. Not traced.

710. WALKER, THOMAS (1724–1804). *Dayton (Ohio). John G. Lowe* (1933). 30 × 25 in. (Mrs Walker sale, Robinson, Fisher & Harding, 11/xii/1924 (198) bt. Leggatt: with Knoedler, 1925/33.) London work.

711. WALMESLEY, CAPTAIN JOHN. *St Louis, Mo. City Art Museum.* 30 × 25 in. (With John Levy Galls., New York, 1931: Sydney M. Shoenburg, St Louis: presented, 1952.) Probably late Bath work.

712. WARREN, DR RICHARD (1731–97). 49 × 39 in. (Mrs Warren-Codrington sale 27/v/1949 (6) bt. Leggatt.) Exh.: at Schomberg House, 1784 (Whitley, p. 228): engraved in mezzotint by J. Jones, 1792.

713. WARWICK, FRANCIS, 1ST EARL OF (1719–73). *Cincinnati. Art Museum.* 50½ × 40½ in. (Passed to his daughter, Mrs Finch-Hatton: Finch-Hatton sale 27/iv/1917 (126) bt. Wertheimer: with Knoedler, 1927: with John Levy, New York, 1931: presented by Harry S. Leyman, 1943.) Probably 1765: the date 1765 is on the plan he holds and the picture was seen at Warwick Castle by Lord Grimston in 1769.

714. WATSON, HON. MRS (Lady Sondes: 1767–1818). *Russborough (Co. Wicklow). Sir Alfred Beit, Bart.* 50 × 40 in. (Descended to Lord Sondes *c.* 1900: with Colnaghi & Knoedler: in Beit collection soon after 1900.) Painted 1786 (Whitley, p. 257): engraved in mezzotint by Thomas Park.

715. WAYTH, DANIEL (1729–85). A receipt, signed by Gainsborough and dated 1 Aug. 1758, for a half-length of Daniel Wayth for 15 guineas was found in a lawyer's office at Bury St Edmunds in April 1928.

716. WESTMORLAND, THOMAS, 8TH EARL (1700–71). *Shottesbrooke. Miss Oswald Smith* (1928). 50 × 40 in. Probably about 1760.

717. WHICHCOTE, SIR CHRISTOPHER, BART. (1738–86). *Burghley House. Marquess of Exeter.* 50 × 40 in. Inscribed with the date 1775, which may refer to the painting. Two unfinished

portraits of the same sitter were in the 1797 sale (29) and (30).

718. WHICHCOTE, JANE, LADY (d. 1812). *Burghley House. Marquess of Exeter.* 50 × 40 in. Companion to no. 717 and also inscribed with the date 1775.

719. WHICHCOTE, SIR THOMAS, BART. (1763–1828). *Sleaford Hall. Whichcote Trustees.* 50 × 40 in. Inscribed with the date 1786, which seems correct.

720. WHITBREAD, SAMUEL (1764–1815). *Southill. Simon Whitbread.* 35½ × 27¾ in. (Passed to Lord Eversley: sale 9/v/1896 (55) bt. for S. H. Whitbread.) Traditionally painted 1788.

720a. WHITE, STEPHEN. *Barningham Hall, Sir Charles Mott-Radclyffe.* 30 × 25 in. (By descent through the Saunderson family.) About 1765.

721. WHITEHEAD, PAUL. Engraved in line by J. Collyer, 1776.

722. WILKINSON, JOHN (1728–1808). *Berlin. Kaiser Friedrich Museum* (1638). 91½ × 57¼ in. (Bt. from W. E. Denison by Agnew, 1902: Edmund Davis, 1903/4: with Agnew: bt. Alfred Beit and given to Berlin, 1904.) Probably soon after 1776. Pl. 170.

723. WILKINSON, PINKNEY (1693–1784). *Boconnoc. G. G. Fortescue.* 30 × 25 in. Probably about 1759/60: not finished.

724. WILLES, SIR EDWARD (1723–87). *Earl's Croome. Lt. Col. O. D. Smith.* 50 × 40 in. Being painted in 1786 (sitter's will). Pl. 233.

725. WILLIAM HENRY, H.R.H. PRINCE (William IV: 1765–1837). *New York. John S. Phipps* (1942). 30 × 25 in. (Duke of Cambridge sale 11/vi/1904 (86) bt. A. Wertheimer: John F. Talmage sale, New York, 20/ii/1913 (24) bt. Scott & Fowles: Scott & Fowles sale, New York, 17/i/1922 (15) bt. Knoedler.) Painted 1781 (Whitley, p. 177). Engraved in mezzotint by Gainsborough Dupont.

726. *The same. Windsor Castle. H.M. The Queen.* 22 × 16 in. R.A. 1783 (134): painted September, 1782. Pl. 214.

"WILLOUGHBY, MISS". *See* EVANS, MISS.

WILLOUGHBY, MRS JAMES. *See* HOBSON, MISS.

727. WISE, HENRY (1706–78). 30 × 25 in. (Passed to Sir Wathen Waller, Bart.: sale 12/xii/1947 (147) bt. Hunter.) Painted at Bath in 1760 (*cf.* Whitley, p. 36). A companion portrait of his wife was too repainted for judgment.

728. WISE, HENRY CHRISTOPHER (1738–1805). 30 × 25 in. (Passed to Sir Wathen Waller, Bart.: sale 12/xii/1947 (146) bt. Wells.) From the early 1760s.

729. WISE, MRS HENRY CHRISTOPHER. *Cleveland* (Ohio). *Museum of Art.* 30 × 25 in. (Descended to Sir Wathen Waller, Bart.: with Duveen, 1913: Mrs F. F. Prentiss, Cleveland: bequeathed, 1944.) Alleged, on unknown evidence, to be R.A. 1778 (118).

730. WOLFE, GENERAL JAMES (*called*). *London. Mrs J. B. Ismay (bequeathed to National Gallery).* 30 × 25 in. (Lord President Inglis, Edinburgh, 1883: Arthur Sanderson sale 3/vii/1908 (60) bt. Agnew: Mrs J. B. Ismay: bequeathed to National Gallery, 1955, by T. Bruce Ismay.) Late Bath work: presumably unconnected with Wolfe.

731. *The same (so-called). Manchester. City Art Galleries.* 30 × 25 in. (Private family in Prussia: James Price sale 15/vi/1895 (75) bt. Colnaghi: bt. from Agnew, 1900.) Bath period: different sitter from no. 730 and equally not General Wolfe.

732. *The same (so-called).* 30 × 25 in. (Said to have been painted for Miss Lowther after Wolfe's death: Mrs Gibbons sale 5/v/1883 (23) bt. T. Woolner: Woolner sale 18/v/1895 (113) bt. Noble: Major C. E. Pym, Foxwold Chase, 1924.) Bath period: quite unlike the admitted portraits of Wolfe.

733. WOLLASTON, WILLIAM (1730–97). *Ipswich. Christchurch Mansion Museum.* 47½ × 38½ in. (F. Wollaston, 1888: E. J. Wythes sale 1/iii/1946 (4) bt. for Ipswich.) Late 1750s. Pl. 49.

734. *The same. Rugby. H. C. Wollaston.* 85 × 58 in. Late Ipswich work: perhaps later than no. 733. Pl. 61.

735. WOOD, MRS HENRY. *Garrowby. Earl of Halifax.* 30 × 25 in. About 1759/60.

736. WOODWARD, REV. RICHARD (1720–94) (?). *Castletown (Ireland). Lord Carew.* 30 × 25 in. From the 1760s. Woodward is the probable sitter, as it is traditionally called a Bishop of Cloyne.

737. WROTTESLEY, MISS ELIZABETH (Duchess of Grafton: 1745–1822). *Woburn Abbey. Duke of Bedford.* 30 × 25 in. About 1764/5.

738. *The same. Melbourne. National Gallery of Victoria.* 30 × 25 in. (Given by Lady Elizabeth Fitzroy to Viscountess Churchill, 1837: Viscount Churchill sale 12/v/1888 (23) bt. Agnew: Sir William Agnew, 1928: Count John McCormack, 1931: bt. from Agnew's, 1933.) About 1764/5.

739. WROTTESLEY, MISS MARY (1740–69). *Woburn Abbey. Duke of Bedford.* 30 × 25 in. About 1764/5.

WYCOMBE, LORD. *See* LANSDOWNE, 2ND MARQUESS OF.

740. WYNDHAM, MISS HENRIETTA (1738/40–1810). *Orchard Wyndham. George Wyndham.* 30 × 25 in. Inscribed with the date 1769. Pl. 109.

741. WYNN, SIR JOHN, 2ND BT. (1701–73). *Lent to Cardiff by Trustees of Glynllifon estate.* 49½ × 39½ in. It bears the date of 1768 on the frame, which seems correct.

742. WYNNE, ROBERT (1732–98). *Garthewin. B. A. Wynne.* 30 × 25 in. Probably a marriage portrait of about 1765: companion to no. 743.

743. WYNNE, MRS ROBERT (Elizabeth Dymoke: 1741?–1816). 30 × 25 in. (Descended with no. 742 until bt. Agnew *c.* 1914: Agnew sale 7/vi/1918 (20) bt. Sulley—*repd.*) Probably a marriage portrait about 1765.

744. YORK, H.R.H. FREDERICK, DUKE OF (1763–1827). *Cowdray. Viscount Cowdray.* 31 × 26 in. (E. Bicknall sale 25/iv/1863 (40) bt. Hogarth: C. F. Huth sale 19/iii/1904 (55) bt. Agnew: Viscount Cowdray, 1904.) Late London work: there is some doubt of the identity of the sitter since Bate-Dudley says Gainsborough never painted the Duke of York.

745. YORKE, HON. MRS CHARLES (Agneta Johnson: d. 1820). 30 × 25 in. (Earl of Hardwicke: with Agnew *c.* 1890: James Price: bt. from Agnew by Knoedler, 1893.) From the 1770s.

746. YORKE, PHILIP (1743–1804). *Erthig. Simon Yorke.* 49 × 39 in. Reputed to be 1779. It is possible that Gainsborough may have painted his second wife, Diana Wynne.

747. PETER DARNAL MUILMAN, CHARLES CROCKETT AND WILLIAM KEEBLE. *Sotterley. Lt.-Col. Michael Barne.* 29½×24½ in. (It has descended from P. D. Muilman through the Boucherett family.) From the middle 1750s: in spite of an old label on the back to the effect that only the landscape is by Gainsborough and the figures are by William Keeble, there can be no doubt the whole picture is Gainsborough's. Pl. 19.

748. THE IPSWICH MUSICAL CLUB. 15×20 in. (Acquired by Mr Strutt, Sr., at Gains-borough's sale, 1759: J. G. Strutt, 1856.) Fulcher (p. 56) gives an account of this sketch and says that the sitters are: Gainsborough himself, Captain Clarke, Wood, playing the fiddle, and Mills, playing the 'cello, and Joseph Gibbs asleep.

749. "THE FAMILY OF GEORGE III" (Eleven figures). *Mertoun. Earl of Ellesmere.* Paper, mounted on canvas: 17½×23½ in. A study for a large group of which no trace otherwise survives. It seems to date from the 1770s, but is somewhat too domestic for a royal family group and neither likeness nor ages fit.

UNIDENTIFIED SITTERS

PORTRAITS FROM THE SUFFOLK PERIOD

750 MOTHER AND DAUGHTER WITH SHEEP AND LAMB. *Glemham. Lady Blanche Cobbold.* 29 × 24 in. About 1750. In J. D. Cobbold coll., by 1899.

751. GIRL IN PINK WITH DOG. *San Marino (Calif.). Henry E. Huntington Library and Art Gallery.* 29½ × 24½ in. (C. Fairfax Murray: with Leggatt: Lord Brocket until 1946: bt. 1946.) A year or so later than no. 750.

752. LADY AND GENTLEMAN IN LAND-SCAPE. *Paris. Louvre.* 30 × 26½ in. (Anon. sale, by Peter Coxe, 24/vi/1806 (66): and G. Watson Taylor sale, at Erlestoke Park, 25/vii/1832 (128) as *Gainsborough and his wife*: Rev. Dr Burney, 1834: bt. from Archdeacon Burney by Sedelmeyer in 1890s: Camille Groult, Paris, 1905: presented by Pierre Groult, 1952.) Perhaps 1746: it has also been called *Thomas Sandby and wife*, but it may well be the painter and his wife. Pl. 17.

753. HUSBAND AND WIFE IN A LAND-SCAPE. *Dulwich College. Gallery* (588). 29½ × 25½ in. (John Doherty, Birmingham, 1858: Doherty, Foxlydiate House, Redditch, 1880: with L. Lesser: presented by C. Fairfax Murray, 1911.) Middle 1750s: companion to no. 754.

754. GIRL SEATED IN A PARK. *Lent from Cook collection to Fitzwilliam, Cambridge.* 28½ × 25½ in. (John Doherty, Birmingham, 1858: Doherty, Foxlydiate House, Redditch, 1880: Sir Francis Cook, Bart., Richmond.) Companion to no. 753.

755. YOUNG MAN IN GREEN SHOOTING-JACKET. *Arbroath. Hospitalfield Trustees.* 14 × 10½ in. (Patrick Allan Fraser bequest, 1890.) Early 1750s.

756. GENTLEMAN WITH DOG IN A WOOD. *Lawford Hall. Sir Philip Nichols.* 26 × 19½ in. (Sale at Weston Underwood Hall, 1827, bt. Stamp Garrard: thence to Walter Buchanan and F. M. Nichols.) Early 1750s. It has been called the poet *Cowper*, but perhaps represents a Throckmorton of Weston Underwood. Pl. 18.

757. MAN WITH BOOK SEATED IN A LANDSCAPE. 23 × 19½ in. (Anon. sale 20/v/1927 (78) bt. P. M. Turner: L. H. Hayter sale, Sotheby's, 15/iv/1953 (39) bt. A. Tooth.) One of the earliest of this style.

758. YOUNG MAN WITH DOG BY PED-ESTAL ("Horace Walpole"). 30½ × 22½ in. (Bt. at Brighton from B. Button, 1879, by H. G. Bohn: sale 28/iii/1885 (1611) bt. Philpot: Earl of Rosebery sale 5/v/1939 (146) bt. Spink: Anon. sale, Sotheby's, 19/v/1954 (102) bt. Bagnell: with C. G. Doward, New York, 1956.) Probably a Gainsborough of the 1750s: it bore a spurious signature by Benjamin Wilson.

759. SPORTSMAN WITH GUN AND TWO DOGS. 30 × 25½ in. (Anon. (?= Sir Philip Sassoon) sale 6/v/1927 (125) bt. Pawsey & Payne: with Agnew, Knoedler & Leggatt, 1928.) Middle 1750s.

760. ELDERLY MAN IN BROWN (1). *Shrubland Park. Hon. J. V. B. Saumarez.* 30 × 25 in. From earlier 1750s.

761. YOUNG MAN IN SILVER. *Shrubland Park. Hon. J. V. B. Saumarez.* 30 × 25 in. Later 1750s: from Broke Hall, Nacton, and perhaps a member of the Broke family.

762. ELDERLY MAN IN BROWN (2). *New York. Herbert Daniel Stone.* 29½ × 24½ in.

(W. A. Coats sale 10/vi/1927 (107) bt. Colnaghi: with Contini, 1929: with Knoedler, 1929/48: A. P. Good sale, Sotheby's, 15/vii/1953 (17) bt. Appleby: with J. Weitzner, New York, 1956.) From later 1750s.

763. YOUNG MAN (*called* "Captain Wade"). 30×25 in. (G. Hulin de Loo, Ghent, 1929.) From later 1750s.

764. GENTLEMAN IN BLUE. *London. Mrs H. Isherwood Kay.* 30×25 in. (From near St Albans: Anon. sale, Foster's, 18/i/1933 (108) bt. H. I. Kay.) Mid 1750s: possibly a member of the Gibbs family. Pl. 29.

765. AN OFFICER OF THE 1ST DRAGOON GUARDS. 30×25 in. (Anon. sale 13/iii/1936 (52) bt. Mrs Sykes: with Newhouse Galls., New York, 1937, as *Philip Thicknesse*.) Signed: *TG* (monogram) / 1756. A portrait of a man in blue with the same signature and called *Philip Thicknesse* is said formerly to have belonged to Sir Cuthbert Quilter. Pl. 26.

766. ELDERLY LADY IN RED WITH BLACK SHAWL. *Indianapolis. John Herron Art Museum.* 30×25 in. (Mrs E. F. Thompson sale 23/vi/1939 (31) bt. Feldman: with Newhouse Gall., New York: Percy R. Pyne: John G. Rauch, Indianapolis, 1941.) Later Ipswich work.

767. LADY IN BLUE. 30×25 in. (Anon. sale 17/vi/1912 (85) bt. Knoedler: A. Kann, Paris, 1912: Private collection, Paris, till 1956: with Knoedler, 1957.) Later Ipswich work.

768. LADY AGAINST FOLIAGE. 30×25 in. (Rodman Wanamaker, Philadelphia, 1904.) Very close in style to *Lady Innes* (no. 395).

769. GIRL IN PINK RIDING HABIT AND HAT. 40×30 in. (?). (A. Sanderson, Edinburgh: with Trotti, Paris: James Stillman, 1907.) Late Ipswich work: *repd. L'Art et les Artistes*, May, 1907.

UNIDENTIFIED PORTRAITS OF 1760 AND LATER

770. FULL-LENGTH MAN HOLDING SNUFF BOX. *Raleigh (N.C.). Museum of Art* (1956). 90×58 in. (Anon. sale, Sotheby's, 20/v/1953 (95) bt. Croft.) Middle Bath period. The sitter is now called *John Scrimgeour*.

771. FULL-LENGTH YOUTH IN VANDYCK COSTUME. *London (in store). Princess Labia.* 63½×42½ in. (Earl of Egremont sale 21/v/1892 (82) bt. C. J. Wertheimer: Comte Boni de Castellane, Paris: Sir Joseph B. Robinson sale 6/vii/1923 (7) bt. in: thence to his daughter.) Late work, unfinished: wrongly listed by Armstrong as *Jonathan Buttall*.

772. FULL-LENGTH OFFICER OF 4TH REGIMENT OF FOOT. *Melbourne. National Gallery of Victoria.* 88½×59 in. (Alleged to have come from studio of Sir William Beechey: Mr Tarner, Brighton, 1867: Anon. (=Tarner) sale 18/iii/1921 (35) bt. Peacock: bt. from Buttery, 1922.) Probably from the 1770s: it has wrongly been identified as *Lord Rawdon* and *Capt. Richard Bullock*, for neither of which is there any evidence. Pl. 138.

773. OFFICER OF THE 20TH FOOT. 30×25 in. (Bt. from R. Partridge by Knoedler, 1923: with John Levy, New York, 1924.) Probably Bath period.

774. NAVAL OFFICER (?). 30×25 in. (Anon. sale 9/vii/1926 (127) bt. Winkley.) Early Bath work.

775. YOUNG MAN. 30×25 in. (Bt. from Spiller by Knoedler, 1922: with Howard Young, New York, 1922.) Bath period.

776. UNKNOWN YOUTH (*called* "Edward Gardiner"). 14½×12½ in. (Anon. sale 25/vi/1904 (52) bt. M. Colnaghi: C. T. D. Crews sale 1/vii/1915 (100) bt. Colnaghi: with Knoedler: with John Levy, New York.) Perhaps Bath period.

777. UNKNOWN MAN (*called* "Samuel Foote"). 30 × 25 in. (Perhaps Wiltshire sale 28/v/1867 (130) bt. Whitehead. Lord Abinger sale, Glasgow, 17/ii/1932 (168): with A. Tooth: with Newhouse Galls., New York: Booth Tarkington, Indianapolis: with John Levy, New York, 1949.) From the early 1760s.

778. MAN IN MEDLAR-RED COAT. 30 × 25 in. (Anon. sale 26/ii/1937 (113) bt. Pawsey & Payne: Anon. sale 10/vii/1953 (133) bt. Dyson.) From the 1760s.

779. "THE PITMINSTER BOY". *Barton. Major J. G. Newton.* 23 × 20 in. Painted for Francis Milner Newton, probably in the 1760s.

780. MAN IN RED COAT (*called* "Marquess of Lansdowne"). 30 × 25 in. (C. W. Mansel Lewis, 1885: with Fischof & Sedelmeyer, 1902: Fritz von Gans, 1903: Sedelmeyer, 1905 (IX Series no. 76): with Fischof, 1907: P. A. B. Widener, Philadelphia, sale, Philadelphia, 21/vi/1944 (430): Mixed sale, Plaza Galls., New York, 21/2 Nov. 1952.) Inscribed with Gainsborough's name and dated 1773.

781. MAN (*called* "James Bourchier"). *Pittsburgh. Carnegie Institute.* 30 × 25 in. (Bt. from J. W. R. Crawfurd by Knoedler, 1917: with John Levy, New York, 1917: Mrs J. Willis Dalzell, Pittsburgh, 1918: bequeathed, 1929.) From the 1770s.

782. ELDERLY MAN IN BLUE. 30 × 25 in. (Bt. from Colnaghi by Sedelmeyer, 1900 (VI Series, no. 86): J. Jaffé, 1900: Jaffé sale, Nice, 12/vii/1943 (113).) Probably from the 1770s.

783. ELDERLY MAN IN BLUE. *Parham. Hon. Clive Pearson.* 30 × 25 in. (Burdett-Coutts sale 4/v/1922 (27) bt. for Hon. B. C. Pearson.) Bath period.

784. MAN IN GREEN. 30 × 25 in. (Anon. sale 13/v/1893 (103) bt. in: bt. from Wallis by Charles Stewart Smith, New York: sale, New York, 5/i/1935 (53) bt. Keppel & Co.) From the 1770s or 1780s.

785. ALLEGED SELF-PORTRAIT. *Ascott. Anthony de Rothschild.* 20½ × 16 in. (Probably Gainsborough Dupont sale, Sudbury, 29/v/1874 (130) bt. Hogarth: Lord R. Sutherland Gower, 1877: Anon. sale 13/v/1893 (122) bt. Meade: C. F. Meade: with Knoedler: bt. by 1927.) This might be Dupont, but its date is puzzling.

786. LADY IN WHITE WITH BLUE CLOAK. *Bath. Holburne of Menstrie Museum* (34). 28½ × 23½ in. From the 1760s. Now a ruin.

787. GIRL (*called* "Mary Gainsborough"). *Boston. Museum of Fine Arts.* Oval: 24 × 19¾ in. (Eben B. Jordan, Boston, 1903: given by R. Jordan, 1924.) From the 1760s. Now a ruin.

788. GIRL WITH FLOWERS. *Columbus (Ohio). Frederick W. Schumacher* (1950). 30 × 25 in. (Col. W. Pinney sale, by Arber & Waghorn, 21/vii/1898 (24) bt. Agnew: Viscount Leverhulme sale, New York, 17/ii/1926 (105): Joseph J. Kerrigan, New York, 1930: Mrs Slater (Kerrigan) sale, New York, 22/iv/1948 (18).) Perhaps from the 1770s.

789. LADY IN ROSE. *Bruern Abbey. Hon. Michael Astor.* 30 × 25¼ in. (H. A. J. Munro sale 11/v/1867 (143) bt. S. Addington: sold *c.* 1870 to Baron Bischoffsheim, Paris: bt. in Paris by A. Tooth, 1953: bt. 1953.) From the 1770s. Pl. 177.

790. LADY IN BLUE. 29½ × 24½ in. (Samuel S. Joseph, 1885: bt. from Mrs Joseph by Agnew *c.* 1916: J. Chrissoveloni sale 8/vi/1928 (115) bt. Sampson: Miss H. Glendenning, New York, 1939.) From the middle or later 1770s.

791. ELDERLY LADY (*called* "Countess of Bristol"). *Chicago. Art Institute.* 35 × 28 in. (Viscount Hampden, 1884: Louis Huth, 1885: sale 20/v/1905 (97) bt. Agnew: W. W. Kimball, Chicago: bequeathed, 1922.) Late work: originally called *Viscountess Hampden*. She may be *Theodosia, Viscountess Crosbie. c.* 1776.

792. LADY IN A BLUE SHAWL (*called* "Duchess of Beaufort"). *Leningrad. Hermitage.* 29½ × 24½ in. (Bt. from C. J. Wertheimer (?) by Alexis de Hitroff, Paris, before 1892: bequeathed, 1912.) Late work.

793. LADY IN WHITE (*called* "Mrs Sheridan"). *Kenwood. Iveagh Bequest* (*not shown*). 30×25 in. (Lord Brougham: bt. from Agnew, 1889.) A Bath period Gainsborough may lurk under the present overpaint.

794. LADY (*called* "Mrs Thomas Gainsborough"). 29×23 in. (A. Hatton Beebe, 1900: with Agnew: with Reinhardt, Chicago: A. H. Mulliken, Chicago: sale, New York, 12/iv/1935 (151) bt. A. S. Verney.) Perhaps once a picture of the 1760s.

795. MINIATURE OF OLD LADY (*called* "Mrs John Gainsborough"). *Ipswich. Christchurch Mansion Museum*. Paper, mounted on panel: 4½×3½ in. (Probably descended from a niece of Mrs Gainsborough to her grandson J. Scott: sale 20/vi/1896 (81) bt. Stock. Mrs Emma Joseph: bequeathed by her daughter, Mrs Laura Armstrong, 1955.) Apparently from the 1780s, which would make it impossible as Gainsborough's mother.

796. MINIATURE OF A LADY (*called* "Mrs John Gainsborough"). 6×4½ in. (W. A. Coats. 1904.) Similar in style to no. 795, but a different sitter.

FANCY PICTURES

Note: Nos. 797 to 815 have been placed, as far as possible, in chronological order. A preliminary list, with fuller references and explanations for some of the histories, will be found in *Burlington Magazine*, June 1946. An unusual number of copies exist of some of these designs, but I know of none which is certainly autograph and it is my impression that the various small "engraver's copies" (even when an engraving was not executed) were all the work of Gainsborough Dupont.

797. A SHEPHERD. *Burnt in the fire at Exton Park, 23 May 1810.* 50 × 40 in. (?). (Bought *c.* 1781 by Earl of Gainsborough: passed 1798 to Sir Gerard Noel Noel, Bt., of Exton Park.) R.A. 1781 (176). Engraved in mezzotint by R. Earlom, 1781.

798. A PEASANT GIRL GATHERING STICKS IN A WOOD. *Fredericton (New Brunswick). Beaverbrook Art Gallery.* 67 × 49 in. (Mrs Gainsborough sale 11/iv/1797 (57) bt. Steers. In the possession of the Abdy family for many years before 1873: bt. from the Trustees of the late Sir Anthony Abdy, Bt., by Lord Beaverbrook and presented to Fredericton, 1956.) Being painted 1782 (Whitley, p. 179) and called unfinished in the 1797 sale. A tradition in the Abdy family had it that this was a family portrait but it seems more likely that it is the fancy picture of 1782. Pl. 255.

799. GIRL WITH PIGS. *Castle Howard. George Howard.* 49½ × 58½ in. (Bt. by Sir Joshua Reynolds, 1782 and sold *c.* 1789 to C. A. de Calonne: de Calonne sale, by Skynner & Dyke, 23 ff./iii/1795 (85) bt. in and sold privately soon afterwards through Bryan to the Earl of Carlisle, Castle Howard.) R.A. 1782 (127). Engraved in mezzotint by R. Earlom, 1783. Pl. 245.

800. TWO SHEPHERD BOYS WITH DOGS FIGHTING. *London. Iveagh bequest, Kenwood.*

88 × 62 in. (Bt. before 1786, by Wilbraham Tollemache, later 6th Earl of Dysart: Admiral Tollemache, 1821: sold by Lord Tollemache in 1890s to Earl of Iveagh.) R.A. 1783 (35). Engraved in mezzotint by Henry Birche, 1791: the engraver's copy was by W. R. Bigg.

801. A BEGGAR BOY AND GIRL. *Williamstown (Mass.). Sterling and Francine Clark Art Institute.* 28 × 25 in. (Bt. from Gainsborough by Duke of Dorset, 1784: descended with Knole to Countess Amherst, Countess De la Warr, and then to Lord Sackville: sold in 1911 to J. P. Morgan: with Knoedler in 1940s: Robert Sterling Clark.) Since at least 1817 called *Miss Linley and her brother*, and it may well have been begun as a larger picture of the two Linleys, on which Gainsborough says he was at work in 1768 (Whitley, p. 383). The receipt of 1784 at Knole, however, calls it "one sketch of a Beggar Boy and Girl". On grounds of style 1768 is possible.

802. BEGGAR BOYS. *London. Duke of Newcastle.* 29 × 25 in. (Sold at the 1789 private sale, no. 61, to the Duke of Newcastle.) Painted in the Spring, 1785 (Whitley, p. 238).

803. COTTAGE GIRL WITH DOG AND PITCHER. *Russborough (Co. Wicklow). Sir Alfred Beit, Bart.* 68½ × 49 in. (Bt. 1785 by Sir Francis Basset (Lord de Dunstaneville): passed to A. F. Basset: with Asher Wertheimer, 1907: soon after in Beit collection.) Painted in the Spring, 1785 (Whitley, p. 241): engraved in stipple by John Whessell, 1806, as *The Young Cottager.* Pl. 273.

804. COTTAGE CHILDREN WITH THE ASS. *Burnt in the fire at Exton Park, 23 May 1810.* (Bt. 1787 by the Earl of Gainsborough: passed to Sir Gerard Noel Noel, Bt., Exton Park.) Painted in the Winter, 1785 (Whitley, p. 250). Engraved in mezzotint by Henry Birche, 1791.

805. COTTAGE GIRL WITH A BOWL OF MILK. *Capetown. South African National Gallery.* 59 × 47 in. (Sold to Macklin for his *Poets' Gallery* as *Lavinia*, 1788: Lord Robert Spencer sale 31/v/1799 (91) bt. Willett: Willett sale 1/vi/1813 (88): Samuel Rogers, 1814: sold to Sir George Phillips *c.* 1816: passed to Earl of Camperdown: bt. by Sir Abe Bailey *c.* 1918: bequeathed to Capetown, 1941.) Painted 1786 (Whitley, p. 264). Engraved in stipple by Bartolozzi, 1790, as *Lavinia*: and by John Whessell, 1806, as *The Cottage Girl*. Pl. 284.

806. THE WOODMAN. *Burnt in the fire at Exton Park, 23 May 1810.* 92¾ × 61½ in. (Bt. from the 1789 sale at Schomberg House (82) by the Earl of Gainsborough: passed to Sir Gerard Noel Noel, Bart., Exton Park.) Painted in the Summer, 1787 (Whitley, p. 285). Engraved in stipple by P. Simon, 1791.

807. COTTAGE CHILDREN (THE WOOD GATHERERS). *New York. Metropolitan Museum.* 57¼ × 46½ in. (Bt. 1787 by Lord Porchester (Earl of Carnarvon): Earls of Carnarvon till 1924: Edward S. Harkness, New York, 1924: bequeathed by Mrs Harkness, 1950.) Painted 1787 (Whitley, p. 292). Pl. 281.

808. A BOY AT A COTTAGE FIRE AND A GIRL EATING MILK. 58½ × 46½ in. (1789 cat. for private sale (49): R. B. Sheridan by 1807: Sheridan sale by P. Coxe, 6/x/1813 (i)—not sold: Alexander Copland sale 12/iii/1836 (44) bt. Seguier: Sir W. W. Knighton by 1845: Knighton sale 23/v/1885 (459) bt. M. Colnaghi: perhaps H. G. Marquand sale, New York, 23/i/1903 (23) bt. S. P. Avery.) Painted at the close of 1787 (Whitley, pp. 292/3) and companion to the next. Engraved in mezzotint by C. Turner, 1809, as *Interior of a Cottage*.

809. A BOY WITH A CAT—MORNING. *New York. Metropolitan Museum.* 58½ × 46½ in. (1798 cat. for private sale (51): R. B. Sheridan by 1807: Sheridan sale, by P. Coxe, 6/x/1813 (iii) —not sold: Alexander Copland sale 12/iii/1836 (45) bt. Seguier: Sir W. W. Knighton by 1845: Knighton sale 23/v/1885 (46) bt. M. Colnaghi:

presented to New York by Henry G. Marquand, 1888.) Painted at close of 1787 (Whitley, pp. 292/3) and companion to the last. Engraved in mezzotint by C. Turner, 1809, as *The Little Cottager*. Now a ruin. Pl. 282.

810. YOUNG HOBBINOL AND GANDE-RETTA. *Los Angeles. Mrs Mildred Browning Green.* 49½ × 39½ in. (Sold to Macklin for his *Poets' Gallery*, 1788: John Knight, 1814: sale 23/iii/1819 (73) bt. Sir R. C. Hoare: sold from Stourhead, 1883, to Samson Wertheimer: Baron Albert von Rothschild, Vienna: Baron Louis Rothschild, New York: with Rosenberg & Stiebel, New York, 1954.) Presumably painted 1788: engraved in stipple by P. W. Tomkins, 1790. The engraver's copy in Macklin sale, 1800. Pl. 283.

811. A HOUSEMAID (unfinished). *London. Tate Gallery* (2928). 99 × 57¾ in. (In 1797 sale (41) bt. Bryan: Earl of Carlisle: given by Rosalind, Countess of Carlisle, 1913.) Probably 1782/86, from appearance of same figure in no. 1001.

812. GIRL GATHERING MUSHROOMS (unfinished). *London. Colonel E. J. S. Ward.* 50 × 40 in. (In 1797 sale (58) bt. Mitchell: Sir Francis Freelimg sale 15/iv/1837 (59) bt. Prowett: A. Levy sale 6/iv/1876 (292) bt. for Lord Dunmore: Anon. (=Dunmore) sale 17/iii/1877 (83) bt. Ross: A. Levy sale 3/v/1884 (19) bt. Grindlay: W. C. Alexander, 1887: bt. by Colnaghi, 1905: Hon. Sir John Ward by 1932.) Presumably a late work.

813. GIRL HOLDING A PENNY (unfinished). *London. Colonel E. J. S. Ward.* 50 × 40 in. (Perhaps Rev. H. S. Trimmer sale 17/iii/1860 (75) bt. Flack: Hon. Sir John Ward by 1932.) Perhaps a late Ipswich work and a study of one of the painter's daughters.

814. A NYMPH AT THE BATH ("Musidora"). *London. Tate Gallery* (308). 73 × 59½ in. (Mrs Gainsborough sale 11/iv/1797 (82) bt. Earle. Given to the National Gallery by Robert Vernon, 1847.) Very late work: unfinished. The figure is based on an Antique design also

used by Adriaen de Vries (G. Sawyer, *Journal of Courtauld & Warburg Institutes*, 1951, p. 134).

815. HAYMAKER AND SLEEPING GIRL. *Boston. Museum of Fine Arts.* 88 × 57 in. (Given to Gainsborough Dupont, 1788: Dupont sale 11/iv/1797 (103) bt. in: Dupont sale 23/v/1891 (60) bt. Agnew: Lord Joicey: sold *c.* 1907 to E. M. Hodgkins, Paris: Samuel G. Archibald, Paris: Archibald sale, New York, 31/iii/1951 (249) bt. C. G. Doward: bt. from Vose Galleries, Boston, 1953.) Very late work, not quite completed. Pl. 277.

816. BOY WITH BIRD'S NEST (Jack Hill). 30 × 24½ in. (Descended in Gainsborough family to Miss Clarke (1859): thence to the Misses Lane: sold *c.* 1896: George J. Gould, New York: with Duveen: Mrs B. F. Jones, Jr., Pittsburgh, 1931: sale, New York, 4/xii/1941 (69)—*repd.* bt. Charles Sessler.) Probably from the 1780s.

816a. OLD PEASANT WITH A DONKEY ("The Schoolmaster!"). *Warwick. Mrs H. W. Standring.* 20½ × 15½ in. (Rev. Bolton: sold by Mrs Somers Smith, 1896, to R. S. Bond, Surbiton: Anon. sale, Knight, Frank & Rutley, 21/v/1954 (222): bt. from Drown, 1955.) Early 1750s: engraved with variations by W. Woollett. The picture seems to have been slightly cut. Pl. 35.

817. BUMPER—A BULL TERRIER. *Raveningham. Sir Edmund Bacon, Bt.* 13¾ × 11¾ in. (Passed with nos. 368/9 to Anon. sale 6/v/1910 (102) bt. Grenlow: bt. from Shepherd by Sir Hickman Bacon, Bt., 1910.) Inscribed on the back of the relining canvas: *Thos Gainsborough/ Pinxit Anno/1745.* Pl. 5.

817a. A FAVOURITE DOG. *Little Wenham Hall. Major A. T. C. Binny.* 45 × 62½ in. (Painted for Edgar family, Ipswich: sold c. 1898 to Mr Maund: E. W. Gilbert.) Probably later 1750s.

818. DOG BELONGING TO MRS DOWNES. *Tockenham. Major J. G. Buxton.* 19 × 23 in. Early 1760s: it has descended through the Jacob family.

819. A SPITZ DOG. 24 × 29 in. (A. W. Gould, 1895: E. R. Gould sale, Sotheby's, 28/iii/1928 (54) bt. Morrison: A. Morrison sale, Sotheby's, 20/iii/1946 (171) bt. Adams: Marcus Wickham Boynton: with Adams Gallery, 1951.) Probably Bath period.

820. A SETTER DOG. *Petworth. John Wyndham.* 39 × 49 in. Fairly late work: probably painted for Earl of Egremont.

821. TWO FOX DOGS. *London. National Gallery* (5844). 32¾ × 44 in. (C. F. Abel sale, Greenwood's, 13/xii/1787 (44): bt. by John Crosdill from whom it passed to Miss Thoyts, sale 6/v/1910 (94) bt. for J. Arthur James: bequeathed by Mrs Arthur James, 1948.) Painted

for Abel, perhaps at the time Gainsborough did his portrait (1777). Pl. 290.

822. TRISTRAM AND FOX. *London. Tate Gallery* (1483). 24 × 20 in. (Passed from Margaret Gainsborough via Henry Briggs to Miss Clarke and Mrs Lane: presented by the Misses Lane, 1896.) London period: it hung over Gainsborough's London chimney piece. Pl. 292.
See also no. 107 (A GREYHOUND: a fragment).

823. GREYHOUNDS COURSING A FOX. *Mentmore. Earl of Rosebery.* 70 × 93 in. (Exhibited for sale at Schomberg House, 1789 (109) bt. Sir John Leicester: Samuel Whitbread, 1814: Eleanor, Duchess of Northumberland, 1867: Anon. (= Colnaghi) sale 10/v/1873 (111) for Baron Meyer de Rothschild: thence to Hannah, Countess of Rosebery.) Very late work: in 1789 it had a companion (108) *A landscape with deer.* Pl. 289.

824. AN OLD HORSE. *London. Tate Gallery* (1484). 21¾ × 25½ in. (Passed from Margaret Gainsborough via Henry Briggs to Miss Clarke and Mrs Lane: presented by the Misses Lane, 1896.) Bath period.

825. A HEN AND CHICKENS. 23 × 24 in. (Passed from Gainsborough to Rev. Gainsborough Gardiner and Mrs E. N. Harward: sale 11/v/1923 (106) bt. Francis Howard.) Probably Bath period.

LANDSCAPES

LANDSCAPES OF THE EARLIER SUFFOLK PERIOD

Note: It has seemed that the least inconvenient order for cataloguing the early landscapes is according to size, in a series according to the height of the pictures.

826. "DRINKSTONE PARK" (*called*). *São Paulo (Brazil). Museum of Art.* 56 × 60½ in. (Descended with Drinkstone Park, perhaps from Joshua Grigby, to H. Powell, 1814: bt. from Harcourt Powell estate *c.* 1935, by A. Tooth: Sir Kenneth Clark, 1935: with F. Partridge, 1951: bt. 1951.) Early 1750s: it is not, as usually stated, a view of Drinkstone Park, but a free variation on a picture by J. Ruisdael (Louvre), of which Gainsborough made a chalk copy (Woodall, no. 227). Pl. 46.

827. BEND OF A RIVER, WITH PEASANTS AND CATTLE WATERING. 49 × 39 in. (Probably came to Thompson family with Mary Spencer of Hart Hall, Suffolk, 1769: Lord Knaresborough (Sir H. Meysey-Thompson): Anon. sale 20/vi/1913 (87) bt. A. Wertheimer: with A. Tooth: with J. W. Anderson, Detroit, 1916: with Hirschl and Adler, New York, 1957.) Probably from the middle 1750s. Pl. 37.

828. GAINSBOROUGH'S FOREST. *London. National Gallery* (925). 48 × 60 in. (Said to have changed hands "twenty times" before 1788: R. Morrison sale, by Greenwood, 8/iii/1788 (78) bt. Boydell: Josiah Boydell, 1808: D. P. Watts (d. 1816), 1814: J. Watts Russell sale 3/vii/1875 (32) bt. for National Gallery.) According to Gainsborough himself, finished in 1748 (Whitley, pp. 296/302). Pl. 22.

829. WOODCUTTER COURTING A MILK-MAID. *Woburn Abbey. Duke of Bedford.* 42¾ × 51 in. Signed: *TG.* Bought from the artist

by the Duke of Bedford for 21 guineas: receipt 24/v/1755 (*Burl. Mag.*, July 1950, p. 201). Pl. 41.

830. WOODY SLOPE WITH CATTLE AND FELLED TIMBER. *Minneapolis. Institute of Arts.* 40 × 36 in. (Engraved as in Desenfans collection, 1796: R. Roe (Fulcher, ed. ii, p. 236): Dr Turton sale 14/iv/1864 (228) bt. Cox: W. Cox sale, Foster's 14/xii/1865 (186) bt. Nathan: F. Cook, Richmond, 1885: bt. from Cook collection by Agnew *c.* 1946: H. F. P. Borthwick-Norton, 1950: with Agnew, 1953: bt. 1953.) From the early 1750s. Pl. 36.

831. ROAD THROUGH WOOD, WITH BOY RESTING AND DOG. *Philadelphia. Pennsylvania Museum.* 39½ × 57½ in. Signed and dated 1747. (F. Perkins, 1852: G. Perkins sale 14/vi/1890 (51) bt. C. F. Murray: bt. for Wilstach collection, Pennsylvania Museum, 1895.) Pl. 23.

832. DROVER'S CART AND LOVERS ("The Broken Egg"). Original probably 37½ × 49½ in. (What may have been the original was: R. Westall (?): C. Meigh sale 21/vi/1850 (162) bt. in: Anon. sale 30/vi/1877 (73) bt. Cox.) Only known from an early copy: the design must be Gainsborough's from the early 1750s.

833. PEASANT WITH TWO HORSES: HAY CART BEHIND. *Woburn Abbey. Duke of Bedford.* 37¼ × 41¼ in. Signed: *TG.* Bought from the artist by the Duke of Bedford: receipt for 15 guineas dated 24/vii/1755 (*Burl. Mag.*, July 1950, p. 201). Pl. 39.

834. RIVER, WITH HORSE DRINKING, LOVERS, etc. *St Louis (Mo.). City Art Museum.*

$37 \times 49\frac{1}{2}$ in. (M. Mitchell sale 8/iii/1819 (97) bt. Pinney: Col. W. Pinney sale, by Arber & Waghorn, 21/vii/1898 (22) bt. Agnew: John Fowler, St Louis: bequest of Cora Liggett Fowler, 1928.) Probably middle 1750s. Pl. 47.

835. FARMYARD WITH MILKMAID, COWS, DONKEYS, etc. *Shrubland Park. Hon. J. V. B. Saumarez.* $36\frac{1}{2} \times 48\frac{1}{2}$ in. (Probably by descent from Lee-Actons of Livermere.) A little before 1755. Pl. 21.

836. SHEPHERD BOY AND FIVE SHEEP. *Toledo (Ohio). Museum of Art.* Oval: $32\frac{3}{4} \times 25\frac{3}{4}$ in. (Painted for Robert Edgar, Ipswich: bt. from Mrs M. G. Edgar in 1890s by (?) Sir G. Donaldson: H. Darrell Brown, 1900: H. D. Brown sale 23/v/1924 (20) bt. Blaker: bt. from Croal Thomson by A. J. Secor, Toledo, 1926: given 1933.) From the earlier 1750s. Pl. 34.

837. RIVER VALLEY WITH RUIN ON HILL TO RIGHT: SHEPHERD WITH CATTLE, SHEEP AND GOATS: GIRL ON DONKEY. $32\frac{1}{2} \times 38$ in. (S. Woodburn sale 24/vi/1853 (26) bt. Norton: Benjamin Gibbons, Boddington Manor: Gibbons family till 20th century: with A. Tooth, 1944/54: Anon. sale 10/xii/1954 (40) bt. Leger.) An exercise in the style of Berghem, from the end of the 1740s.

838. VIEW NEAR THE COAST. *Ipswich. Christ Church Mansion Museum.* $30\frac{3}{4} \times 41$ in. (Possibly Anon. (= Williams) sale 23/iv/1831 (86) bt. Pinney: Cdr. F. V. Stopford sale 18/vii/1941 (96) bt. for Ipswich.) Hardly later than 1750/55. Pl. 25.

839. RIVER WITH A WEIR, SHEEP AND FIGURES. *Guildtown. Hon. Mrs Burnett.* $30\frac{1}{2} \times 37\frac{1}{2}$ in. (Bt. at London auction by Gooden & Fox *c.* 1939: Lord Woodbridge, 1939/50.) Very early work: engraved in reverse, 1764, by W. Austin, when in possession of Panton Betew, Ipswich. This is the original: a smaller version, perhaps a copy by Ibbetson, was in the 1936 Exh. (92).

840. RIVER SCENE WITH FIGURES AND DOG BARKING AT A SWALLOW. *Edinburgh. National Gallery of Scotland.* $30 \times 60\frac{1}{2}$ in. (formerly enlarged to $39 \times 60\frac{1}{2}$ in.). (Bt. in London by W. H. Fuller in 1890s: Fuller sale New York, 25/ii/1898 (33): James W. Ellsworth, Chicago: with Knoedler: Kenneth Wilson, 1927: bt. by Knoedler from his daughter, Countess of Munster: A. P. Good sale, Sotheby's, 15/vii/1953 (15) bt. Tooth: bt. 1953.) From the earlier 1750s. Pl. 24.

841. A TRAMP ASLEEP UNDER A SAND-BANK. *Los Angeles. University of California.* $30\frac{1}{2} \times 24\frac{1}{2}$ in. (Anon. sale 12/iii/1926 (21) bt. Arnot: Arthur Morrison sale, Sotheby's, 20/iii/1946 (173) bt. Spink: H. A. C. Gregory sale, Sotheby's 10/v/1950 (123) bt. Spooner: Lord Mackintosh: with Leggatt, 1953: bt. 1954 by Mrs James Kennedy for the James Kennedy Memorial collection.) Late 1740s: a dog disappeared in cleaning about 1951 (C. H. C. Baker, *The Connoisseur*, Oct. 1954, p. 143).

842. STREAM WITH BRIDGE, CART, LOVERS AND DONKEYS. $29\frac{1}{2} \times 57\frac{1}{2}$ in. (Duchess of Hamilton, 1856, as *The Lakes of Cumberland*: Hamilton sale 6/xi/1919 (19) bt. Agnew (with wrong size): bt. from Duveen by Sir Philip Sassoon *c.* 1928: Sassoon sale 27/iv/1934 (102) bt. Tooth: William A. Coolidge, Boston.) From the earlier 1750s.

843. SHIPPING ON A NORFOLK BROAD. *Faringdon. G. H. Berners.* $29 \times 55\frac{1}{2}$ in. Probably a little after 1755: obtained from the artist in a raffle in the 1750s by Mr Berners of Wolverstone. Pl. 38.

844. RUSTIC COURTSHIP (MILKING TIME). *Montreal. Art Association* (57). $29 \times 47\frac{1}{2}$ in. (Probably Anon. sale 15/vii/1893 (91) bt. Dowdeswell: bt. from French Gallery, London, by David Morrice, Montreal, 1895: presented, 1915.) Probably, but not quite certainly, the original. It was engraved in 1760 by Vivares when in possession of Panton Betew, Ipswich, and a number of copies exist. Pl. 40.

845. GIRL AT A STILE, CATTLE AND GIPSIES. *Penn House. Earl Howe.* 28 × 53½ in. (Charles Jennens, London, 1761: bequeathed to Admiral Lord Howe.) Not far from 1750.

846. LANE WITH WOODY BANKS, CATTLE AND FIGURES. 27 × 36 in. (William Garnett, 1888: with Agnew, 1921: Robert Cluett sale, New York, 26/v/1932 (90) bt. L. Miller—*repd.*) About 1748.

847. RIVER VIEW WITH MAN DRINKING AT BROOK, CATTLE AND BOATS. 25 × 42 in. (Rev. R. Longe, 1856: Anon. (= F. W. Longe,) sale 9/xii/1905 (109) bt. C. F. Murray: Barnet Lewis sale 28/ii/1930 (90) bt. Leggatt—*repd.*: with Agnew, 1937.) Probably from earlier 1750s.

848. TWO PEASANTS WITH A DOG ON A SANDY ROAD. 25 × 30 in. (F. E. Hills sale, Redleaf, by Knight, Frank & Rutley, 27/vi/1929 (23)—*repd.*) Probably 1750/55.

849. POOL IN WOODS WITH BOY ON DRINKING HORSE, COTTAGE, etc. *Hilborough Hall. Major Charles Mills.* 25 × 30 in. (J. C. Cankrien sale 4/vi/1853 (66) bt. Cherry: John Remington Mills (d. 1879).) Earlier 1750s.

850. WOODY BANK WITH WHITE HORSE AND SLEEPING PEASANT. *Fifehead Magdalen. C. R. Sutton.* 25 × 30 in. (Probably bequeathed 1838 by Francis Chaplin to Sir Richard Sutton.) The remains of a very early picture.

851. RUSTIC LOVERS (GIRL SEATED ON FAGGOTS) WITH DOG, etc. *Fifehead Magdalen. C. R. Sutton.* 25 × 30 in. (Probably bequeathed 1838 by Francis Chaplin to Sir Richard Sutton.) The remains of a very early picture.

852. ELMSETT CHURCH. *Barnard Castle. Bowes Museum.* 25 × 30 in. (Presented by F. J. Nettlefold, 1949.) Probably 1750/55: *repd.* in Nettlefold Catalogue, 1935.

853. WOODY LANDSCAPE WITH SEATED FIGURE ("View of Dedham"). *London.* National Gallery (1283). 24½ × 30½ in. (Possibly S. Boddington sale 29/vi/1881 (31) bt. Martin Colnaghi. David P. Sellar, 1885: Anon. (= Sellar) sale 12/v/1888 (51) bt. Agnew: bt. 1889.) Probably about 1750.

854. RUINED ABBEY ON HILL, FIGURES, DONKEYS AND DISTANT STREAM. *London (in store). Princess Labia.* 24½ × 29½ in. (Duke of Marlborough, Whiteknights, 1828: C. Turner, Norwich: Mrs Gibbons sale 5/v/1883 (25): resold, 26/v/1894 (26) bt. A. Smith: Sir J. C. Robinson, 1897: Sir J. B. Robinson, Bt., sale 6/vii/1923 (13) bt. in.) About 1750.

855. RUINED ABBEY ON HILL, FIGURES, DONKEYS, etc. *Raleigh (N.C.). North Carolina Museum of Art.* 24½ × 30 in. (Anon. sale 28/iii/1952 (95) bt. Bellesi.) A battered variant of no. 854, with an additional baby donkey. It appeared to be signed and dated 1750.

856. RUSTIC LOVERS, TWO COWS, MAN ON DISTANT BRIDGE. *Chestnut Hill (Pa.). Wharton Sinkler.* 24 × 29 in. (One of a pair said to be painted for Francis Hayman (Fulcher. ed. 2, p. 74): John Heywood, 1814: John Heywood Hawkins, 1844: C. H. T. Hawkins sale 11/v/1896 (12) bt. Colnaghi: H. Pfungst, 1898: Pfungst sale 15/vi/1917 (88) bt. A. Wertheimer—*repd.*: with D. H. Farr, Philadelphia, 1928.) Probably 1755/59. Companion to 857. Pl. 54.

857. WOODY LANE WITH FARM CART, MILKMAID AND CATTLE. *Castlehill (Ayr.). L. H. Wilson.* 24 × 29 in. (One of a pair said to have been painted for Francis Hayman: John Heywood, 1814: J. Heywood Hawkins, 1844: Mrs J. E. Hawkins sale 30/x/1936 (102) bt. Agnew—*repd.*: with Agnew, 1937: with Lockett Thompson.) Probably 1755/59. Companion to no. 856. Pl. 53.

858. FIGURES AND DONKEYS ON A ROAD, DISTANT WINDMILL. *Arundel Castle. Duke of Norfolk.* 24 × 42 in. Probably 1750/55. Already at Arundel in 1856.

859. SANDY LANE THROUGH WOODS WITH COTTAGE AND DONKEYS. *Vienna.*

Kunsthistorisches Museum (1723). 24 × 36 in. (Humphrey Roberts sale 22/v/1908 (193) bt. Agnew: Anon. (= Agnew) sale 10/v/1912 (74) bt. in: bt. from Agnew, 1913.) From the early 1750s.

860. A LANE IN THE WOODS WITH FIGURES. *Cambridge. Fitzwilliam Museum.* 22½ × 29 in. (E. Peel: Anon. sale 28/vii/1933 (49) bt. for Cambridge.) The remains of a picture of about 1750.

861. THE CHARTERHOUSE. *London. Foundling Hospital.* Circle: 22 in. Presented by the artist in 1748. Pl. 1. Colour plate.

862. DROVER'S CART WITH CALVES RECEDING DOWN A SANDY LANE. 20 × 25 in. (E. W. Lake sale 11/vii/1845 (32) bt. Smith: Beriah Botfield, 1848: with Martin Colnaghi: W. H. Fuller sale, New York, 25/ii/1898 (22): Private coll., Newport, L.I., sale, New York, 3/xii/1936 (42)—*repd.*) Probably from the late 1740s.

863. WOODLAND GLADE WITH FELLED TIMBER (No figures). *Balcaskie. Sir Ralph Anstruther, Bt.* 20 × 19 in. About 1750/55.

864. GIPSIES UNDER A TREE. *London. Tate Gallery* (5845). 19 × 24 in. (Given by artist to Joshua Kirby: descended to Rev. H. Scott Trimmer, sale 17/iii/1860 (35) bt. Rutley: G. A. F. Cavendish-Bentinck sale 11/vii/1891 (553) bt. Martin Colnaghi: Arthur James: bequeathed by Mrs Arthur James, 1948.) Unfinished first version for the engraved picture (*see* no. 887)—*see* W. Thornbury, *Life of Turner*, 1862, II. pp. 59/60.

865. A MAN PLOUGHING, A CHURCH AND A WINDMILL. *London (in store). Princess Labia.* 19 × 23½ in. (J. Salusbury Muskett: Mrs William Unthank: Col. C. J. Unthank sale, Robinson & Fisher, 28/v/1897 (179) bt. Agnew: Sir J. B. Robinson sale 6/vii/1923 (11) bt. in.) Very early work: engraved in reverse by S. Middiman, 1782, when in possession of Panton Betew, Ipswich. A version is in the J. G. Johnson collection, Philadelphia (834): 25 × 30 in.

866. PEASANT PLOUGHING WITH TWO HORSES, WINDMILL ON A HILL. 19 × 23 in. (Possibly Susan, Countess of Guildford, 1833: Baroness North: Anon. (= Lord North) sale 13/v/1895 (54) bt. Tooth. Anon. sale 31/v/1946 (150) bt. Leger. A. P. Good sale, Sotheby's, 15/vii/1953 (16) bt. Gooden & Fox.) About 1750. The North picture was presumably the original: the above history may refer to the original and to one, or even two, copies.

867. A WAGGON RECEDING DOWN A SANDY LANE. *Wimborne. Col. Solly.* 19 × 23¼ in. (Bt. by Rev. Thomas Rackett (1780–1840): thence by descent.) Very early work: companion to no. 869.

868. *Replica of no.* 867. *New York. John M. Schiff* (1955). 18 × 25 in. (J. Salusbury Muskett: Mrs W. Unthank: C. J. Unthank sale, Robinson & Fisher, 28/v/1897 (177) bt. Agnew: Dr Paul Müller sale, Paris, 25/v/1910 (23) bt. Williamson.) I have not seen this, but it should be an original, from its history (*cf.* no. 865).

869. EDGE OF WOOD, WITH FIGURES, CATTLE AND DISTANT CHURCH. *Wimborne. Col. Solly.* 18 × 25 in. (Bt. by Rev. Thomas Rackett (1780–1840): thence by descent.) Very early work: companion (?) to no. 867.

870. SAND PIT BY A SANDY ROAD: VILLAGE IN DISTANCE. *Dublin. National Gallery of Ireland* (191). 18 × 23½ in. (J. H. Reynolds: bt. at F. W. Reynolds sale 10/iv/1883 (109).) Very early work.

871. OLD PEASANT WITH ASSES AND DOG OUTSIDE HUT. *Idsworth. Major A. F. Clarke-Jervoise.* 18 × 23½ in. (Bt. by Jervoise Clarke (1734–1808): thence by descent.) From the end of the 1740s. Pl. 20.

872. THREE FIGURES AT FOOT OF WOODY BANK TO RIGHT. 10 × 13½ in. (With P. M. Turner: with A. Tooth: Private collection, Argentina.) Very early work.

873. WOODY STREAM WITH BOY SHOOTING DUCK. *London. Private collection.*

15 × 18¾ in. (With A. Tooth, 1946.) Very early
indeed.

**874. GIRL TALKING TO TWO YOUTHS
UNDER BANK AT LEFT.** 14 × 11½ in.
(Descended from Joshua Kirby to Rev. H. S.
Trimmer: Trimmer sale 17/iii/1860 (51) bt.
Rutley: Cavendish-Bentinck sale 11/vii/1891
(549) bt. Gooden: Mrs S. D. Warren sale, New
York, 8/i/1903 (66): E. McMillin sale, New York,
20/i/1913 (192): with Knoedler, 1931: Thomas
Frederick Cole, New York: Fricke etc. sale,
New York, 15/iii/1945 (14)—*repd.*) Probably
1750/55.

875. A POOL IN THE WOODS (No figures).
13¾ × 11¼ in. (J. G. Fordham, 1856: A. R.
Fordham sale, Sotheby's, 21/xi/1934 (90) bt.
Colnaghi: with P. M. Turner, 1936: P. M.
Turner estate, 1951.) From the middle 1750s.

876. THE PATH THROUGH THE WOODS
(No figures). *Russborough (Co. Wicklow). Sir
Alfred Beit, Bt.* 13½ × 10¼ in. (Descended from
Joshua Kirby to Rev. Henry S. Trimmer:
Trimmer sale 17/iii/1860 (85) bt. Rutley: G. A.
Cavendish-Bentinck sale 11/vii/1891 (550) bt.
Agnew: Alfred Beit: Sir Otto Beit, Bt.) Un-
finished: from early 1750s.

877. ANIMALS CROSSING A FORD. *Upton
House. National Trust.* 12¾ × 14 in. (Presumably
descended from Joshua Kirby to Rev. Henry
Scott Trimmer. Trimmer sale 17/iii/1860 (93)
bt. Rutley. G. A. F. Cavendish-Bentinck sale
11/vii/1891 (551) bt. Martin Colnaghi: Mrs M.
Colnaghi sale, Robinson & Fisher, 20/xi/1908
(183) bt. Banks: Viscount Bearsted: given to
National Trust, 1948.) From the late 1740s.

878. THE DROVER'S CART. *Ipswich. Hon.
Mrs Douglas Tollemache.* 12½ × 15¾ in. (Said to
have been given by Gainsborough to Dr Scafe.)
Very early work indeed.

**879. GIPSIES AND DONKEYS IN A WOOD-
LAND CLEARING.** 12¼ × 14¼ in. (Presumably
descended from Joshua Kirby to Rev. Henry

Scott Trimmer: Trimmer sale 17/iii/1860 (45)
bt. J. H. Anderdon: Anderdon sale 31/v/1879
(147) bt. Philpot: Lord Ronald Gower, 1885:
Anon. sale 20/vi/1896 (127) bt. Agnew: bt. from
Wallis, 1909, by Mrs Robert Paterson, New York:
sale, New York, 17/iii/1938 (24)—*repd.*) From the
end of the 1740s.

880. EDGE OF A WOOD (No figures). *Hove.
Art Gallery.* 11¾ × 13¾ in. (George Frost, Ipswich,
1821: passed to Thomas Green estate, 1856:
Green sale 20/iii/1874 (113) bt. Noseda: J. P.
Heseltine, 1878: Heseltine sale, Sotheby's,
27/v/1935 (38) bt. for Ernest Cook: bequeathed through N.A.C.F., 1955.) Not far from
1750.

**881. WOODY LANE WITH COTTAGE AND
SHEEP.** *Cardiff. Irene, Countess of Plymouth.*
11½ × 13½ in. (Probably William Beckford:
Duchess of Hamilton, 1856: Hamilton Palace
sale 8/vii/1882 (1104) bt. Agnew: Earl of
Plymouth, 1888.) Late 1740s.

882. PEASANT AND SHEEP ON A ROAD.
10½ × 8¾ in. (Possibly one of the pictures which
descended from Joshua Kirby to Rev. Henry
Scott Trimmer: Trimmer sale 17/iii/1860 (41)
bt. Rutley. Sir John Leslie sale, Sotheby's,
20/viii/1941 (29) bt. P. M. Turner: with Tooth,
1945 and 1950: Private collection, London.)
From the later 1740s.

883. A POOL IN THE WOODS. *Ipswich.
Christchurch Mansion Museum.* 9½ × 11½ in. (Dr
Kilderbee: Mr Churchyard, Woodbridge: Countess of Hardwicke, 1856: Earl of Hardwicke sale
27/vi/1924 (132) bt. for Ipswich.) Probably
1750/55.

884. VIEW AT WOLVERSTONE, SUFFOLK.
9¼ × 12¼ in. (Col. Hamilton, 1788: R. Loyd
Anstruther, 1887: sold to Colnaghi's, 1895:
"Eastern Art Museum" sale, New York,
7/ii/1950 (16)—*repd.*) Engraved by W. Birch,
1788 as "View at Wolverstone". Very early
work indeed.

885. TWO SHEEP AND TWO LAMBS BY SOME PALINGS. *Hatfield Peverel. Master of Kinnaird.* 9×10½ in. (With Colnaghi, 1955: bt. 1955.) From the early 1750s.

The following pictures are known only from engravings at present:

886. LANDGUARD FORT WITH FIGURES, etc., IN FOREGROUND. Painted for Philip Thicknesse and destroyed by damp in his lifetime. It measured 33½×58 in. Engraved by T. Major and published 1754.

887. GIPSIES IN A WOOD. Engraved by J. Wood, 1759. This was the final version of the picture for which no. 864 was the first, unfinished, version. It may have measured 29×24½ in.: and it is possible that the following pedigree (or parts of it) may refer to the original picture: **Earl** of Lichfield sale, at Shugborough Hall, **by** Robins, 10/viii/1842 (77) bt. Burland, Liverpool: Wiltshire sale 25/v/1867 (131) bt. Cox: W. Cox sale, by Foster, 1/v/1879 (221) bt. Williams: H. Graves & Co. sale 27/v/1882 (165) bt. in: Anon. sale 23/iii/1895 (92) bt. McLean.

888. POOL AND LANE NEAR WOODS, WITH CATTLE, A GIRL WITH A BASKET AND A SMALL BOY. Engraved by F. Vivares, 1765, when in the possession of Panton Betew. Probably a picture of 1750/55. This could have been the picture Exh. B.I. 1814 (28) as *View near Sudbury*, lent Lord Chief Baron Thomson: in his sale, by Squibb, 21/vi/1819 (93) as "engraved".

888a. FIGURES AT A STILE: SLEEPING PIGS, etc. Engraved when in possession of Panton Betew, 1765. About 1750/55.

LATE SUFFOLK AND BATH PERIOD LANDSCAPES (*c. 1758–1774*)

Note: These are listed in a provisional chronological order as far as possible, or in groups of related pictures.

889. THE BOY AT THE STILE. *Balcaskie. Sir Ralph Anstruther, Bt.* Oak panel: 14×12 in. (Given by Gainsborough to Col. James Hamilton, whose daughter married General Anstruther.) Engraved by James Stow, 1796: see Whitley, p. 365, for story of the gift. Late Ipswich or early Bath work: being on panel it is exceptional.

890. WOODY STREAM WITH PASTORAL FIGURES AND DISTANT BRIDGE. *Villa Nova (Pa.). Mrs Robert L. Montgomery.* 47¼×57¼ in. (J. Longe, 1856: Longe sale 1/v/1866 (38) bt. Agnew for John Heugh: Heugh sale 10/v/1878 (239) bt. Agnew: J. S. Morgan, 1885: bt. from G. Morgan by Knoedler *c.* 1916: Colonel R. L. Montgomery.) Possibly very late Ipswich work: at one time wrongly called *A view in Shropshire*. Pl. 81.

891. *The same. Elton Hall. Sir Richard Proby, Bart.* 48½×57 in. Signed *T. G.* (Traditionally bought by George Coyte (d. 1781) of Ipswich: passed to Samuel Tolver: D. B. Preston: with Agnew, 1905: Earl of Carysfort, 1905: thence by descent.) Its pedigree suggests it may have been painted at Ipswich, but I find it puzzling. Yet a third version, which I have not seen: ex. Sulley & Co.: bt. from Knoedler, 1897 by A. M. Byers, Pittsburgh: has descended to Mrs J. Denniston Lyon, Pittsburgh.

892. POND AT EDGE OF WOOD, WITH HERDSMAN AND CATTLE. *Oxford. Ashmolean Museum* (170). 32×26¾ in. (Bequeathed by Rev. Thomas Penrose, 1851.) Unfinished: perhaps very late Ipswich work.

893. LANE AT EDGE OF WOOD WITH WALKING PEASANT. *London. Tate Gallery* (1485). 8¾×6¾ in. (Passed from Gainsborough to Miss Clarke and Mrs Lane: presented by the Misses Lane, 1896.) A battered and slight object,

presumably genuine, from its history: if so, very late Suffolk work. Companion to no. 894.

894. WOODLAND GLADE WITH THREE FIGURES. *London. Tate Gallery* (1486). 8¾ × 6¾ in. Companion to no. 893 (*q.v.*): unfinished and trivial little work.

895. EDGE OF A WOOD WITH COTTAGE AND DISTANT FIGURES. *Hartley Wintney. H. W. J. Ferrand.* (Has descended to present owner from Ralph Allen (d. 1764) of Prior Park, Bath.) Probably a very early Bath study. Pl. 56.

896. WOODY VALLEY WITH PEASANT, MILKMAID AND COWS. *Tockenham. Major J. G. Buxton.* 25 × 30 in. (Has descended to present owner from John Jacob (1723–1776) of The Rocks, near Bath.) Called *The Rocks, near Bath*: probably very early Bath work. Pl. 55.

897. SUNSET: CARTHORSES DRINKING AT A STREAM. *London. Tate Gallery* (310). 56 × 59¼ in. (Said to have hung for "a great portion of 80 or 90 years" over a chimneypiece in Bedford Square (*Art Union*, 1847, p. 366, and *Art Journal*, 1849, p. 72): J. Ewer, 1814: Anon. (= Ewer) sale 12/v/1832 (8) bt. Vernon: bequeathed, 1847.) Probably a very early Bath work. Pl. 65.

898. WOODY LANDSCAPE WITH HORSE-MAN AND FLOCK OF SHEEP. *Worcester (Mass.). Art Museum.* 57 × 62 in. (Thomas Todd, Aberdeen, 1857: bt. in at sale, Foster's, 30/iii/1859 (32): Todd sale, by Foster, 28/iv/1869 (102) bt. for Joseph Gillott: Gillott sale 27/iv/1872 (284) bt. W. Cox: Sir Horatio Davies, 1892: Anon. sale 20/vi/1896 (95) bt. Tooth: C. P. Taft, Cincinnati, 1902/07: C. L. Fischer, Roehampton, 1918: with Knoedler: with Scott & Fowles: bt. 1919.) Probably one of his most ambitious works of the early 1760s. Pl. 66.

899. THE WOODMAN'S RETURN—WITH TWO DONKEYS. 39 × 48½ in. (Painted for Dr Charlton, Bath: Charlton sale 6/iii/1790 (91) bt. Garn: Dr Freckleton, 1823: sale 1/v/1858

(22) bt. in: Mrs Freckleton sale 12/vii/1873 (138) bt. Cox: Earl of Dudley sale 16/vi/1900 (39) bt. Agnew: with Colnaghi: bt. from Lawrie by H. O. Watson & Co., New York: John Henry Smith sale, New York, 18–22/i/1910: Senator W. A. Clark sale, New York, 11/i/1926 (101): Whitney sale, New York, 30/iv/1946 (346)—*repd.*) Close in date to the portrait of Dr Charlton, which was S.A. 1766. Not seen: in spite of its history, I doubt that it is by Gainsborough.

900. WOODY LANDSCAPE WITH MILK-MAID AND DROVER. *Scampston. Mrs M. L'Estrange Malone.* 57 × 47 in. (Has descended from Sir William St Quintin, who bought it in 1766 for £43/11/6.) S.A. 1766 (53). Pl. 92.

901. WOODY LANE WITH RUINED CASTLE, PEASANT AND HORSE. *Ipswich. H. L. Fison.* 15¾ × 20¾ in. (Passed from the artist to the Misses Lane, one of whom became Mrs Green (1835): through Lane family to Sir Thomas Devitt, Bt.: sale 16/v/1924 (81) bt. Eyre: Anon. sale 5/vii/1926 (57) bt. Leggatt: bt. 1927.) Probably from the middle 1760s.

902. WOODY LANDSCAPE WITH CHURCH AND GIRL WALKING WITH DOG. *Glasgow. Art Gallery (Hamilton Trust collection).* 25 × 30 in. (Bt. *c.* 1850/1 for Humphry collection: A. P. Humphry sale 4/x/1946 (59) bt. Bernard: bt. from Tooth, 1947.) Probably from the middle 1760s.

903. EDGE OF A WOOD: WOODMAN WITH SCYTHE, etc. *Dell Park. Miss Margot Schroeder.* 15½ × 20½ in. (Col. Hugh Baillie sale 15/v/1858 (20) bt. Farrar: Louis Huth, 1884: sale 20/v/1905 (102) bt. Agnew: Anon. sale 2/xii/1911 (38) bt. Tooth for Baron Bruno Schroeder.) Middle to later 1760s. An inferior repetition is at Chicago.

904. RURAL COURTSHIP. 49 × 39 in. *U.S.A. Private Collection.* (Descended through Rev. Gainsborough Gardiner to Mrs E. N. Harward: sale 11/v/1923 (102) bt. Knoedler: Percy R. Pyne II, New York, 1926: with Newhouse Galls.,

1939: with Agnew 1957.) Probably a picture of the middle 1760s.

905. MILKING SCENE: FOUR COWS AND A COTTAGE. 21¾ × 43 in. (With Lawrie & Co., 1898.) Only known from plate in Armstrong, 1904 ed., opp. p. 16.

906. PEASANTS RETURNING FROM MARKET THROUGH A WOOD. *Toledo (Ohio). Museum of Art.* 47 × 66 in. (Probably Marquess of Lansdowne sale, by P. Coxe, 25/ii/1806 (105): Esdaile family, Cothelestone, till 1955: with E. J. Speelman: bt. 1955.) Engraved by Bartolozzi, 1802: probably 1766/67. Pl. 98.

907. THE HARVEST WAGGON. *Birmingham University. Barber Institute.* 47¼ × 57 in. (Given by artist to W. Wiltshire, 1774: J. Wiltshire sale 25/v/1867 (126) bt. for Sir Dudley Marjoribanks (Lord Tweedmouth): sold 1904 to Sir Samuel Montague (Lord Swaythling): Swaythling sale 12/vii/1946 (20) bt. for Birmingham.) Perhaps S.A. 1767 (61). Pl. 99.

908. REPOSE: HORSES AND COWS AT EDGE OF A WOOD. *Kansas City. William Rockhill Nelson Gallery.* 47 × 58 in. (Given by artist to his daughter, Margaret (d. 1820), from whom it passed to Henry Briggs, 1818: bt. from him by Hogarth, 1846: British Gallery of Art (= Hogarth) sale 13/vi/1851 (100) bt. in and sold to Elhanan Bicknell: Bicknell sale 25/iv/1863 (91) bt. Woods Huth: J. Gillott sale 27/iv/1872 (286) bt. Agnew for K. D. Hodgson: sold to James Price, 1891: Price sale 15/vi/1895 (79) bt. H. Quilter: Quilter sale 7/iv/1906 (66) bt. Agnew for F. B. Sharp: bt. from Sharp by Agnew, 1920: (Sir) A. J. Bennett: bt. through Agnew by Kansas, 1931.) Lithographed in reverse by J. Lane. Probably late 1760s. The tree to the left and certain elements on the right disappeared in cleaning, between 1912 and 1920: it is probable that it now represents Gainsborough's first design, which he himself later altered. Pl. 112.

909. SHEPHERD AND SHEPHERDESS WITH CATTLE AT EDGE OF A WOOD. *Dublin. National Gallery of Ireland.* 49 × 39 in.

(Probably C. F. Abel sale, by Greenwood, 13/xii/1787 (45): J. Crosdill, 1814: by descent to Miss Thoyts: sale 6/v/1910 (93) bt. Lane: A. M. Grenfell sale 26/vi/1914 (45) bt. Lane: bequeathed by Sir Hugh Lane, 1915.) Probably from the end of the 1760s. Pl. 93.

910. WOODY LANDSCAPE: BOY ON HORSE AND WOODMAN RETURNING. *Balcarres. Earl of Crawford and Balcarres.* 40 × 50¼ in. (Probably painted for S. Kilderbee and Kilderbee sale 30/v/1829 (124) bt. Emmerson. W. Wells, 1841: Wells sale 20/v/1852 (55) bt. Fordham: D. T. White, 1856: W. Benoni White sale 23/v/1879 (208) bt. Agnew for Sir Robert Loyd-Lindsay (Lord Wantage): thence by inheritance.) Perhaps near to 1769 in date. Pl. 80.

911. PEASANTS GOING TO MARKET: EARLY MORNING. *Egham. Royal Holloway College.* 48 × 58 in. (Bought from Gainsborough by Henry Hoare before 1776: Stourhead Heirlooms sale 2/vi/1883 (16) bt. for Royal Holloway College.) Probably about 1769. Pl. 115.

912. PEASANTS GOING TO MARKET (ii). *Kenwood. Iveagh bequest* (3). 47 × 57½ in. (Traditionally painted for 2nd Viscount Bateman about 1770: bt. from Lord Bateman by the Earl of Iveagh, 1888: bequeathed, 1928.) Close in style to no. 911 and about the same date. Pl. 114.

913. A POOL IN THE WOODS, WITH CATTLE DRINKING. *Russborough (Co. Wicklow). Sir Alfred Beit, Bart.* 13¼ × 11¾ in. (Said to have been painted as a present to Mr Muskett of Epping: descended to Lt. Col. C. J. Unthank: sale, Robinson & Fisher, 28/v/1897 (172) bt. Agnew: with Colnaghi, 1899: Alfred Beit, 1900: Sir Otto Beit, Bt.) Probably from the later 1760s.

914. THREE COWS ON A KNOLL IN A WOOD. 13½ × 11½ in. (W. Wells, 1841: Wells sale 10/v/1890 (18) bt. Agnew: W. Nicholson, Basing Park, 1909: Anon. (Nicholson) sale, Sotheby's, 19/iii/1947 (157) bt. Bernard.) Probably late Bath work.

915. WOODY LANDSCAPE WITH CATTLE. 24×29 in. (Earl of Normanton, 1898: sold to Duveen, 1934: with Howard Young, New York, 1935.) Only known from illustration in *The Art Journal*, 1898, p. 328. The attribution needs controlling.

916. COTTAGE ON WOODED SLOPE: SHEPHERD AND CATTLE RETURNING. Oval (on squared canvas): 14×19 in. (George Gostling, 1814: Anon. (= Col. Gostling Murray) sale 23/vi/1883 (770) bt. White: F. Fish sale 24/iii/1888 (287) bt. Agnew: William Nicholson, Basing Park, 1909: Anon. (=Nicholson) sale, Sotheby's, 19/iii/1947 (158) bt. Spink: with Tooth, 1953.) Probably late Bath work.

917. SHEEP IN A WOODLAND GLADE. *London. R. W. Lloyd.* 29×35 in. (S. S. Joseph: bt. from Mrs Joseph by Agnew *c.* 1916: bt. 1916.) Probably very late Bath work.

918. PACKHORSES CROSSING A BRIDGE. *Asthall Manor. Mrs T. A. Hardcastle.* Paper, mounted on canvas: 11½×13½ in. Probably later Bath work.

919. WOODY LANDSCAPE WITH GIRLS WITH MILKPAILS, CATTLE, etc. *Boston. Museum of Fine Arts.* 46½×57 in. (Possibly R. B. Sheridan, 1814: Duke of Newcastle, 1844: Earl of Lincoln sale 4/vi/1937 (32) bt. for Sir Bernard Eckstein: Eckstein sale, Sotheby's, 8/xii/1948 (71) bt. Frost & Reed: with J. Mitchell Chapman: bt. 1949.) Probably late Bath work. Pl. 113.

920. *The same. Cincinnati. Institute of Fine Arts* (*Taft collection*). 48½×58½ in. (Possibly W. Pearce sale, by Phillips, 23/iv/1872 (354). Miss Holland, 1910: Viscount D'Abernon: with Duveen, 1923: with Scott & Fowles: Charles P. Taft, Cincinnati.) Almost identical with no. 919: perhaps also an original.

921. *Variant of the same.* 46×58 in. (Hon. Augustus Phipps sale, 19/iv/1834 (3) bt. Sir Eyre Coote, Bt.: in Coote coll., Ballyfin, till *c.* 1914: Anon. sale 26/vi/1914 (75) bt. Amor: said to be in a Buenos Aires private collection.) The principal variation from nos. 919/20 is that the standing milkmaid no longer holds a pail on her head. Possibly a little earlier than the other two.

922. ROCKY WOODLAND GLADE WITH BOY AND GIRL, CATTLE, etc. *Hackwood Park. Viscount Camrose.* 47½×59¼ in. (W. Wiltshire, Shockerwick, in 1770s: Wiltshire sale 25/v/1867 (127) bt. Davis for Sir Dudley Marjoribanks (Lord Tweedmouth): sold privately to Sir Samuel Montague (Lord Swaythling), 1904: Lord Swaythling sale 12/vii/1946 (21) bt. for Lord Camrose.) A vague (but not old) tradition states that this was R.A. 1771: it was in any case probably painted at Bath and the date is plausible. Pl. 123.

923. *The same. Los Angeles. University of California.* 47×58 in. (Conceivably Lord Carysfort, 1814: sale 14/vi/1828 (62) bt. Peacock: bt. from H. Graves by James Price before 1882, and sold *c.* 1891: Sir Julian Goldsmid sale 13/vi/1896 (64) bt. Vokins for Howard Morley: bt. from Morley coll., Shockerwick, by Frost & Reed, 1950: with J. Mitchell Chapman: bt. for James Kennedy Memorial Collection, Los Angeles 1954.) Nearly identical with no. 922, but more lightly handled, perhaps later.

924. VILLAGE SCENE WITH PEASANTS ON HORSEBACK, PIGS, etc. *Hardwicke Court. Miss Olive Lloyd-Baker.* 42×54 in. (Probably from the collection of William Sharp of Fulham, whose daughter married (1800) T. J. Lloyd-Baker.) The curious crayon-like technique is most closely paralleled in the backgrounds of certain portraits of about 1772 (e.g. no. 266). Pl. 134.

925. CATTLE RETURNING AT EVENING: RUSTIC LOVERS. *Brighton. R. C. A. Palmer-Morewood.* 40×50 in. Related in technique to no. 924. It has probably been in the Morewood collection at Alfreton since the 18th century. Pl. 135.

926. CATTLE RETURNING DOWN A WOODY LANE. *Buscot. Lord Faringdon.* Paper, mounted on canvas: 38×48½ in. (S. H. de Zoete sale 8/v/1885 (177) bt. Colnaghi: Walter de Zoete

sale 5/iv/1935 (76) bt. Leggatt: bt. 1935.) The curious technique is related to no. 925 and suggests a date about 1772.

927. CATTLE AND SHEEP NEAR POOL: MAN WATERING A HORSE. 14½ × 17½ in. (S. Rogers, 1814: sale 3/v/1856 (697) bt. for Miss Burdett-Coutts: Burdett-Coutts sale 4/v/1922 (28) bt. Knoedler: sold to Freeman, London, 1937.) Date uncertain.

928. MARKET CART CROSSING A FORD. *Washington. Corcoran Art Gallery (W. A. Clark coll.)* 11½ × 13¼ in. (Marchioness of Thomond: Samuel Rogers, 1814: sale 3/v/1856 (694) bt. for Miss Burdett-Coutts: Burdett-Coutts sale 4/v/1922 (29) bt. L. Davis: bt. by Senator Clark from Knoedler, 1922.) Probably 1780s: long the companion to no. 927.

929. WOODY LANDSCAPE WITH HAGAR AND ISHMAEL. *Dolben. Lt. Col. Sir O. W. Williams-Wynn, Bt.* 30 × 36½ in. (Gainsborough sale 2/vi/1792 (73): Sir Watkin Williams Wynn, 1814.) Probably Bath period: already called *Hagar and Ishmael* in 1792.

930. CATTLE AND SHEEP AT A POOL, WITH PASTORAL FIGURES. *Bruern Abbey. Hon. Michael Astor.* 47 × 59 in. (Earl De La Warr sale 2/v/1857 (148) bt. Pennell: F. H. Huth sale, 14/vi/1907 (101) bt. Agnew: with Sir George Donaldson, 1911: with Knoedler, New York: Horace Harding sale, New York, 1/iii/1941 (64):

with Knoedler: bt. 1953.) Probably late Bath work. Pl. 133.

931. CATTLE, WITH RESTING MILKMAID AND OTHER FIGURES. *Jersey. Earl of Jersey.* 47½ × 58 in. (Probably no. 95 of the Schomberg House sale, 1789, bt. by Mrs Child, mother of the 5th Countess of Jersey.) Probably late Bath work. Pl. 124.

932. WOODY VALLEY WITH COTTAGE, PEASANT GIRLS AND DONKEYS. *Cardiff. National Museum of Wales.* 15½ × 20½ in. (Probably given by Margaret Gainsborough to Henry Briggs, 1818. Graves sale 18/iii/1854 (133) bt. Humphrey: Joseph Humphrey, 1857: Anon. sale 14/v/1920 (76) bt. Hugh Blaker: Miss Gwendoline Davies, Gregynog: bequeathed, 1951.) Bath period.

933. WOODY LANE WITH DROVER'S CART AND MILKMAID. 25 × 30 in. (Said to have been painted for Henry Compton: sale 8/iii/1811 (67) bt. in: passed to Lady Baynes: Anon. (= Lady Baynes) sale 1/iii/1873 (69) bt. in: resold, 29/vi/1878 (62) bt. Agnew: Miss Wild, Spoon Park: with P. M. Turner: with John Levy, New York: Albert R. Jones, Kansas City, 1933: Mr and Mrs Richard V. Nuttall, Pittsburgh: sale, New York, 21/v/1952 (37).) Probably Bath period, which makes it unlikely it was painted for Henry Compton, who was Secretary to Queen Charlotte.

LANDSCAPES OF THE LONDON PERIOD (1774-1788)

934. WOODY LANE, WITH MARKET CART GOING OVER RISING GROUND. *Penrhyn Castle. Lady Janet Douglas-Pennant.* 54 × 74 in. (Caulfield collection (?): bt. 1855/60 from Farrer by Col. Hon. Douglas Pennant (later Lord Penrhyn): thence by descent, 1950.) The main original of this design, with donkeys in the lower left corner. Probably early London work.

935. *The same. Liverpool. Walker Art Gallery (Sudley collection).* 37½ × 52½ in. (William Esdaile (d. 1837): passed to Mrs Rees Goring Thomas: Anon. (= Goring Thomas) sale 16/v/1863 (125) bt. in: R. Goring Thomas sale 12/v/1888 (25) bt. Henson: bt. from Gooden by George Holt, Sudley, Liverpool, 1889: bequeathed by Miss Emma Holt, 1945.) A later, reduced, variant of

no. 931, with cattle in the lower left corner.
Pl. 193.

936. WOODY LANDSCAPE WITH GIPSIES
ROUND A FIRE. *London. Tate Gallery* (5803).
47 × 55½ in. (Possibly Anon. (= Earl of Halifax)
sale 25/vi/1808 (93): Richard Sanderson sale
17/vi/1848 (18) bt. in: resold 20/iii/1858 (15) bt.
Pearce: Wynn Ellis sale 6/v/1876 (55) bt. for
Sir F. T. Mappin: Mappin sale 13/vi/1910 (27)
bt. Agnew: Anon. (= J. R. Harvey) sale
28/iv/1922 (46) bt. Buttery: with A. Tooth,
1929, and bt. by F. J. Nettlefold: presented to
Tate Gallery, 1947.) Probably later 1770s.
Pl. 132.

937. THE WATERING PLACE. *London.
National Gallery* (109). 59 × 72 in. (Possibly
Schomberg House, 1789 (76): 1797 sale (102) bt.
Charles Long (Lord Farnborough): bequeathed,
1827.) R.A. 1777 (136). Pl. 181.

938. *Study for part of no.* 937. *London. Francis G.
Brenton* (1930). 14½ × 12½ in. Study for the pool
and cattle only.

939. POOL IN THE WOODS WITH COT-
TAGE, FIGURES, AND CATTLE. *Biddesden.
Lord Moyne.* 47 × 57 in. (J. Gillott sale 27/iv/1872
(287) bt. Agnew for K. D. Hodgson: bt. from
R. K. Hodgson by Sir Edward Guinness (Earl
of Iveagh): passed to Lord Moyne, 1927.)
Probably from the later 1770s. Pl. 180.

940. COTTAGE DOOR WITH CHILDREN
PLAYING. *Cincinnati. Art Museum.* 47 × 58 in.
(Earl of Mulgrave, 1814: sold by Marquess of
Normanby *c.* 1865 to Earl of Normanton: bt. by
Duveen, 1934: Mr and Mrs Charles Finn Williams,
Cincinnati, 1935: presented, 1948.) Possibly
R.A. 1778 (119): *see* Whitley, p. 157. Pl. 192.

941. THE COTTAGE DOOR. *San Marino
(Calif.). Henry E. Huntington Library and Art
Gallery.* 58 × 47 in. (Bt. by Thomas Harvey of
Catton, 1786: Coppin, Norwich, 1807: Sir John
Leicester (Lord de Tabley) by 1809: sale 7/vii/1827
(52) bt. for Earl Grosvenor: bt. from Duke of
Westminster through Duveen, 1922.) Probably
R.A. 1780 (62). Pl. 203.

941a. WOODY LANDSCAPE WITH CARTS
RECEDING DOWN A LANE. *San Francisco.
De Young Memorial Museum.* 50 × 40 in. (Kilderbee sale 30/v/1829 (125) bt. Emmerson: Brooke
Greville sale 30/iv/1836 (79) bt. Norton: Coote
family till 1923: Countess de Kotzebue sale, New
York, by Plaza Art Galls., 28/i/1956 (352):
presented by Mr Oakes, 1956.) Not far from
1780. Pl. 202.

942. TWO PEASANTS STUDYING A
TOMBSTONE. 11½ × 9 in. (Lord Ronald Sutherland Gower sale 28/i/1911 (41) bt. Parsons.)
Fragment of a large picture shown at R.A. 1780
(319): an aquatint exists after the whole composition.

943. HORSES WATERING AT A FOUN-
TAIN. *Southill. Simon Whitbread.* 49 × 38¼ in.
Probably not far from 1780: at Southill since at
least 1815. Pl. 201.

944. *The same.* 48½ × 39 in. (Sir John Leicester:
J. L. Parker: Earl of Lonsdale, 1814: Lonsdale
sale 8/iii/1879 (7) bt. in: resold 18/vi/1887 (910)
bt. Agnew: Sir Charles Tennant: sold by Lord
Glenconner, 1931: with Howard Young, New
York, 1931: Mr and Mrs Charles Finn Williams,
Cincinnati, 1937.) More or less identical with
no. 943. Probably R.A. 1780 (74).

945. RIVER LANDSCAPE WITH FIGURES
IN A BOAT. *Philadelphia. Pennsylvania Museum.*
46 × 65½ in. (Said to have been painted for Lane
family, King's Bromley: J. Newton Lane, 1854:
bt. from him by William Delafield: sale 30/iv/1870
(87) bt. Agnew for Hemming: R. Hemming
sale 28/iv/1894 (82) bt. Agnew: W. L. Elkins,
Philadelphia, 1898: bequeathed by George W.
Elkins.) Probably early London work, but it
could be earlier. Pl. 122.

946. SHEPHERD BOY DRIVING SHEEP
AND CATTLE HOME. *London. Marchioness
of Dufferin and Ava.* 21½ × 29½ in. (Joseph Smith
of Shortgrove, 1814: bt. from Shortgrove by Sir
Edward Guinness (Earl of Iveagh), 1889: Hon.
Ernest Guinness sale 10/vii/1953 (60) bt. for Lady
Dufferin.) Probably about 1780/81.

947. RETURNING FROM MARKET. *Cincinnati. Art Museum (Hanna collection).* 40 × 50 in. (Rev. John Lucy (1790–1874): sale 1/v/1875 (42) bt. for Earl of Dudley: Anon. (= Lord Dudley) sale 13/vii/1923 (128) bt. Sulley: with Scott & Fowles, New York, 1926: Miss Mary Hanna by 1931: presented, 1946.) Perhaps not far from 1780. Pl. 178.

948. A COUNTRY CART CROSSING A FORD. *London. Mrs. H. Scudamore.* 38½ × 48½ in. (Bt. from artist by Wilbraham Tollemache, later 6th Earl of Dysart: descended to Lord Tollemache: sale 15/v/1953 (110) bt. for Sir James Caird, Bt.) This has always passed as a companion to the other Tollemache Landscape (no. 1001) of 1786, but this must be several years earlier. Pl. 190.

949. *The same. Bethlehem (Pa.). Eugene G. Grace.* 27¼ × 35½ in. (G. Gostling, 1814: descended to Mrs Gostling Murray: Anon. (= Gostling Murray) sale 23/vi/1883 (767) bt. Agnew: D. Jardine by 1899: Jardine sale 16/iii/1917 (96) bt. Sulley: with Knoedler: E. G. Grace, 1927.) Nearly identical in design with no. 948, but the cart is nearer the spectator: probably later than no. 948.

950. A CART RECEDING DOWN A WOODY LANE. *Manchester. City Art Gallery.* 24½ × 29½ in. (Lord Robert Ponsonby Tottenham, Bishop of Clogher, 1832: Col. Robert Tottenham: bt. from C. M. Spink, 1950.) Difficult to date but perhaps not far from 1780.

950a. CART ON SANDY LANE NEAR AN ESTUARY. 25 × 30 in. (Hester (Hall), Countess of Sussex: descended to Francis Hall, Ontario: sold, 1948: sold by David B. Findlay Gall., New York, to American private collector, 1952.) Allegedly of the date (1771) of Gainsborough's portrait of Lady Sussex, but close in style to no. 948: repd. in *The Connoisseur*, Aug. 1952, p. 78.

951. PASTORAL LOVERS AND COWS NEAR WOODLAND STREAM. *Burghley House. Marquess of Exeter.* 43 × 57½ in. (Sir Thomas Whichcote, Bt.: passed to his daughter, Isabella, Marchioness of Exeter, 1902.) Probably acquired from the artist in the 1780s at the time Gainsborough painted the Whichcote portraits.

952. *The same. Petworth. John Wyndham.* 48 × 57 in. (Probably bt. by Earl of Egremont: Lord Leconfield.) Nearly identical with no. 951 but without the sheep. Pl. 179.

953. CATTLE RETURNING HOME AT EVENING. *Bowood. Marquess of Lansdowne.* 38½ × 49½ in. (Probably C. F. Abel sale, by Greenwood, 13/xii/1787 (47): Mrs Thrale (Piozzi), who gave it to her niece, Mrs H. M. Hoare, c. 1807: Anon. sale, by Phillips, 2/vi/1815 (18): Marquess of Lansdowne by 1844.) Apparently one of a pair: for its history see *Thraliana*, ed. K. C. Balderston, 1942, II, p. 1082. Probably about 1780 or earlier. Pl. 125.

954. SEASHORE WITH FISHERMEN AND BOAT SETTING OUT. *Syosset (L. I.). Mrs Robert Mellon Bruce.* 39 × 49 in. (Sir J. F. Leicester (Lord de Tabley), 1814: sale 7/vii/1827 (27) bt. for Sir George Phillips: passed to his daughter, Lady Camperdown: Earl of Camperdown sale 21/ii/1919 (134) bt. Knoedler: Hon. Andrew W. Mellon, 1920.) R.A. 1781. Pl. 224.

955. COAST SCENE: SELLING FISH. *London. Westminster Trustees.* 39½ × 50 in. (Said to have been painted for 1st Earl Grosvenor: first recorded in the collection, 1802: Duke of Westminster.) About 1781. Pl. 225.

956. COAST SCENE WITH FISHERMEN DRAGGING NETS. *Anglesey Abbey. Lord Fairhaven.* 41 × 50½ in. (Descended in Cruttenden family to Mrs J. Clark Kennedy: with Agnew, 1898: George J. Gould, New York, 1900: with Duveen, 1925: given by Lord Duveen to J. Ramsay Macdonald, 1933: Anon. sale 1/vi/1945 (64) bt. Frost & Reed: Sir Edward Mountain, Bt. 1946: with Leggatt, 1952.) Said to have been painted for E. H. Cruttenden (d. 1771), but Gainsborough is well reported (Whitley, p. 176) to have painted no seascapes before 1781 and it

agrees in style with nos. 954/5 and the background is related to no. 959. R.A. 1781 (77). Pl. 226.

957. SAILING VESSELS: CATTLE ON A HIGH BANK. 25 × 30 in. (Samuel Rogers, 1814: sale 3/v/1856 (713) bt. Holloway: John Dillon, 1857: sale 17/iv/1869 (92) bt. Agnew: J. Heugh sale 25/iv/1874 (173) bt. Agnew for K. D. Hodgson: R. K. Hodgson: with Agnew: Pandelli Ralli: with Agnew, 1952.) Probably a little earlier than no. 958 and from the early 1780s.

958. *The same. Glen. Lord Glenconner.* 30 × 25 in. (Probably P. Delme sale 19/ii/1790 (16) bt. Long: Charles Long (Lord Farnborough): Samuel Long sale 11/iii/1882 (155) bt. Agnew: James Price: with Agnew: Sir Charles Tennant, 1890.) An upright variant of no. 957: perhaps a little later. Pl. 200.

959. MOUNTED PEASANT DRIVING CATTLE OVER BRIDGE: LOVERS, etc. *Rycote Park. C. M. Michaelis.* Oval (on rectangular canvas): 48¼ × 64¼ in. (Traditionally exchanged by Gainsborough for a fiddle with Mr Bowles of North Aston: Anon. (= Col. Bowles) sale 25/v/1850 (11) bt. in: H. M. Skrine, Warleigh: sold from there c. 1900: Sir Max Michaelis.) Pretty certainly R.A. 1781 (Whitley, p. 173). Pl. 220.

960. THE WOODCUTTER'S RETURN. *Belvoir Castle. Duke of Rutland.* 58 × 48 in. R.A. 1782 (166). Bought by 4th Duke of Rutland before 1787. Pl. 227.

961. *The same.* 58½ × 47½ in. *Bowdoin College (Maine). Lent by Lady Oakes, 1957.* (Conceivably the picture which passed from Felice de Giardini to Hon. Richard Rigby before 1785: Rigby sale 9/i/1789 (9) bt. Peter: Chandos Leigh (Lord Leigh), 1839: bt. from Stoneleigh Abbey by Duveen before 1931: Sir Harry Oakes, Nassau.) Almost identical with no. 960.

962. HERDSMAN AND GIRL, WITH CATTLE AND SHEEP, IN A WOOD. *Belvoir Castle. Duke of Rutland.* 58 × 48 in. Apparently

the companion to no. 960: bt. by 4th Duke of Rutland before 1787. Pl. 228.

963. SHEPHERD AND SHEEP BY A POOL: TWO CARTHORSES, etc. *Belvoir Castle. Duke of Rutland.* 38½ × 49 in. Bought by 4th Duke of Rutland shortly before his death in 1787.

964. A VIEW AT THE MOUTH OF THE THAMES. *Melbourne (Victoria). National Gallery.* 62 × 75 in. (Probably passed from Robert Palmer (d. 1787) to his daughter, Lady Beauchamp-Proctor: Sir R. Proctor-Beauchamp sale, Sotheby's, 11/vi/1947 (23) bt. Agnew: bt. from Tooth by the Felton Trustees, 1947.) R.A. 1783 (240). Pl. 244.

965. AN ESTUARY WITH SHEPHERD AND SHEEP. *Nawton. Sir Martyn Beckett, Bt.* 25 × 30 in. (Probably bt. in middle 1780s by William Hamilton Nisbet: R. C. N. Hamilton, 1856: Mrs Nisbet Hamilton Ogilvy sale, at Biel, by Dowell's, 16/iv/1921 (1): Sir Gervaise Beckett, Bt., 1936.) Very close in style to no. 964. Pl. 223.

966. ROCKY MOUNTAIN VALLEY WITH SHEPHERD, SHEEP AND WATERFALL. *Sutton Place. Duke of Sutherland.* 45¾ × 56½ in. (Bt. by Lord Gower from the sale at Schomberg House, 1789, no. 72.) R.A. 1783 (34). Pl. 257.

967. *The same. Birmingham. City Art Gallery (lent by Mrs O. S. Ashcroft.)* 27¼ × 36½ in. (Probably W. Coningham sale 9/vi/1849 (22) bt. Smith. F. C. K. Fleischmann, 1904: thence to his son, Oscar Ashcroft.) A finished study for no. 966, with a shepherd in the bottom left foreground added.

968. ROCKY MOUNTAIN VALLEY WITH SHEPHERD, STREAM AND GOATS. *Philadelphia. Pennsylvania Museum.* 38 × 48 in. (C. F. Huth sale 19/iii/1904 (53) bt. Agnew: John H. McFadden, Philadelphia.) Clearly related in style to no. 966. Pl. 258.

969. UPLAND HAMLET WITH FIGURES AND STREAM. *New York. Metropolitan Museum.*

$47\frac{1}{2} \times 59$ in. (Possibly the picture listed in Armstrong as ex. — Smith: Messrs. Tooth (1904). Presented by George A. Hearn, 1906.) Perhaps about 1783. Pl. 191.

970–981. TWELVE LANDSCAPES ON GLASS FOR A PEEP-SHOW. *London. Victoria and Albert Museum.* Each pane: $11 \times 13\frac{1}{4}$ in. (Bt. from Miss Gainsborough by Dr Munro: Monro sale 28/vi/1833 (168) bt. W. White, who bequeathed them to G. W. Reid: Anon. sale 22/iii/1890 (132) bt. in: Leopold Hirsch sale 11/v/1934 (104) bt. for Ernest E. Cook: bequeathed by E. E. Cook through N.A.C.F., 1955.) Dateable about 1783. It is possible that Dr Monro only had ten Gainsborough views and that two of the present ones (*A heath with a windmill* and *A town across a river*) are not from Gainsborough's hand. Pls. 261–268.

982. MOUNTAIN LANDSCAPE WITH RIVER, BRIDGE AND FIGURES. *Cardiff. National Museum of Wales.* 15×25 in. (Bequest of Miss Gwendoline Davies, 1951.) Closely related to one of the views in nos. 970 ff.

983. TWO COWS BY A WOOD, AND RUSTIC LOVERS. *Mertoun. Earl of Ellesmere.* $24\frac{1}{2} \times 30$ in. (Probably Duke of Bridgewater (d. 1803). Certainly Marquess of Stafford, 1816: thence by descent.) Probably related to one of the compositions in nos. 970 ff.

984. WOODY MOUNTAIN LANDSCAPE WITH PEASANT AND CATTLE ON BRIDGE. *London. National Gallery* (2284). $15\frac{3}{4} \times 19$ in. (E. Higginson sale 4/vi/1846 (28) bt. Farrer. Probably Wynn Ellis sale 6/v/1876 (53) bt. Agnew: Mrs Martin Colnaghi, 1892: bequeathed by Martin Colnaghi, 1908.) Probably *c.* 1783: more or less companion to no. 985. Pl. 269.

985. WOODED MOUNTAIN VALLEY WITH PEASANT FIGURES. *Courteenhall. Lady Wake.* $15\frac{3}{4} \times 23\frac{1}{4}$ in. (E. Higginson sale 4/vi/1846 (54) bt. Norton: R. H. Benson, 1887: thence to his daughter.) Probably about 1783: more or less a companion to no. 984.

986. WOODY UPLAND LANDSCAPE WITH SHEPHERD AND SHEEP. $15\frac{1}{2} \times 20\frac{1}{2}$ in. (? Annis sale, by Phillips, 10/vi/1831 bt. Neeld: Sir John Neeld, 1877: Neeld sale 9/vi/1944 (8) bt. Greene: with Roland, Browse & Delbanco, 1946.) Closely related to nos. 984/5.

987. THE MALL. *New York. Henry Clay Frick Collection.* 47×57 in. (1789 sale at Schomberg House (77): Mrs Gainsborough sale 2/vi/1792 (78) bt. in: resold 11/iv/1797 (97) bt. Williamson: Anon. (= Elwin) sale, by Phillips. 12/iv/1799 (68) bt. Howe: for sale on commission by Mr Sparrow, Ipswich, 1807: George Frost (d. 1821), Ipswich, 1809: S. H. Kilderbee sale 30/v/1829 (126) bt. for Joseph Neeld: bt. from Sir Audley Neeld, Bt., 1916.) Painted in 1783 and exhibited at Schomberg House, 1784. Pl. 243.

988. CHARITY RELIEVING DISTRESS. *Putteridge Bury. Sir Francis Cassel, Bt.* 39×30 in. (cut down from 49×39 in.). (Lord Robert Spencer sale 31/v/1799 (92) as *Italian Villa*, bt. Bowyer: Walsh Porter sale 22/iii/1803 (29) bt. Marquis of Hertford: sold from Ragley *c.* 1933 to Sir Felix Cassel, Bt.) Exhibited at Schomberg House, 1784: retouched and improved by Gainsborough, 1787 (Whitley, pp. 228 and 294). A copy (perhaps by Dupont), showing the whole composition, was in the F. C. F. Parker sale 24/vii/1936 (20). Pl. 229.

989. LANDSCAPE WITH A MANSION AMONG TREES. *Middleton Park. Mrs A. C. J. Wall.* $47\frac{1}{2} \times 57\frac{1}{2}$ in. (Anon. sale 20/v/1920 (71) bt. Leger: bt. from Leggatt by Victor Rienaeker *c.* 1920: with Colnaghi, 1937: bt. from F. Partridge, 1938, by A. C. J. Wall (d. 1955).) Perhaps about 1784: reproduced in the Ipswich Exh. Catalogue, 1927 (47) before the 1932 cleaning.

990. WOODY LANDSCAPE WITH A VILLA. *London. National Gallery* (1825). $16\frac{3}{4} \times 21\frac{1}{2}$ in. (Bequeathed by Henry Vaughan, 1900.) Possibly related to no. 989.

991. A LODGE IN A PARK, WITH CHILDREN DESCENDING STEPS, etc. *Kinderhook (N.Y.). Robert Perret.* 60×72 in. (Probably

Schomberg House sale, 1789 (68): Mrs Gains-borough sale 2/vi/1792 (82) bt. in: bt. later by Prince Regent: Anon. (=Prince Regent) sale 29/vi/1814 (21) bt. Rutley: Sir G. Warrender, 1817: Warrender sale 3/vi/1837 (21) bt. Stewart: Sir Thomas Baring sale 2/vi/1848 (61) bt. Nieu-wenhuys: Anon. sale, Robinson & Fisher, 28/v/1897 (191) bt. Colnaghi: do. 21/vi/1900 (109): bt. in Washington c. 1900 by J. Pierpont Morgan: his daughter, Mrs George Nichols, New York, 1924–51: with Coleman Galls., New York: bt. 1951.) Probably from the middle 1780s: a lithograph by Louis Marvy (d. 1850) shows it in undamaged condition.

992. UPLAND VALLEY, WITH SHEPHERD, SHEEP AND CATTLE. *Mayfield House. W. S. Constable Curtis.* 46¼ × 58½ in. Signed: *T. G.* (Painted for Prince of Wales and given to Mrs. Fitzherbert in 1810: bequeathed, 1837, to Hon. Mrs Dawson Damer: Dawson Damer sale 27/iii/1841 (142) bt. in and later sold to Pennell, who sold it to J. Gillott, 1845: Hogarth sale 13/vi/1851 (50) bt. in and sold later to Elhanan Bicknell: Bicknell sale 25/iv/1863 (81) bt. Wallis: bt. from Graves by Thomas Curtis, 1863.) Ex-hibited at Schomberg House, 1784 (Whitley, p. 229): still in Gainsborough's hands at his death and in the 1789 Exhibition (75). Pl. 259.

993. THE HARVEST WAGGON. *Toronto Art Gallery.* 48 × 59 in. Signed: *T.G.* (Bt. by the Prince of Wales and given to Mrs Fitzherbert, 1810: bequeathed to Hon. Mrs Dawson Damer, 1837: Dawson Damer sale 27/iii/1841 (141) bt. in: John Gibbons (d. 1851): Gibbons sale 26/v/1894 (24) bt. in: bt. from Rev. B. Gibbons by Colnaghi, 1898: bt. from Colnaghi by Lionel Phillips, 1898: Sir Lionel Phillips sale 25/iv/1913 (45) bt. Agnew for Judge Gary, New York: Gary sale, New York, 20/iv/1928 (30) bt. Duveen: Mr and Mrs Frank P. Wood, Toronto: presented, 1942.) Painted in the winter, 1784/5 (Whitley, pp. 235 and 258): bt. by Prince of Wales in 1786 but still in Gainsborough's hands at his death and in the 1789 Exhibition (94). Pl. 270.

994. A CART IN FRONT OF A COTTAGE ON A WOODED SLOPE. *Birmingham. City*

Art Gallery. 15¾ × 19½ in. (Descended through the Dupont family to Miss E. S. Browne, High Wycombe: bequeathed to Mansfield College, Oxford, 1906: bt. thence, 1953.) Probably about 1785.

995. HERDSMEN DRIVING CATTLE DOWN A WOODY LANE. 24 × 29 in. (Bt. either by Robert Palmer (d. 1787) or Richard Palmer (d. 1806): Mrs Golding Palmer sale 28/vii/1916 (25) bt. Agnew: with Knoedler, 1916: with Reinhardt, New York.) Perhaps about 1785: companion to no. 996. Pl. 271.

996. BOY DRIVING COWS NEAR POOL: A COTTAGE AMONG TREES. 24 × 29 in. (Bt. either by Robert Palmer (d. 1787) or Richard Palmer (d. 1806): Mrs Golding Palmer sale 28/vii/1916 (26) bt. Agnew: with Knoedler, 1916: with Reinhardt, New York: John N. Willys, New York, 1925: Mrs Van Wie Willys (?).) Companion to no. 995: perhaps about 1785, and one of the landscapes shown at Schomberg House in 1786 (Whitley, p. 256). Pl. 272.

997. *The same* (with park gate instead of cottage). *London. Tate Gallery* (309). (*Loan collection.*) 23 × 30 in. (Probably in Schomberg House sale 1789 (66) bt. Woodhouse: J. Woodhouse sale 14/ii/1801 (32) bt. Esdaile: Esdaile sale 24/iii/1838 (67) bt. Vernon: bequeathed by Robert Vernon, 1847.) A sketchy variant of no. 996.

998. PACKHORSES. THE MIDDAY REST. *London. Rex Benson.* 21½ × 27½ in. (Robert H. Benson, 1902.) Perhaps one of the pictures exhibited at Schomberg House in 1786 (Whitley, p. 255).

999. WOODY LANDSCAPE: CATTLE, SHEEP AND FIGURES AT A FOUNTAIN. *Petworth. John Wyndham.* 24½ × 29½ in. (Earl of Egremont, 1814: Lord Leconfield.) Probably about 1786.

1000. WOODY LANDSCAPE: PEASANT & TWO HORSES CROSSING POOL. *Hartford (Conn.). Wadsworth Atheneum.* 25 × 30 in. (Charles

Meigh sale 22/vi/1850 (133) bt. Lenox: bequeathed by James Lenox to New York Public Library: sale New York 17/x/1956 (42) bt. Nicholson: bt. 1957.) Perhaps about 1786.

1000a. MOUNTAIN LANDSCAPE WITH SHEEP. *Sutton Place. Duke of Sutherland.* c. 25 × 30 in. Close in style to no. 1000.

1001. THE COTTAGE DOOR WITH GIRL WITH PIGS. *London. Mrs H. Scudamore.* 38¾ × 48¾ in. (Bt. c. 1786 by Wilbraham Tollemache, later Earl of Dysart: descended to Lord Tollemache: Tollemache sale 15/v/1953 (109) bt. for Sir James Caird, Bt.) Painted 1786 (Whitley, p. 262). Pl. 246.

1002. THE MARKET CART. *London. Tate Gallery (80).* 72½ × 60½ in. (Bt. 1787 by Sir Peter Burrell, later Lord Gwydyr: Lord Gwydyr sale 9/v/1829 (87) bt. for Governors of the British Institution and given to National Gallery, 1830.) Painted 1786 and exhibited at Schomberg House: the woodman and faggots added 1787 (Whitley, pp. 263, 270–273). Pl. 286 and colour plate.

1003. *The same. Detroit. Mr and Mrs Charles T. Fisher* (1939). 48 × 40 in. (Possibly 1797 sale (96) bt. William Neave (or Williamson?). Sir Thomas Neave, 1817: Anon. (= S. H. M. Neave) sale 27/vi/1885 (27) bt. in: resold 15/v/1886 (85) bt. in: resold 2/iv/1887 (113) bt. Martin: Lord Michelham (?): C. T. Fisher, 1927.) For various problems connected with this see H. I. Kay in W. R. Valentiner, *Unknown Masterpieces*, 1930, no. 97.

1004. THE BULLOCK WAGGON. *New York. Mrs Jeremiah D. Maguire* (1931). 38 × 51 in. (Joseph Gillott sale 27/iv/1872 (285) bt. Agnew: Louis Huth sale 20/v/1905 (101) bt. Tooth: Senator W. A. Clark sale, New York, 11/i/1926 (102): with Scott & Fowles, New York, 1927.) It bears an old inscription: *T. Gainsborough/Pinx.* 1787.

1005. TREES BY A POOL (a fragment). 41 × 30 in. (For history up to 1920 see no. 622: with Agnew, 1931 cut down to 54½ × 30½ in.: with Leggatt, 1947 (43 × 30 in.): Anon. sale 9/iv/1954 (99) bt. Soames (41 × 30 in.): Anon. sale, Sotheby's, 20/iv/1955 (107) bt. Leggatt.) A fragment of the portrait group of the *Sloper family* (see no. 622), painted 1787/8.

1006. WOODY MOUNTAIN VALLEY WITH RUSTIC FIGURES, SHEEP, etc. *Mayfield House. W. S. Constable Curtis.* 47½ × 58 in. (Conceivably no. 48 in Schomberg House sale 1789: Rev. J. Coles, Basingstoke, 1840: bt. from him by Constable Curtis, 1850.) Probably 1787/8. Pl. 260.

1007. ROCKY MOUNTAIN VALLEY: SHEPHERD AND SHEEP AT A SPRING. *London. Royal Academy (Diploma Gallery).* 60½ × 73½ in. (Presented by Miss Margaret Gainsborough, 1799.) Perhaps the picture Gainsborough was intending for the chimney of the Council Room at Somerset House in 1787 (Whitley, p. 294): no. 87 in exhibition for sale at Schomberg House, 1789.

1008. MOUNTAIN LANDSCAPE WITH PEASANTS CROSSING A BRIDGE. *Washington. National Gallery of Art.* 44½ × 52½ in. (Perhaps Mrs Gainsborough sale 11/iv/1797 (69) bt. Sir J. Leicester (Lord de Tabley). Bt. from Lady Lindsay by A. Wertheimer: Sir Edgar Vincent (Lord D'Abernon) 1912: with Duveen, 1926/31: given by Hon. Andrew W. Mellon, 1937.) Seemingly a very late unfinished work. Pl. 287. Colour plate.

1009. TWO WOODMEN LOADING AN ASS. *Stourhead. National Trust.* 39½ × 49 in. (1789 sale at Schomberg House (71) bt. Lady Hoare: Hugh Hoare, 1814: passed from Wavendon to Stourhead, 1913: bequeathed to National Trust by Sir Henry Hoare, 1947.) Painted 1787 (Whitley, pp. 293/4.).

1010. GIPSIES ROUND A FIRE IN A RUINED ABBEY (Sketch). *London. Private collection.* 34 × 28½ in. (Probably Earl of Aldborough: W. H. Trant sale, Foster's, 11/vi/1832 (184) bt. Thompson, Bt., from Tooth, 1955.) Probably an unfinished picture of 1788. Pl. 230.

1011. THE COTTAGE DOOR, WITH A PEASANT SMOKING. *Los Angeles. University of California.* 77 × 62 in. (Mrs Gainsborough sale 2/vi/1792 (83) probably bt. in: Sir George Beaumont by 1808: bt. from Coleorton about 1935 by Spink and others: with Spink, 1954: bt. by J. Mitchell Chapman for the James Kennedy Memorial collection, 1954.) The last landscape of importance painted by Gainsborough and designed as a companion to the *Market Cart* (no. 1002): exhibited for sale at Schomberg House, 1789 (60). Pl. 285.

1012. LANDSCAPE WITH DIANA AND ACTAEON. *Buckingham Palace. H.M. The Queen.* 61 × 73 in. (1797 sale (43) bt. Hammond for Prince of Wales.) Very late unfinished work. Pl. 288.

COPIES AFTER THE OLD MASTERS

Note: With one or two exceptions, our only certain information about these is their being recorded in the early Gainsborough sales—that by private contract at Schomberg House in 1789 and that in 1797 (10/11 April).

1013. After CUYP. "*A conversation*". Sale 11/iv/1797 (17)—with others: bt. Hammond.

1014. After DU JARDIN. "*A landscape with cattle*". Sale 11/iv/1797 (16)—with another: bt. Smith.

1015. After VAN DYCK. THE PEMBROKE FAMILY. *Castle Ashby. Marquess of Northampton* 37½ × 49 in. (1789 cat. no. 17 as "Painted by Memory, after having seen the original at Wilton": sale 2/vi/1792 (75): bt. from Mrs Gainsborough by Capt. Thomson, who sold it to Richard Lane: bt. from Lane, 1828, by Hon. G. Agar Ellis (Lord Dover): thence to Viscount Clifden: Clifden sale, by Robinson & Fisher, 25/v/1895 (785) bt. C. Davis: Van Andre, 1898: Lady Ashburton: Lord Spencer Compton.) A smaller version, bearing Dupont's signature, passed from Sir Sidney Herbert to Viscountess Hambleden.

1016. After VAN DYCK. JAMES, DUKE OF RICHMOND AND LENNOX. 71½ × 50½ in. (1789 cat. no. 41: bt. in at sales 2/vi/1792 (72) 11/iv/1797 (93) and 25/iv/1801 (81).) Whole length. Presumably after the picture now at New York, which was then at Corsham Court.

1017. After VAN DYCK. LORD JOHN AND LORD BERNARD STEWART. *St. Louis (Mo.). City Art Museum.* 93 × 57 in. (1789 cat. no. 92: sold to Earl of Darnley: Darnley sale 1/v/1925 (20)—*repd.*: bt. Bromhead Cutts: Mrs Jackson Johnson, St. Louis: passed to Art Museum, 1943.) A copy of the picture belonging to Countess Mountbatten, then in the Earl of Darnley's possession.

1018. After VAN DYCK. LORD BERNARD STEWART. 29 × 23½ in. (Possibly 1789 cat. no. 65 as *A man's portrait*, sale 2/vi/1792 (69) and 1797 sale (34) bt. Bryan (26 × 21 in.): Earl of Darnley sale 1/v/1925 (21) bt. Agnew: still with Agnew, 1934.) Detail of head from the last. Exh.: Cincinnati, 1931 (21)—*repd.*

1019. After VAN DYCK. "*A Portrait*". (1789 cat. no. 94—22½ × 17¾ in.)

1020. After VAN DYCK. DUC D'AREN-BERG. *Gateley Hall. C. G. Hoare.* 38¼ × 33 in. (1789 cat. no. 73: sale 2/vi/1792 (71) it passed by descent to the family of Gainsborough's sister, Mrs Gardiner, and was bequeathed by Rev. E. R. Gardiner to Mrs Edward Netherton Harward: Harward sale 11/v/1923 (104) bt. Agnew: bt. by C. G. Hoare *c.* 1924.) Equestrian whole length after the picture at Holkham—which Gainsborough visited in 1785 with a view to painting a companion equestrian portrait of the Prince of Wales (which was never achieved).

1021. After VAN DYCK. INIGO JONES. (1789 cat. no. 57: 28 × 23½ in.) Presumably after the picture now at Leningrad.

1022. After VAN DYCK. THREE CHILDREN OF CHARLES I. (Sale 11/iv/1797 (16)—with another: bt. Smith.) It is not certain that this was by Gainsborough. Presumably after the picture at Windsor.

1023. After MICHAUD. "*A small landscape*". (Sale 11/iv/1797 (2)—"Michaud: a small landscape and figures with the *imitation* of ditto by Gainsborough": bt. Garvey.)

1024. After MURILLO. ABRAHAM AND ISAAC. 33½ × 41¼ in. (1789 cat. no. 97, sold to Mr Cornewall. Probably P. Hinds sale 5/iv/1856 (58) bt. Watson: Anon. (= Sir J. Hawley) sale 14/v/1858 (42) bt. Waters: W. Cox sale, Foster's, 26/ii/1862 (48) bt. in.: [Cox] sale 16/v/1863 (156) bt. in: Vokins sale 30/i/1864 (265) bt. in: Cox sale 8/ii/1884 (76). With C. G. Doward, New York, 1951.) A copy of a picture now at Aynhoe Park.

1025. After MURILLO. THE GOOD SHEP-HERD. *Southill. Simon Whitbread.* 63¾ × 44¾ in. (1789 cat. no. 50: probably bt. soon after by Samuel Whitbread: certainly at Southill by 1815.) It bears an inscription, signed by Dupont: "The Good Shepherd, painted from memory by Mr Gainsborough in 1780, after having seen the original in the possession of the Duke of Bridge-water." The Bridgewater picture was in fact a copy by Grimou after an original by Murillo later in Lord Rothschild's possession. *Repd.* in *Country Life*, 12 July 1930, p. 65.

1026. After REMBRANDT. HEAD OF A RABBI. *Hampton Court Palace. H.M. The Queen.* 29 × 24 in. (1789 cat. no. 93.) After the Rembrandt now in the National Gallery, London (190): then in the collection of the Duke of Argyll.

1027. After RUBENS. DESCENT FROM THE CROSS. *Bruern Abbey. Hon. Michael Astor.* 48 × 38½ ins. (Sale 11/iv/1797 (63) bt. Steers as "unfinished, after the celebrated one of Rubens": J. W. Steers sale 3/vi/1826 (52) as "after Vandyke", bt. Bond: W. R. G. Bond, Tyneham House, 1935: Anon. (= Bond) sale, Sotheby's 25/vi/1947 (22) bt. Sinclair: Hon. Michael Astor by 1950.) In reverse from the original in Antwerp Cathedral: perhaps made from the version in Lord Lee's collection, which was then at Corsham. Pl. 291.

1028. After RUBENS. HEADS OF TWO FRIARS. *Oxford. Ashmolean Museum.* 21 × 18½ in. (Bt. from Miss Gainsborough by Farington, 1799 (*Diary* under 28/i/1799): S. H. Kilderbee sale 30/v/1829 (108) bt. Seguier for Hon. G. Agar Ellis (Lord Dover): passed to Viscount Clifden: Clifden sale 6/v/1893 (3) bt. Long for Henry

Pfungst: sold by Pfungst to Leggatt's and by them to T. K. Stubbins, 1905: Stubbins sale 29/xi/1918 (20) bt. for Mrs Weldon: bequeathed by her, 1937.) After a picture which belonged to Gainsborough, which was no. 35 in the 1789 cat., sold to the Earl of Warwick. It is still at Warwick Castle.

1029. After TENIERS. THE RETURN FROM SHOOTING. (a) 45 × 59 in. (Perhaps sale 11/iv/1797 (17)—with others: bt. Hammond: William Smith, 1814: John Allnutt, 1843: Allnutt sale 20/vi/1863 (485) bt. in: bt. from Rutley by Edward Wheler Mills, before 1865: passed to Mrs Edward Cooper (*née* Mills): Cooper sale 12/xii/1947 (3) bt. Leggatt: with Leggatt, 1951.) This is a faithful copy of the original by Teniers still at Longford Castle, as it was then.

1030. (b) *Dublin. National Gallery of Ireland.* 44½ × 58½ in. (Probably descended from Gains-borough's friend Joshua Kirby, to Rev. Henry Scott Trimmer: Trimmer sale 17/iii/1860 (93*) bt. Rutley: John Clarke sale 8/vi/1895 (95) bt. Lawrie: T. G. Arthur, Glasgow, 1904: Arthur sale 20/iii/1914 (146) bt. Martin for Lane: be-queathed to Dublin by Sir Hugh Lane, 1915.) This is a variant copy, in which a log replaces the two dogs in the right foreground.

1031. After TITIAN. "THE CORNARO FAMILY". 22½ × 36½ in. (1789 cat. no. 47: sale 2/vi/1792 (70): Marquess of Lansdowne sale 19/iii/1806 (28): Samuel Rogers, 1814: Rogers sale 2/v/1856 (575) bt. Morant—possibly for Sir John Ramsden.) After the picture now in the National Gallery, London.

1032. After VELASQUEZ. "THE CONSPI-RATORS". 31½ × 38 in. (1789 cat. no. 36: Lord de Dunstanville, 1814.) Copied in 1785 (Whitley, p. 249) from a picture ascribed to Velasquez then belonging to Lord Grantham and now to Baroness Lucas (Mayer, no. 143).

ILLUSTRATIONS

CHARTER
HOUSE.
Gainsborough, 1748.

1 [861] The Charterhouse. *Foundling Hospital Offices, London.*

2 [416] John Kirby. *Fitzwilliam Museum, Cambridge.*

3 [417] Mrs John Kirby. *Fitzwilliam Museum, Cambridge.*

4 [275] John Gainsborough. *Dublin.*

5 [817] "Bumper", 1745. *Sir Edmund Bacon, Bt.*

6 [291] The Painter. *E. G. Spencer-Churchill.*

7 [297] The Painter's wife. *Owner unknown.*

8 [290] The Painter, 1754. *Marchioness of Cholmondeley.*

9 [418] John Joshua Kirby. *Victoria and Albert Museum.*

10 [18] Mr and Mrs Robert Andrews. *National Gallery, London.*

11 [86] Mr and Mrs John Browne and child. *Marchioness of Cholmondeley.*

12 [659] Philip Thicknesse. *St Louis, Mo.*

13 [546] John Plampin. *National Gallery, London.*

14 [454] Richard Savage Lloyd and Cecil Lloyd. *Mrs Harman Hunt.*

15 [452] Heneage Lloyd and sister. *Fitzwilliam Museum, Cambridge.*

17 [752] The painter and his wife (?). *Louvre.*

16 [420] Mr and Mrs John Joshua Kirby. *National Portrait Gallery, London.*

19 [747] P. D. Muilman, C. Crockett and W. Keeble. *Lt.-Col. Michael Barne.*

18 [756] Gentleman with dog. *Sir Philip Nichols.*

20 [871] Peasant with donkeys. *Major A. F. Clarke-Jervoise.*

21 [835] Farmyard with milkmaid. *Hon. Victor Saumarez.*

22 [*828*] "Gainsborough's Forest", 1748. *National Gallery, London.*

23 [*831*] Road through a wood, 1747. *Philadelphia.*

24 [840] River bank with figures. *Edinburgh.*

25 [838] Estuary with church, cattle and figures. *Ipswich.*

26 [765] Officer of 1st Dragoon Guards, 1756. *Owner unknown.*

27 [340] Hon. Charles Hamilton. *Earl of Haddington.*

28 [313] Joseph Gibbs. *National Portrait Gallery, London.*

29 [764] Gentleman in blue. *Mrs Isherwood Kay.*

30 [6] Mrs Nathaniel Acton. *Hon. Victor Saumarez.*

31 [369] Mrs Henry Hill. *Lady Stewart.*

32 [40] Lambe Barry. *F. B. Hart-Jackson.*

33 [41] Lambe Barry. *Hon. Victor Saumarez.*

35 [816a] Old peasant with donkey. *Mrs H. W. Standring.*

34 [836] Boy with sheep. *Toledo (Ohio).*

36 [830] Woody slope with felled timber. *Minneapolis.*

37 [827] River with cattle and peasants. *Formerly Messrs Tooth.*

38 [*843*] Shipping on a Norfolk Broad. *G. H. Berners.*

39 [*833*] Peasant with two horses. *Duke of Bedford.*

40 [844] "Rustic courtship". *Montreal.*

41 [829] Woodcutter courting a milkmaid. *Duke of Bedford.*

43 [1184] Rev. Richard Canning. *With S. Sabin.*

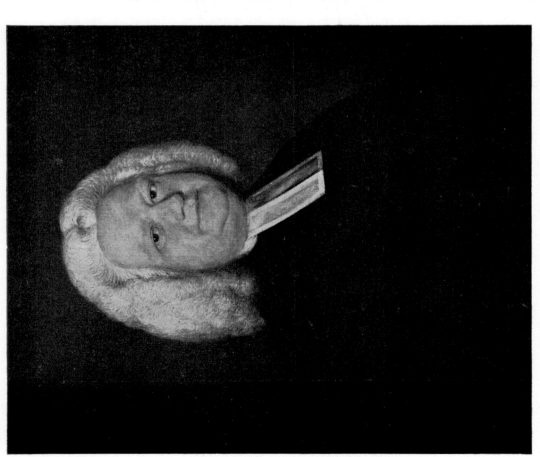

42 [389] Rev. Henry Hubbard. *Emmanuel College, Cambridge.*

45 [692] Admiral Edward Vernon. *National Portrait Gallery, London.*

44 [407] Samuel Kilderbee. *De Young Museum, San Francisco.*

46 [826] "Drinkstone Park". São Paulo, Brazil.

50 [284] The Painter's daughters. *Victoria and Albert Museum.*

51 [286] The Painter's daughters. *National Gallery, London.*

52 [285] The Painter's daughters. *National Gallery, London.*

53 [857] Farm cart and cattle in a woody lane. *L. H. Wilson.*

54 [856] Woody lane with rustic lovers. *Wharton Sinkler, Philadelphia.*

55 [*896*] "The Rocks, near Bath". *Major J. G. Buxton.*

56 [*895*] Woody landscape. *H. W. J. Ferrand.*

58 [169] Thomas (?) Coward. *Birmingham.*

57 [522] Robert, Earl Nugent, 1760. *City Estates Committee, Bristol.*

60 [556] Uvedale Tomkyns Price. *Munich.*

59 [595] Sir William St Quintin, 4th Bt. *Mrs L'Estrange-Malone.*

61 [734] William Wollaston. *H. C. Wollaston.*

62 [660] Mrs Philip Thicknesse, 1760. *Cincinnati (Emery coll.).*

63 [554] William Poyntz. S.A. 1762. *Earl Spencer.*

64 [523] Robert, Earl Nugent. S.A. 1761. *Sir Guy Nugent, Bt.*

65 [897] Sunset: carthorses drinking. *Tate Gallery, London.*

66 [898] Woody landscape with horseman and sheep. *Worcester, Mass.*

67 [*13*] Lady Alston. *Louvre*.

69 [567] James Quin. S.A. 1763. *Dublin.*

68 [477] Thomas John Medlycott. S.A. 1763. *H. J. Watlington, Bermuda.*

70 [552] Mrs Portman. *Lent to Tate Gallery by Viscount Portman.*

71 [202] James Donnithorne. *Colonel H. J. Cator.*

73 [438] William Leyborne (?). Bristol.

72 [439] Mrs William Leyborne (?). Bristol.

75 [478] Welbore, Lord Mendip, 1763. *Christ Church, Oxford.*

74 [350] Philip, 2nd Earl of Hardwicke, 1763. *Owner untraced.*

77 [*34*] Hon. Mrs George Baillie. *Earl of Haddington.*

76 [*631*] Lady Georgiana Spencer, 1763. *Earl Spencer.*

78 [628] John, 1st Earl Spencer. *Earl Spencer.*

79 [605] Sir John Sebright, Bt. *Sir Hugo Sebright, Bt.*

80 [910] Woody landscape with figures. *Earl of Crawford and Balcarres.*

81 [890] Woody landscape with figures. *Mrs R. L. Montgomery, Villa Nova, Pa.*

82 [*108*] The Byam family. *Marlborough College.*

83 [375] General Honywood. S.A. 1765. *Sarasota, Florida.*

85 [676] Charles Tudway. *Viscountess Lee of Fareham.*

84 [677] Mrs Charles Tudway. *Baltimore (Jacob Epstein coll.).*

87 [136] *Dr Rice Charlton. S.A. 1766. Holburne of Menstrie Museum, Bath.*

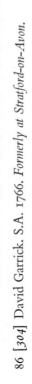

86 [304] *David Garrick. S.A. 1766. Formerly at Stratford-on-Avon.*

88 [*387*] Mary, Countess Howe. *Kenwood*.

89 [524] Hon. Edmund Craggs Nugent. S.A. 1765. *Fredericton (N.B.) University.*

91 [505] Dr Abel Moysey. C. F. Moysey.

90 [287] The Painter's daughters. Worcester, Mass.

92 [900] Woody landscape with milkmaid and drover. S.A. 1766. *Mrs L'Estrange-Malone.*

93 [909] Cattle and peasants at edge of a wood. *Dublin.*

95 [19] John, 4th Duke of Argyll. S.A. 1767. Scottish National Portrait Gallery.

94 [227] Lady Eardley. Oscar B. Cintas, Havana.

97 [693] George, 2nd Lord Vernon. S.A. 1767. *Southampton.*

96 [403] General James Johnston. *Dublin.*

98 [906] Peasants returning from market. *Toledo, Ohio.*

99 [907] The Harvest Waggon. S.A. 1767 (?). *Barber Institute, Birmingham University.*

101 [490] George, Duke of Montagu, 1768. *Duke of Buccleuch.*

100 [491] Mary, Duchess of Montagu, 1768. *Duke of Buccleuch.*

103 [152] Sir Robert Clayton, Bt, 1769. *Liverpool.*

102 [331] Joshua Grigby. *Viscountess Kemsley.*

104 [*514*] Hon. Thomas Needham. S.A. 1768. *Ascott (National Trust)*.

105 [82] 3rd Earl of Bristol. S.A. 1768. *Ickworth (National Trust)*.

107 [446] Thomas Linley, Sr. *Dulwich College.*

106 [235] Mrs Scroope Egerton, 1768. *R. F. Angus, Montreal.*

109 [740] Miss Henrietta Wyndham, 1769. *George Wyndham.*

108 [388] Miss Isabella Howland. *Mrs McLane van Ingen, New York.*

110 [577] Lord Rivers. R.A. 1769. *G. H. Lane-Fox-Pitt-Rivers.*

111 [606] Isabella, Countess of Sefton. R.A. 1769. *Earl of Sefton.*

112 [908] "Repose". *Kansas City.*

113 [*919*] Woody landscape with milkmaids. *Boston.*

114 [912] Peasants going to market. *Kenwood.*

115 [911] Peasants going to market. *Royal Holloway College, Englefield Green.*

116 [411] John, 10th Viscount Kilmorey. *Tate Gallery, London.*

117 [*674*] Sir Benjamin Truman. *Messrs Truman, Hanbury & Co.*

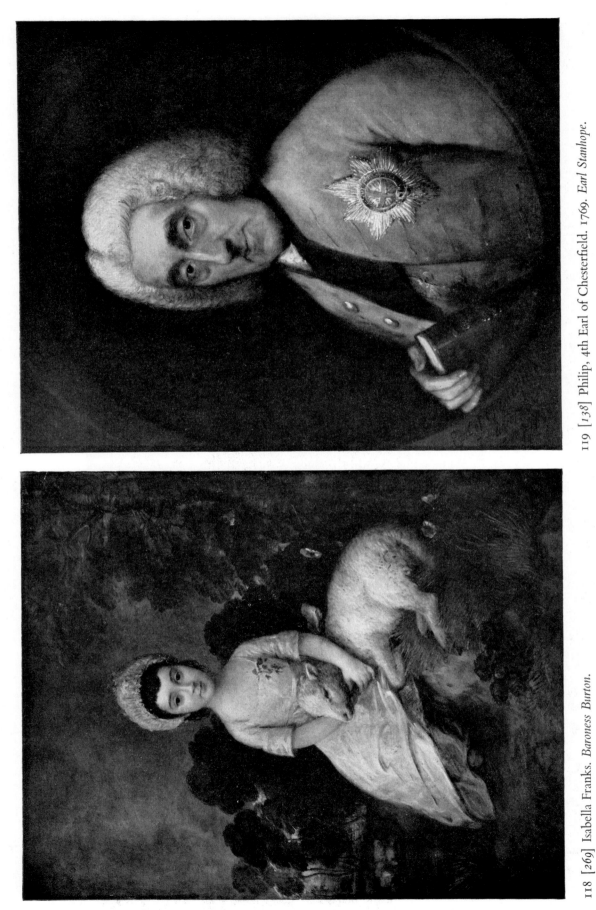

119 [138] Philip, 4th Earl of Chesterfield. 1769. *Earl Stanhope.*

118 [269] Isabella Franks. *Baroness Burton.*

121 [569] William, 1st Earl of Radnor, 1770. *Earl of Radnor.*

120 [88] Henry, 3rd Duke of Buccleuch, 1770. *Duke of Buccleuch.*

122 [945] River landscape with cattle and boat. *Philadelphia.*

123 [922] Woodland gorge with cattle and figures. *Viscount Camrose.*

124 [*931*] Landscape with cattle and milkmaid. *Earl of Jersey.*

125 [953] Cattle returning home at evening. *Marquis of Lansdowne.*

126 [228] Lady Eardley and daughter. R.A. 1770. *Earl of Crawford.*

127 [*106*] Jonathan Buttall ("The Blue Boy"). R.A. 1770 (?). *H. E. Huntington Art Gallery, San Marino (Calif.).*

129 [*697*] Captain Wade. R.A. 1771. *Baroness Burton.*

130 [443] Edward, 2nd Viscount Ligonier. R.A. 1771. H. E. Huntington Art Gallery, San Marino (Calif.).

131 [*444*] Penelope, Viscountess Ligonier. R.A. 1771. *H. E. Huntington Art Gallery, San Marino (Calif.).*

132 [*936*] Woody landscape with gipsies. *Tate Gallery, London.*

133 [*930*] Cattle and sheep at a pool. *Hon. Michael Astor.*

134 [*924*] Village landscape. *Miss Olive Lloyd-Baker.*

135 [*925*] Cattle returning at evening. *R. C. A. Palmer-Morewood.*

137 [506] Abel Moysey. *C. F. Moysey.*

136 [266] Lady Margaret Fordyce. *Earl of Crawford and Balcarres.*

139 [95] Colonel John Bullock. *Baroness Burton.*

138 [772] Officer of 4th Regiment of Foot. *Melbourne.*

141 [458] William Lowndes, 1771. *Hon. Mrs Talbot-Rice.*

140 [333] Francis, 1st Earl of Guilford, 1773. *Earl of Guilford.*

142 [187] Frances, Countess of Dartmouth, 1771. *Earl of Dartmouth.*

143 [264] Alexander Fordyce. *Earl of Crawford and Balcarres.*

144 [565] Sir William Johnstone-Pulteney. *Lord Kinnaird.*

145 [450] Elizabeth and Mary Linley. R.A. 1772 (?). *Dulwich College.*

146 [604] Dr Ralph Schomberg. *National Gallery, London.*

147 [237] John Eld, 1772. *Boston.*

148 [358] John Heathcote. *Alvan T. Fuller, Boston.*

149 [137] Robert and Susannah Charlton. *Richmond, Virginia.*

151 [473] Captain Thomas Matthew, 1772. *Boston.*

150 [474] Mrs Thomas Matthew, 1772. *Boston.*

152 [221] Gainsborough Dupont. *National Gallery, London.*

153 [280] Margaret Gainsborough. *National Gallery, London.*

154 [656] Tenducci. *Barber Institute, Birmingham University.*

155 [447] Thomas Linley, Jr. *Dulwich College.*

156 [570] William, 1st Earl of Radnor, 1773. *Earl of Radnor.*

157 [75] Hon. Bartholomew Bouverie, 1773/4. *Earl of Radnor.*

158 [77] Hon. William Henry Bouverie, 1773. *Earl of Radnor.*

159 [76] Hon. Edward Bouverie, 1773. *Earl of Radnor.*

161 [664] Sir Charles Thompson, 1774. *National Gallery, London.*

160 [257] Hon. William Fitzwilliam, 1775. *Fitzwilliam Museum, Cambridge.*

162 [216] Hon. Frances Duncombe, 1773. *Earl of Radnor.*

163 [460] Mrs Lowndes. *Estate of R. W. Reford, Montreal.*

164 [696] Mrs William Villebois, 1777. *Viscount Cowdray.*

165 [81] Lady Brisco, 1776. *Kenwood.*

167 [482] Paul Cobb Methuen, 1776. *Lord Methuen.*

166 [262] Elizabeth, *Viscountess Folkestone. Liverpool.*

169 [469] Hon. Harriott Marsham. *Barber Institute, Birmingham University.*

168 [32] Johann Christian Bach, 1776. *Lord Hillingdon.*

171 [1] Carl Friedrich Abel. R.A. 1777. H. E. Huntington Art Gallery, San Marino (Calif.).

170 [722] John Wilkinson. Berlin.

173 [323] Hon. Mrs Graham. R.A. 1777. *Edinburgh.*

172 [272] William, 2nd Viscount Gage. R.A. 1777. *Viscount Gage.*

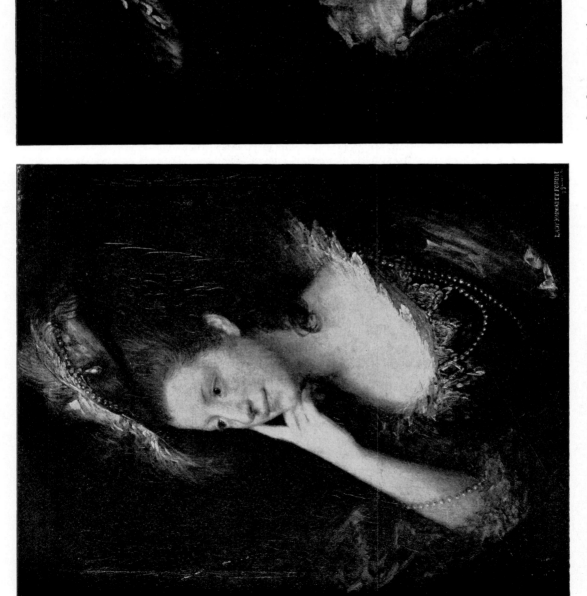

174 [265] Lady Margaret Fordyce. *Earl of Rosebery.*

175 [289] Mary Gainsborough, 1777. *National Gallery, London.*

177 [789] Lady in rose dress. *Hon. Michael Astor.*

176 [151] Miss Clarges. *Richmond, Virginia.*

178 [*947*] Returning from market. *Cincinnati (Hanna coll.)*.

179 [*952*] Woodland stream with figures. *Petworth (National Trust)*.

180 [*939*] Woodland pool with figures. *Lord Moyne.*

181 [*937*] The Watering Place. R.A. 1777. *National Gallery, London.*

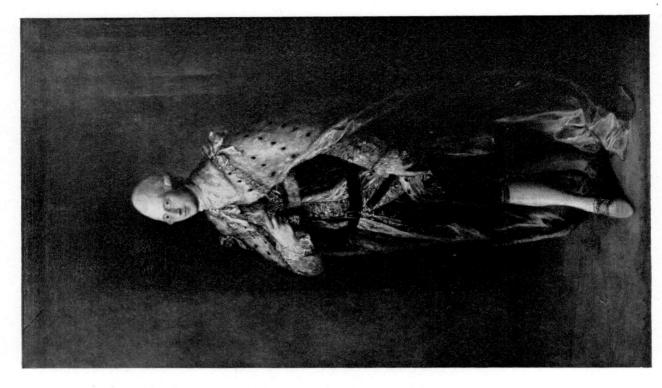

183 [176] Henry Frederick, Duke of Cumberland. R.A. 1777.
Buckingham Palace.

182 [180] Anne, Duchess of Cumberland. R.A. 1777.
Buckingham Palace.

185 [130] Queen Charlotte. R.A. 1781. *Windsor Castle.*

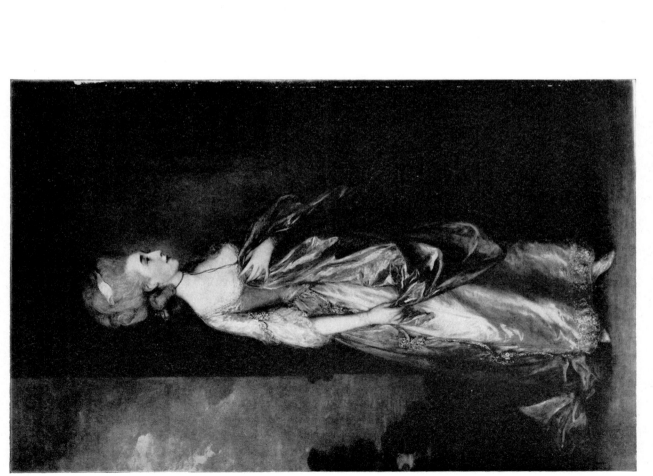

184 [239] Mrs Elliott. R.A. 1778. *Metropolitan Museum, New York.*

186 [661] Robert Thistlethwayte. *Mrs Borthwick-Norton.*

187 [662] Mrs Robert Thistlethwayte. *Mrs Borthwick-Norton.*

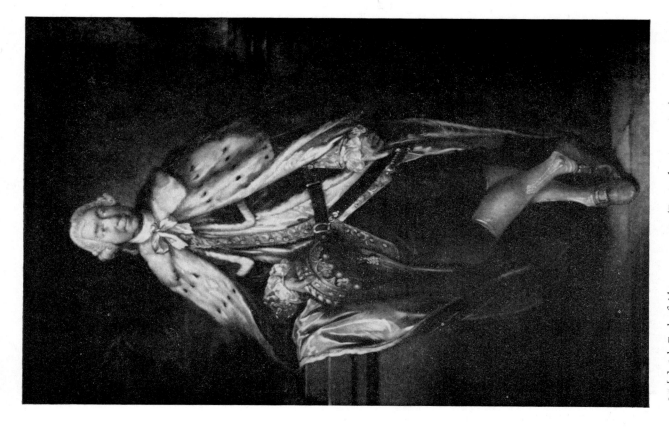

189 [4] 8th Earl of Abercorn, 1778. (From the mezzotint.)

188 [5] 4th Earl of Abingdon. *Anonymous loan to Birmingham.*

190 [948] A country cart crossing a ford. *Mrs H. Scudamore.*

191 [969] Upland hamlet with figures and stream. *Metropolitan Museum, New York.*

192 [*940*] Cottage door with children playing. *Cincinnati.*

193 [*935*] Woody lane with market cart. *Liverpool.*

194 [147] James Christie. R.A. 1778. *J. Paul Getty Museum, Malibu.*

195 [571] Anne, Countess of Radnor, 1778. *Earl of Radnor.*

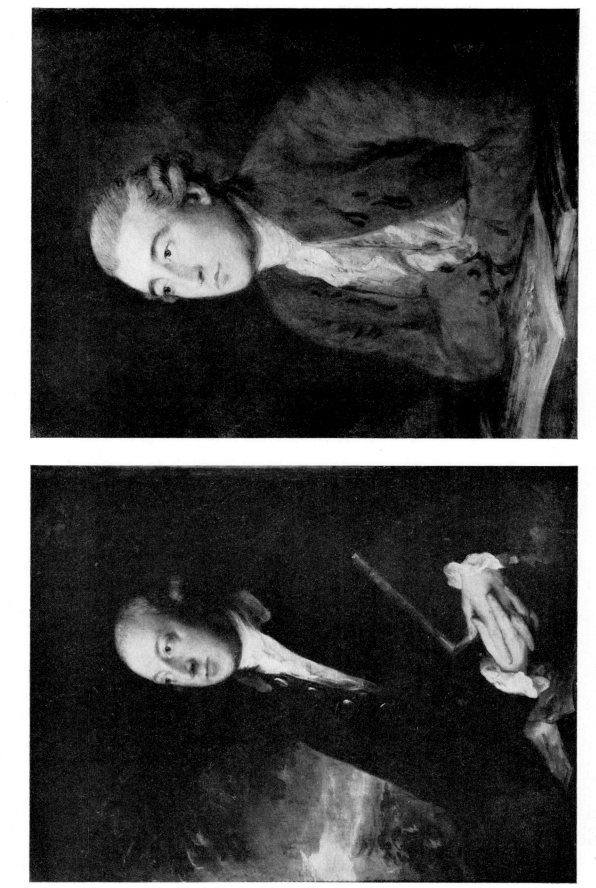

197 [456] Philip James de Loutherbourg. R.A. 1778. *Dulwich College.*

196 [540] Thomas Pennant, 1776. *Cardiff.*

198 [*336*] Duke of Hamilton. *Mrs Horace Dodge, Detroit.*

199 [337] Duchess of Hamilton. *Mrs Horace Dodge, Detroit.*

201 [943] Horses watering at a fountain. *Simon Whitbread.*

200 [958] Sailing vessels: cattle on a high bank. *Lord Glenconner.*

203 [941] The Cottage Door. R.A. 1780. H. E. Huntington Art Gallery, San Marino (Calif.).

202 [941a] Carts receding down a woody lane. De Young Museum, San Francisco.

205 [363] John Augustus, Lord Hervey. *Ickworth (National Trust)*.

204 [45] Sir Henry Bate-Dudley. R.A. 1780. *Baroness Burton*.

207 [51] Mrs Henry Beaufoy. R.A. 1780. *H. E. Huntington Art Gallery, San Marino (Calif.)*.

206 [194] Georgiana, Duchess of Devonshire. *Washington (Mellon coll.)*.

208 [292] The artist. *Royal Academy of Arts, London.*

209 [299] The artist's wife. *Courtauld Institute, London.*

210 [629] Georgiana, Countess Spencer, 1781. *Earl Spencer.*

211 [240] Mrs Elliott. R.A. 1782 (?). *Frick Collection, New York.*

212 [*109*] Adolphus Frederick, Duke of
Cambridge, 1782. *Windsor Castle.*

213 [*703*] George, Prince of Wales (George IV),
1782. *Windsor Castle.*

214 [*726*] William Henry, Duke of Clarence
(William IV), 1782. *Windsor Castle.*

215 [*406*] Edward, Duke of Kent, 1782.
Windsor Castle.

217 [50] Henry Beaufoy, 1785. *H.M. Beaufoy.*

216 [252] Johann Christian Fischer. R.A. 1780. *Buckingham Palace.*

219 [211] Mrs George Drummond. *Montreal.*

218 [210] George Drummond. *Ashmolean Museum, Oxford.*

220 [959] Cattle crossing a bridge. R.A. 1781. C. M. Michaelis.

222 [675] John and Henry Truman-Villebois. *Mrs Carll Tucker, New York.*

221 [667] Edward and William Tomkinson, 1784. *Taft Museum, Cincinnati.*

223 [965] Estuary with shepherd and sheep. *Sir Martyn Beckett, Bt.*

224 [954] Fishermen setting out. R.A. 1781. *Mrs Robert Mellon Bruce, L.I.*

225 [955] Coast scene: selling fish. *The Westminster Trustees.*

226 [956] Fishermen dragging nets. R.A. 1781. *Lord Fairhaven.*

227 [960] The woodcutter's return. R.A. 1782. *Duke of Rutland.*

228 [962] Woody scene with cattle and figures. *Duke of Rutland.*

229 [988] Charity relieving distress, 1784. *Sir Francis Cassel, Bt.*

230 [1010] Gipsies in a ruined abbey. *London, Private collection.*

231 [52] Mark Beaufoy, 1780/81. *H. M. Beaufoy.*

232 [481] Paul Methuen, 1784. *Lord Methuen.*

233 [724] Sir Edward Willes, 1786. *Lt.-Col. O. D. Smith.*

234 [145] Nathaniel Cholmley, 1785. *Hon. Mrs I. M. H. Strickland.*

236 [36] Mrs Peter William Baker, 1781. *Frick Collection, New York.*

235 [29] Giovanna Baccelli. R.A. 1782. *Countess of Swinton.*

238 [579] Mrs "Perdita" Robinson, 1781/2. *Wallace Collection, London.*

237 [206] Mrs John Douglas, 1784. *Waddesdon (National Trust.)*

240 [707] George, Prince of Wales (George IV). R.A. 1782. *Waddesdon (National Trust).*

239 [594] Colonel St Leger. R.A. 1782. *Buckingham Palace.*

241 [515] Master Nicholls ("The Pink Boy"). R.A. 1782. *Waddesdon (National Trust).*

242 [519] Hugh, Duke of Northumberland. R.A. 1783. *Middlesex Guildhall.*

243 [987] The Mall, 1783. *Frick Collection, New York.*

244 [964] View of the mouth of the Thames. R.A. 1783. *Melbourne.*

245 [*799*] Girl with pigs. R.A. 1782. *George Howard.*

246 [*1001*] Cottage door with girl and pigs, 1786. *Mrs H. Scudamore.*

247 [250] Hon. Mrs Henry Fane, 1786. *Oscar Yerburgh.*

248 [249] Hon. Mrs Henry Fane. R.A. 1782. *H. E. Huntington Art Gallery, San Marino (Calif.).*

249 [124] William, 1st Earl Cathcart, 1784. *Earl Cathcart.*

250 [617] Mrs Siddons, 1783/5. *National Gallery, London.*

251 [203] John Frederick, 3rd Duke of Dorset, 1782. *Lord Sackville.*

252 [7] Sir Robert Adair. *Baltimore (Jacob Epstein coll.).*

253 [647] Edward Swinburne, 1785. *Detroit.*

254 [646] Sir John Edward Swinburne, 6th Bt., 1785. *Detroit.*

255 [798] Peasant girl gathering sticks, 1782. *Fredericton University (N.B.)*.

256 [*613*] Mrs Sheridan. R.A. 1783. *Washington (Mellon coll.).*

257 [966] Mountain valley with sheep. R.A. 1783. *Duke of Sutherland.*

258 [968] Mountain valley with sheep and goat. *Philadelphia.*

259 [*992*] Upland valley with sheep, 1784. *W. S. Constable Curtis.*

260 [*1006*] Mountain valley with figures and sheep. *W. S. Constable Curtis.*

262 [971] Peepshow Landscape no. 2.

264 [973] Peepshow Landscape no. 4.

261 [970] Peepshow Landscape no. 1.

263 [972] Peepshow Landscape no. 3.

Victoria and Albert Museum, London.

266 [976] Peepshow Landscape no. 6.

265 [974] Peepshow Landscape no. 5.

268 [978] Peepshow Landscape no. 8.

Victoria and Albert Museum, London.

267 [977] Peepshow Landscape no. 7.

269 [*984*] Woody landscape with bridge. *National Gallery, London.*

270 [*993*] The Harvest Waggon, 1784/5. *Toronto.*

271 [*995*] Herdsmen driving cattle. *Owner untraced.*

272 [*996*] Boy driving cows near a pool. *Owner untraced.*

273 [*803*] Cottage girl with dog and pitcher, 1785. *Sir Alfred Beit, Bt.*

274 [335] Mr and Mrs William Hallett ("The Morning Walk"), 1785. *National Gallery, London.*

276 [542] Juliana, Lady Petre, 1788. H. E. Huntington Art Gallery, San Marino (Calif.).

275 [576] Mary, Duchess of Richmond. Ascott (National Trust).

278 [47] *Lady Bate-Dudley, 1787. Baroness Burton.*

277 [815] Haymaker and sleeping girl. *Boston.*

280 [583] Lord Rodney, 1783/6. *Earl of Rosebery.*

279 [97] Sir Peter Burrell (Lord Gwydyr), 1787. *Mrs James B. Duke, New York.*

281 [807] Cottage children (The Woodgatherers), 1787. *Metropolitan Museum, New York.*

282 [809] Boy with a cat—Morning, 1787. *Metropolitan Museum, New York.*

283 [810] Young Hobbinol and Ganderetta, 1788. *Mrs. Mildred Browning Green, Los Angeles.*

284 [805] Cottage Girl with bowl of milk, 1786. *Capetown.*

286 [*1002*] The Market Cart, 1786/7. *Tate Gallery, London.*

285 [*1011*] Cottage door with a peasant smoking, 1788. *University of Southern California, Los Angeles.*

287 [1008] Mountain landscape with bridge. *Washington (Mellon coll.).*

288 [1012] Diana and Actaeon. *Buckingham Palace.*

289 [823] Greyhounds coursing a fox. *Earl of Rosebery.*

290 [821] Two fox dogs. *National Gallery, London.*

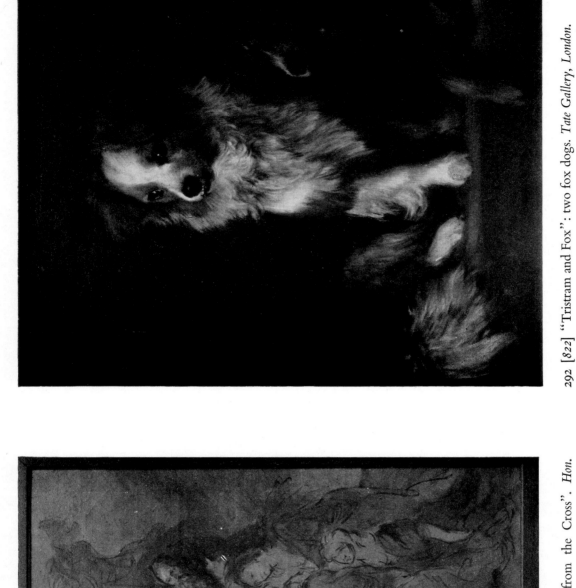

291 [1027] Copy from Rubens' "Descent from the Cross". *Hon. Michael Astor.*

292 [822] "Tristram and Fox": two fox dogs. *Tate Gallery, London.*

Index of the Present Owners of Paintings

Note: This index includes all public collections and what one may call "genuine" private collections. Pictures at present in the art trade or whose present ownership is unknown to me are not included. Where helpful I have added the catalogue number.

GREAT BRITAIN

Her Majesty The Queen
Prince Alfred
Princess Augusta Sophia
Duke of Cambridge
Queen Charlotte (2)
Princess Charlotte Augusta Matilda
The Three Princesses (135)
Lord Cornwallis
Ernest Augustus, Duke of Cumberland
Henry, Duke of Cumberland (2)
Duchess of Cumberland (2)
Princess Elizabeth
J. C. Fischer
George III (2)
Bishop Hurd
Duke of Kent
Princess Mary
Prince Octavius
John Quin
Mrs Robinson
Colonel St Leger
Princess Sophia
Duke of Sussex
Prince of Wales
Prince William Henry
Diana and Actaeon (1012)
Copy of Rembrandt (1026)

PUBLIC COLLECTIONS: LONDON

Courtauld Institute
Thomas Gainsborough
Mrs Thomas Gainsborough
Charles Tudway (Lee collection)

Drapers' Company
John Smith

Equitable Life Assurance Company
Sir Charles Morgan

Foundling Hospital Offices
The Charterhouse (861)

Guildhall
Rev. H. Burrough

Middlesex Guildhall
Duke of Northumberland

Haberdashers' Company
Jerome Knapp

Ironmongers' Company
Lord Hood

Kenwood
Lady Brisco
Miss Brummell
Countess Howe
Lady (793)
Landscape (912)

Lincoln's Inn
Sir John Skynner

Marine Society
John Thornton

National Gallery
Baillie family
Sir W. Blackstone
Gainsborough Dupont
Margaret and Mary Gainsborough (2)
Mary Gainsborough
Mr and Mrs Hallett
Lord Kilmorey
John Plampin
Dr Schomberg
Mrs Siddons
Miss Singleton
Sir C. Thompson
"General Wolfe"
Fox dogs (821)
Gainsborough's Forest (828)
Dedham vale (853)
Landscape (984)
Landscape (990)
Market Cart (1002)

Tate Gallery
Sir Henry Bate-Dudley
Sir F. Gregg
Abel Moysey
Mrs Portman (Loan)
Housemaid (811)
Nymph at the Bath (814)
Tristram and Fox (822)
Old Horse (824)
Gipsies—sketch (864)
Landscape (893)
Landscape (894)

Sunset (897)
Gipsies (936)
Landscape (997)

National Portrait Gallery
Lord Amherst
Duke of Bedford
George Colman
Lord Cornwallis
J. Gibbs
J. Henderson
John Joshua Kirby and wife
General Stringer Lawrence
Admiral Vernon

National Maritime Museum
Lord Sandwich

Royal Academy of Arts
Thomas Gainsborough
Landscape (1007)

Royal Society of Arts
Lord Folkestone

Victoria and Albert Museum
Margaret and Mary Gainsborough
John Joshua Kirby
Twelve Landscapes on glass (970–981)

Wallace Collection
Miss Haverfield
Mrs Robinson

PUBLIC COLLECTIONS OUT-SIDE LONDON

Arbroath, Hospitalfield Trustees
Man (755)

Barnard Castle, Bowes Museum
Landscape (852)

Bath, Holburne of Menstrie Museum
Dr Charlton
Lady (786)

Birmingham, City Art Gallery
Lord Abingdon (Loan)
T. Coward
Sir Charles Holte
Landscape (994)

Birmingham University, Barber Institute
Hon. H. Marsham
G. F. Tenducci
Harvest Waggon (907)

Bristol, Art Gallery
W. Leyborne Leyborne
Mrs W. Leyborne

Bristol, City Estates Committee
Earl Nugent

Cambridge, Emmanuel College
Rev. H. Hubbard
Bishop Hurd
Bishop Jackson

Cambridge, Fitzwilliam Museum
Philip Dupont
Hon. W. Fitzwilliam
John Kirby
Mrs John Kirby
John Joshua Kirby
Heneage Lloyd and sister
Landscape (860)

Cardiff, National Museum of Wales
Sir Richard Lloyd
Thomas Pennant
Sir John Wynn (Loan)
Landscape (932)
Landscape (982)

Dulwich College
Samuel Linley
Thomas Linley, Sr
Thomas Linley, Jr
Elizabeth and Mary Linley
P. J. de Loutherbourg
Mrs Moodey and children
Man and wife (753)

Edinburgh, National Gallery
Hon. Mrs Graham
Mrs Hamilton Nisbet
Landscape (840)

Edinburgh, National Portrait Gallery
4th Duke of Argyll

Glasgow
Landscape (902)

Hartlebury Castle (Bishops of Worcester)
Bishop Hurd

Royal Holloway College
Landscape (911)

Hove
Landscape (880)

Ipswich
Miss Edgar (Loan)
Samuel Kilderbee
William Wollaston
"Mrs Gainsborough" (795)
Landscape (838)
Landscape (883)

Leeds, Temple Newsam
Mrs Prowse

Liverpool
Sir R. Clayton
Lady Folkestone
Landscape (935)

Manchester
"General Wolfe"
Landscape (950)

Marlborough College
Byam family

National Trust
(1) *Ascott*
Hon. Thomas Needham
Duchess of Richmond
(2) *Blickling*
Lord Buckinghamshire
Lady Buckinghamshire
(3) *Charlecote*
George Lucy (2)
(4) *Ickworth*
Earl of Bristol
Augustus Hervey
Lord Hervey
(5) *Lacock Abbey*
John Talbot
(6) *Stourhead*
Landscape (1009)
(7) *Upton House*
Landscape (877)
(8) *Waddesdon*
Mrs John Douglas
10th Duke of Hamilton
Lord Archibald Hamilton
Master Nicholls
Mrs Robinson
Lady Sheffield
Prince of Wales
(9) *Wallington Hall*
Susannah Trevelyan

Norwich
Lord Suffield

Oxford, All Souls
Benjamin Buckler

Oxford, Ashmolean Museum
George Drummond
Landscape (892)
Copy of Rubens (1028)

Oxford, Christ Church
Lord Mendip
Sir John Skynner

Port Sunlight. Lady Lever Art Gallery
Princess Augusta Sophia (?)
Mrs Frere

Southampton
Lord Vernon

Stratford-on-Avon, Town Hall (formerly)
David Garrick

GREAT BRITAIN: PRIVATE COLLECTIONS
(Alphabetically under owners, regardless of location.)

Duke of Abercorn
Earl of Abercorn

Hugh L. Agnew
Thomas Gainsborough

Lord Allendale
Sir Thomas Blackett

G. W. Andrews
Mr and Mrs Andrews

Col. G. H. Anson
Christopher Horton
Lady Littleton

Sir Ralph Anstruther, Bt.
Landscape (863)
Boy at the stile (889)

Duke of Argyll
5th Duke of Argyll
Lord Frederick Campbell
Henry Seymour Conway

Mrs F. N. Ashcroft
William Pearce

Mrs O. S. Ashcroft
Miss Butler
David Garrick
Landscape (967)

Hon. Michael Astor
J. C. Middleton
Lady (789)
Landscape (930)
Copy of Rubens (1027)

Princess Alice, Countess of Athlone
Queen Charlotte

Earl of Aylesford
Earl of Aylesford
Lady Charlotte Finch

Sir Edmund Bacon, Bt.
"Bumper" (817)

Miss Selina L. Baker
Peter Baker
Mrs Peter Baker

Lt.-Col. Michael Barne
Mrs Muilman and others (747)

A. Edgell Baxter
Thomas Prowse

Lord Bearsted
Mrs Carr
Margaret Gainsborough

Jocelyn Beauchamp
Robert Palmer

H. M. Beaufoy
Henry Beaufoy
Mark Beaufoy

Sir Martyn Beckett, Bt.
Coast scene (965)

Duke of Bedford
Duke of Bedford (2)
Duchess of Bedford
Duchess of Marlborough
Miss Elizabeth Wrottesley
Miss Mary Wrottesley
Landscape (829)
Landscape (833)

Mrs D. M. M. Bell
Mrs Robert Hingeston

Major Rex Benson
The midday rest (998)

Estate of late Earl of Berkeley
Captain G. C. Berkeley

G. H. Berners
Norfolk broad (843)

Major A. T. C. Binny
Dog (817a)

Mrs Borthwick-Norton
Countess of Chesterfield
Robert Thistlethwayte
Mrs Thistlethwayte

F. E. S. Bowlby
Lady Mary Bowlby

Earl of Bradford
Lady Torrington

Duke of Buccleuch
Duke of Buccleuch
Duchess of Buccleuch
Duke of Montagu
Duchess of Montagu (2)

Hon. Mrs Burnett
Landscape (839)

Baroness Burton
Sir Henry Bate-Dudley
Lady Bate-Dudley
Colonel John Bullock
Miss Franks
Lady Sussex and niece
Lord Tracy
Captain Wade

Marquess of Bute
Marquess of Bute

Major G. J. Buxton
David Garrick
Dog (818)
Landscape (895)

Marquess Camden
Marquess Camden

Lord Camrose
Landscape (922)

Hon. Mrs Cartwright
Thomas Cartwright

Sir Francis Cassel, Bt.
Charity relieving distress (988)

Earl Cathcart
Earl Cathcart

Col. H. J. Cator
James Donnithorne

Chafy family
Mr Chafy

Marchioness of Cholmondeley
Mr and Mrs Browne
Thomas Gainsborough
Thomas Gainsborough and family

John Christie
Miss Shuckborough

Earl of Clarendon
3rd Earl of Jersey

Major A. F. Clarke-Jervoise
Landscape (871)

Lady Blanche Cobbold
Mother and daughter (750)

Dennis Cohen
Lord Bristol

W. S. Constable-Curtis
Landscape (992)
Landscape (1006)

Sir Francis Cook, Bt.
Girl (754)

Lord Cowdray
Francis Bennett
Miss Talbot
Mrs Villebois
Duke of York

Martin Crabbe
John Ord

Earl of Crawford
Lady Eardley and child
Alexander Fordyce
Lady Margaret Fordyce
Landscape (910)

Capt. B. Hutton Croft
Mrs Croft

Earl of Dartmouth
Earl of Dartmouth
Countess of Dartmouth (2)

Earl of Derby
Earl of Derby

Duke of Devonshire
Countess Spencer
Countess Talbot

Lady Janet Douglas-Pennant
Landscape (934)

Col. J. W. S. Drummond-Moray
Lord Douglas

Marchioness of Dufferin
Landscape (946)

Sir William Dugdale, Bt.
Mrs Cradock
Mrs Richard Dugdale
Mr and Mrs Francis Stratford
Miss Maria Stratford
Miss Sarah Stratford

Earl of Durham
W. H. Lambton

Sir Timothy Eden, Bt.
Sir John Eden

Earl of Ellesmere
Family group (749)
Landscape (983)

Sir Arthur Elton, Bt.
Mrs Durbin

Marquess of Exeter
Sir Christopher Whichcote
Lady Whichcote
Landscape (951)

Lord Fairhaven
Coast scene (956)

F. W. Fane
Henry Fane

Lord Faringdon
Landscape (926)

H. W. J. Ferrand
Landscape (895)

H. L. Fison
Landscape (901)

Mrs Louis Fleischmann
Margaret or Mary Gainsborough

Sir Ian Forbes-Leith, Bt.
Major W. Tennant

G. G. Fortescue
Marquis of Buckingham
Pinkney Wilkinson

Viscount Gage
Lord Gage

Miss Gainsborough Gardiner
Edward Gardiner

Lord Glenconner
Coast scene (958)

Dr Gosset
Isaac Gosset

Mrs Green
Sir Edward Turner

Earl of Guilford
Earl of Guilford

Earl of Haddington
Hon. Mrs Baillie
Hon. Charles Hamilton

Earl of Halifax
Mrs Henry Wood

Miss Mary Graves Hamilton
Walwyn Graves

Sir E. Hanmer, Bt.
Sir Thomas Hanmer

Mrs T. A. Hardcastle
Landscape (918)

Earl of Harewood
George Canning

Mrs Geoffrey Hart
William Lee

F. B. Hart-Jackson
Lambe Barry

Mrs Arden Haworth-Booth
Lewis Bagot

General Hibbert
Thomas Hibbert

Lord Hillingdon
J. C. Bach
Thomas Tickell

Estate of Adolph Hirsch
Margaret Gainsborough
(see also *Major and Mrs Pinto*)

C. G. Hoare
Copy of Van Dyck (1020)

Earl of Home
Lady Douglas

Major A. J. G. Hope
General Leslie

C. W. L. Penrhyn-Hornby
Rev. G. Hornby
Mrs G. Hornby

Mrs Stella Hotblack
Lady Clarges

George Howard
Countess of Carlisle
Girl with pigs

Earl Howe
Earl Howe
Landscape (845)

Mrs Harman Hunt
R. S. and Miss C. Lloyd

Lord Hylton
Thomas Jolliffe

Earl of Ilchester
Lady Mary Fitzpatrick

Mrs L. P. Irby
Mrs Casberd

Earl of Jersey
Landscape (931)

E. Peter Jones
Frederick Cornewall

Mrs H. Isherwood Kay
Man (764)

Viscountess Kemsley
Joshua Grigby

Lord Kenyon
Ralph Leycester

Lord Kinnaird
Sir W. Johnstone Pulteney

Master of Kinnaird
Landscape (885)

Princess Labia
Dehaney family
Mrs Drummond
Miss Katherine Edgar
Lord Graves
Boy in Van Dyck costume (771)
Landscape (854)
Landscape (865)

Marquis of Lansdowne
Landscape (953)

Earl of Leicester
T. W. Coke
Thomas Gainsborough

Sir John Leigh, Bt.
Earl of Chesterfield
Countess of Chesterfield

Marquess of Linlithgow
Countess of Hopetoun

R. W. Lloyd
Landscape (917)

Miss Olive Lloyd-Baker
Landscape (924)

Mrs L'Estrange Malone
Sir William St Quintin, 4th Bart.
Sir William St Quintin, 5th Bart.
Landscape (900)

Rev. G. W. Markham
2nd Marquis of Lansdowne

Hon. Mrs Marten
Mrs Sturt

Sir Hubert Medlycott, Bt.
W. Tugwell
Mrs W. Tugwell
W. Tugwell, Jr.
Mr Tugwell

Lord Methuen
Paul Methuen
Paul Cobb Methuen

C. M. Michaelis
Landscape (959)

Major Charles Mills
Landscape (849)

Miss Minet
Daniel Minet
Mrs Daniel Minet

Sir Charles Mott-Radclyffe
Stephen White

Lord Moyne
Mrs William Russell
Miss Tyler
Landscape (939)

C. F. Moysey
Dr Abel Moysey
Abel Moysey

Sir Arundel Neave, Bt.
Sir Richard and Lady Neave

Bruce Nelson
Rev. Robert Hingeston (?)
Mrs Robert Hingeston

Duke of Newcastle
Beggar boys (802)

Major J. G. Newton
Pitminster boy (779)

Sir Philip Nichols
Man with dog (756)

Duke of Norfolk
11th Duke of Norfolk
12th Duke of Norfolk
Landscape (858)

Marquess of Normanby
Lord Mulgrave (2)

Marquess of Northampton
Copy of Van Dyck (1015)

Lord Northbourne
Lord Camden

Helen, Duchess of Northumberland
Hon. Henry Drummond
Hon. Mrs Drummond
Earl of Kinnoull
Duke of Northumberland

Sir Guy Nugent, Bt.
Earl Nugent

Lord O'Neil
Miss Rodes

R. C. A. Palmer-Morewood
Landscape (925)

Hon. Clive Pearson
Col. Norton Knatchbull
Capt. Charles Phipps
Man in blue (783)

General Peck
Dr Ditcher

Major and Mrs R. J. Pinto
Rev. Wadham Pigott
G. A. Vestris

G. H. L. F. Pitt-Rivers
Lord Rivers

Miss M. E. Pleydell-Bouverie
Countess of Radnor

Irene, Countess of Plymouth
Landscape (881)

Earl of Powis
Earl of Powis

Mrs G. E. R. Prior
Humphrey Gainsborough

Sir Richard Proby, Bt.
John Proby
Landscape (891)

Earl of Radnor
Hon. Bartholomew Bouverie
Hon. Edward Bouverie
Hon. William Henry Bouverie
Hon. Frances Duncombe
Earl of Radnor (2)
Countess of Radnor

Hon. Mrs B. M. Talbot Rice
William Lowndes

Earl of Rosebery
Lady Margaret Fordyce
Lord Rodney
Lord Rosebery
Greyhounds coursing a fox (823)

Anthony de Rothschild
"Selfportrait" (785)
(see also *National Trust: Ascott*)

Mrs Dorothy de Rothschild
Lord Bateman

Duke of Roxburghe
Capt. Roberts

Capt. C. E. A. L. Rumbold
Sir Thomas Rumbold and son

Duke of Rutland
Woodcutter's return (960)
Landscape (962)
Landscape (963)

Lord Sackville
Duke of Dorset
F. Giardini
Lord George Sackville

Hon. Victor Saumarez
Mrs Acton
Lambe Barry
Thomas Vere
Mrs Vere
Man (760)
Young man (761)
Landscape (835)

Lord Saye and Sele
Lady Saye and Sele

Miss Margot Schroeder
Landscape (903)

Mrs H. Scudamore
Country cart (948)
Landscape (1001)

Sir Hugo Sebright, Bt.
Sir John Sebright

Earl of Sefton
Countess of Sefton

Mrs Vivian Seymer
Benjamin Buckler

Mrs Shuttleworth
Mr Giardini (?)

Lt.-Col. O. D. Smith
Sir Edward Willes

Miss Oswald Smith
Earl of Westmorland

Col. Solly
Landscape (867)
Landscape (869)

Earl Spencer
William Poyntz
Earl Spencer
Countess Spencer
Lady Georgiana Spencer

E. G. Spencer-Churchill
Thomas Gainsborough

Mrs H. W. Standring
Peasant with donkey (816a)

Earl Stanhope
Lord Chesterfield
Lord Stanhope

Lady Stewart
Col. Thomas Fletcher
Margaret Gainsborough
Mrs Hill

Hon. Mrs I. M. H. Strickland
N. Cholmley

Lord Suffield
J. Modyford Heywood

Duke of Sutherland
Landscape (966)
Landscape (1000a)

C. R. Sutton
Landscape (850)
Landscape (851)

Lady Swinburne
Sir Edward Swinburne

Countess of Swinton
Mme Baccelli
David Garrick

Lord Templemore
Marquess of Donegall (2)
Marchioness of Donegall

Hon. Mrs D. Tollemache
Landscape (878)

Messrs Truman, Hanbury & Co.
Sir Benjamin Truman

J. C. C. Vowler
Dr William Walcot
Mrs William Walcot
Mr Walcot

Lady Wake
Landscape (985)

Earl Waldegrave
Duke of Gloucester
Lord Waldegrave
Lady Waldegrave

Mrs A. C. J. Wall
Prince of Wales
Landscape (989)

Col. E. J. S. Ward
Girl with mushrooms (812)
Girl with a penny (813)

Trustees of late Duke of Westminster
Lord Belgrave
Countess Grosvenor
Coast scene (955)

Whichcote Trustees
Sir Thomas Whichcote

Simon Whitbread
Margaret and Mary Gainsborough
Samuel Green
B. Massey
John Smeaton
Samuel Whitbread
Horses watering (943)
Copy of Murillo (1025)

Sir O. W. Williams-Wynn, Bt.
Hagar and Ishmael (929)

L. H. Wilson
Mrs Davenport
Landscape (857)

H. C. Wollaston
William Wollaston

Capt. V. M. Wombwell
Mrs Modyford Heywood

George Wyndham
Miss Henrietta Wyndham

John Wyndham
Countess of Egremont
J. A. Ernst
Dog (820)
Landscape (952)
Landscape (999)

B. A. Wynne
Robert Wynne

Col. Wynne-Finch
Earl of Aylesford
Countess of Aylesford

Oscar Yerburgh
Hon. Mrs Henry Fane

Simon Yorke
Philip Yorke

Gerard M. Young
William Jackson

Marquess of Zetland
Prince of Wales

EIRE
Dublin Gallery
Duchess of Cumberland
John Gainsborough
General Johnstone
Mrs King
Duke of Northumberland
John Quin
Landscape (870)
Landscape (909)
Copy of Teniers (1030)

Trinity College, Dublin
Duke of Bedford

Sir Alfred Beit, Bt.
Mme Baccelli
Hon. Mrs Watson
Cottage Girl (803)
Landscape (867)
Landscape (913)

Lord Carew
Rev. R. Woodward

T. B. Ponsonby
Mrs Ponsonby

Major Shirley
Lord Chesterfield
Lady Chesterfield

EUROPEAN COLLECTIONS
Vienna
Landscape (859)

Paris. Louvre
Lady Alston
Elizabeth Anne Gosset
Lady and Gentleman (752)

Paris. M. Groult
Lady Mulgrave

Paris. M. Routhier
Lord Sandwich

Paris. Baronne Edouard de Rothschild
Mrs Hibbert
Mrs Puget

Berlin
J. Wilkinson

Munich
U. T. Price

Stuttgart
Prince Octavius

Budapest
C. Hotchkiss

Bologna. Liceo Musicale
J. C. Bach

Vaduz (Liechtenstein)
Thomas Linley

Lisbon. Gulbenkian Foundation
Mrs Lowndes-Stone
Miss Rowley

Madrid
Robert Butcher
Dr Sequeira

Stockholm
Thomas Haviland

Leningrad
Lady (792)

BRITISH COMMONWEALTH COLLECTIONS

Australia

Elizabeth Bay. F. Penfold Hyland
Mme Le Brun

Melbourne
Miss Wrottesley
An officer (772)
Landscape (964)

Perth
W. Mayhew

Auckland (N.Z.)
John Sparrowe

Dunedin (N.Z.)
Henry Lowndes

Bermuda
H. J. Watlington
T. Medlycott

Canada
Fredericton (N.B.). University
E. C. Nugent
Girl with sticks (798)

Montreal
Mrs Drummond
Landscape (844)

Montreal. R. F. Angus
Mrs Egerton

Montreal. Mrs Reford
Mrs Lowndes

Montreal. A. J. Nesbitt
Mrs Unwin

Ottawa
Ignatius Sancho
Rev. W. Stevens

Toronto
Harvest Waggon (993)

Vancouver
G. Montgomerie

South Africa
Capetown
Girl with milk (805)

PUBLIC COLLECTIONS IN THE UNITED STATES

Albany (N.Y.)
Lady Mostyn

Amherst (Mass.). Amherst College
Lord Amherst

Baltimore (Md.)
Robert Adair
Mrs Charles Tudway

Boston
John Eld
Captain Matthew
Mrs Matthew
Mrs E. M. Pleydell
John Taylor
Girl (787)
Haymaker and sleeping girl (815)
Landscape with milkmaids (919)

Buffalo (N.Y.)
Miss Evans (probably Dupont)

Cambridge (Mass.). Fogg Art Museum
Sir Benjamin Thompson

Chicago
Lady (791)

Cincinnati
Lord Downe
Miss Fitzpatrick
Mrs William Hammond
Mrs Provis
Mrs Thicknesse
Earl of Warwick
Cottage door (940)
Returning from market (947)

Cincinnati. Taft Museum
Duchess of Gloucester
Tomkinson boys
Landscape (920)

Cleveland
Mrs Jolliffe
Mrs H. C. Wise

Detroit
Sir John Swinburne
Edward Swinburne

Hartford (Conn.)
Landscape (1000)

Indianapolis
Lady in red (766)

Kansas City
"Repose" (908)

Los Angeles. County Museum
Duchess of Gloucester

Los Angeles. University of California
Mrs Burrough
Landscape (841)
Landscape (923)
Cottage door (1011)

Malibu (Calif.). J. Paul Getty Museum
James Christie

Minneapolis
Landscape (830)

Muskegon (Mich.)
William Lynch

New York. Frick collection
Mrs Baker
Hon. Frances Duncombe
Mrs Elliott
Lady Innes
J. P. Jodrell
The Mall

New York. Metropolitan Museum
C. R. Burney
Nathaniel Burrough
Queen Charlotte (Bache)
Mrs Elliott
Miss Sparrow
Mrs Tennant
Cottage children (807)
Boy with cat (809)
Landscape (969)

Philadelphia
Miss Linley (Elkins)
John Palmer (Elkins)
Mrs Clement Tudway (Elkins)
Landscape (Elkins) (945)
Mr Coyte (Johnson)
Landscape (Johnson) (see 865)
Lady Rodney (McFadden)
Landscape (McFadden) (968)
Landscape (Wilstach) (831)

Pittsburgh
Gentleman (781)

Raleigh (N.C.)
J. Scrimgeour (see 770)
Landscape (855)

Richmond (Va.)
Charlton children
Miss Clarges

Rochester (N.Y.). University
Mrs William Provis

St Louis (Mo.)
Philip Thicknesse
Captain Walmesley
Landscape (834)
Copy of Van Dyck (1017)

San Francisco. California Palace of the Legion of Honour
Mrs Fitzherbert

San Francisco. De Young Memorial Museum
Sir W. Draper
S. Kilderbee
Landscape (941a)

San Marino (Calif.). Huntington Gallery
C. F. Abel
Mrs Beaufoy
J. Buttall
Duchess of Cumberland
Hon. Mrs Fane
Lord Ligonier
Lady Ligonier
Mrs Meares
Lady Petre
Girl in pink (751)
Cottage door (941)

Sarasota (Fla.)
General Honywood

Toledo (Ohio)
Lady Frederick Campbell
Shepherd boy (836)
Landscape (906)

Washington. Corcoran Gallery
Lord de Dunstanville
Lady de Dunstanville
Landscape (928)

Washington. National Gallery
Lord Darnley (Widener)
Duchess of Devonshire (Mellon)
Hon. Mrs Graham (Widener)
Mrs Methuen (Widener)
Mrs Sheridan (Mellon)
Miss Tatton (Mellon)
Mrs Taylor (Mellon)
Landscape (Mellon) (1008)

Williamstown (Mass.). Williams
College
Robert Butcher

Williamstown (Mass.). Clark
Foundation
Lord Hampden
Beggar children (810)

Worcester (Mass.)
Margaret and Mary Gainsborough
Landscape (898)

PRIVATE COLLECTION IN THE UNITED STATES
(Alphabetically under owners, regardless of location.)

Bailey Aldrich
Mary Hamond

Harry Payne Bingham estate
Lady Carr
Sir Paul Pechell

Mrs Robert Mellon Bruce
Seascape (954)

Walter P. Chrysler, Jr.
Miss Montagu

Mrs W. R. Coe
W. Y. Davenport

Jefferson Coolidge
Mr Hood

Mrs Horace Dodge
Duke of Hamilton
Duchess of Hamilton

Mrs James B. Duke
Sir Peter Burrell

E. W. Edwards
Lady Blackstone
Lord Lauderdale

Estate of A. W. Ericson
Lady Eden

Charles T. Fisher
Market cart (1003)

A. Leo Flesh
Thomas Sheridan

Miss Helen Clay Frick
R. B. Sheridan

Alvan T. Fuller
Master Heathcote

Eugene G. Grace
Landscape (949)

Mrs Mildred Browning Greene
Hobbinol and Ganderetta (810)

Mrs Mabel S. Ingalls
Duchess of Devonshire

Paul B. Jamison
Mrs Lascelles

Kay Kimbell
Miss Sarah Buxton
Mrs Oswald
The Misses Sloper

John G. Lowe
Thomas Walker

Mrs J. Denniston Lyon
Mrs Kinloch
Landscape (see no. 891)

Mrs Jeremiah D. Maguire
Landscape (1004)

Mrs Robert L. Montgomery
Landscape (890)

John M. Morehead
E. Morton Pleydell

Lady Oakes
Woodcutter's return (961)

Robert Perret
Landscape (991)

John S. Phipps
Prince William Henry

E. F. Price
Lady Dundonald

Private collection
Miss Mott

Mrs Ogden Reid
Lady Glenorchy

Mrs Samuel P. Rotan
Miss Heberden

John M. Schiff
Landscape (868)

Frederick W. Schumacher
Girl (788)

Wharton Sinkler
Landscape (856)

Wm. Skinner
Sir John Skynner

Herbert Daniel Stone
Man (762)

Mrs William R. Timken
General Bligh

Henry J. Topping
George Chad

Daniel Topping
Mrs George Chad

Mrs Carll Tucker
Truman-Villebois children

Mrs McLane Van Ingen
Miss Howland

Mrs John Wendell, Jr.
James Bourchier

Henry S. Williams
Mrs Fisher

SOUTH AMERICA
Havana. Oscar B. Cintas
Lady Eardley
Prince of Wales

São Paolo. Museum
Marquis of Hastings
Landscape (826)

São Paulo. Dr Chateaubriand
Mrs Bolton

Index of Previous Owners of Gainsborough's Landscapes

Note: This is intended rather as a concordance than as a complete index, so that Landscapes cited in other books or appearing in sale catalogues can readily be identified. This presents little difficulty with the portraits and with the other small categories of pictures, so that it has been limited to the Landscapes. Only genuine private owners have been included.